QUANTITATIVE

REVIEW

The only study guide

nearly 300 real GM

questions—and answers—

by the creators

of the test.

THE OFFICIAL GUIDE FOR
GMAT® QUANTITATIVE REVIEW

- The -
OFFICIAL
Guide

- Real questions from past GMAT® tests
- Nearly 300 real questions, answers, and explanations in:
  Arithmetic · Algebra · Geometry · Problem Solving · Data Sufficiency
- NEW organization of questions in order of difficulty saves study time

From the Graduate Management Admission Council®

THE OFFICIAL GUIDE FOR GMAT® QUANTITATIVE REVIEW

For additional information contact:
Graduate Management Admission Council
1600 Tysons Blvd., Ste. 1400
McLean, VA 22102 USA
www.gmac.com

ISBN: 0-9765709-2-0

10 9 8 7 6 5 4 3 2 1

Produced by Blanche Brann LP, Lawrenceville, NJ
Charles Forster, Designer
Mike Wilson, Production Designer

Printed in the United States of America

Table of Contents

1.0   What Is the GMAT®?

1.0 What Is the GMAT®?

The Graduate Management Admission Test® (GMAT®) is a standardized, three-part exam delivered in English. The test was designed to help admissions officers evaluate how suitable individual applicants are for their graduate business and management programs. It measures basic verbal, mathematical, and analytical writing skills that a test taker has developed over a long period of time through education and work.

The GMAT® exam does not measure a person's knowledge of specific fields of study. Graduate business and management programs enroll people from many different undergraduate and work backgrounds, so rather than test your mastery of any particular subject area, the GMAT® exam will assess your acquired skills. Your GMAT® score will give admissions officers a statistically reliable measure of how well you are likely to perform academically in the core curriculum of a graduate business program.

Of course, there are many other qualifications that can help people succeed in business school and in their careers—for instance, job experience, leadership ability, motivation, and interpersonal skills. The GMAT® exam does not gauge these qualities. That is why your GMAT® score is intended to be used as one standard admissions criterion among other, more subjective, criteria, such as admissions essays and interviews.

1.1 Why Take the GMAT® Test?

GMAT® scores are used by admissions officers in roughly 1,800 graduate business and management programs worldwide. Schools that require prospective students to submit GMAT® scores in the application process are generally interested in admitting the best-qualified applicants for their programs, which means that you may find a more beneficial learning environment at schools that require GMAT® scores as part of your application.

Because the GMAT® test gauges skills that are important to successful study of business and management at the graduate level, your scores will give you a good indication of how well prepared you are to succeed academically in a graduate management program; how well you do on the test may also help you choose the business schools to which you apply. Furthermore, the percentile table you receive with your scores will tell you how your performance on the test compares to the performance of other test takers, giving you one way to gauge your competition for admission to business school.

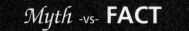

Myth -vs- FACT

M – **If I don't score in the 90th percentile, I won't get into any school I choose.**

F – **Very few people get super-high scores.**

Fewer than 50 of the more than 200,000 people taking the GMAT® exam each year get a perfect score of 800. Thus, while you may be exceptionally capable, the odds are against your achieving a perfect score. Also, the GMAT® exam is just one piece of your application packet. Admissions officers use GMAT® scores in conjunction with undergraduate record, application essays, interviews, letters of recommendation, and other information when deciding whom to accept into their programs.

Schools consider many different aspects of an application before making an admissions decision, so even if you score well on the GMAT® exam, you should contact the schools that interest you to learn more about them and to ask about how they use GMAT® scores and other admissions criteria (such as your undergraduate grades, essays, and letters of recommendation) to evaluate candidates for admission. School admissions offices, school Web sites, and materials published by the school are the best sources for you to tap when you are doing research about where you might want to go to business school.

For more information about how schools should use GMAT® scores in admissions decisions, please read the Appendix A of this book. For more information on the GMAT®, registering to take the test, sending your scores to schools, and applying to business school, please visit our Web site at www.mba.com.

1.2 GMAT® Test Format

The GMAT® exam consists of four separately timed sections (see the table on the next page). You start the test with two 30-minute Analytical Writing Assessment (AWA) questions that require you to type your responses using the computer keyboard. The writing section is followed by two 75-minute, multiple-choice sections: the Quantitative and Verbal sections of the test.

The GMAT® is a computer-adaptive test (CAT), which means that in the multiple-choice sections of the test, the computer constantly gauges how well you are doing on the test and presents you with questions that are appropriate to your ability level. These questions are drawn from a huge pool of possible test questions. So, although we talk about the GMAT® as one test, the GMAT® exam you take may be completely different from the test of the person sitting next to you.

Here's how it works. At the start of each GMAT® multiple-choice section (Verbal and Quantitative), you will be presented with a question of moderate difficulty. The computer uses your response to that first question to determine which question to present next. If you respond correctly, the test usually will give you questions of increasing difficulty. If you respond incorrectly, the next question you see usually will be easier than the one you answered incorrectly. As you continue to respond to the questions presented, the computer will narrow your score to the number that best characterizes your ability. When you complete each section, the computer will have an accurate assessment of your ability.

Myth -vs- **FACT**

M – **Getting an easier question means I answered the last one wrong.**

F – **Getting an easier question does not necessarily mean you got the previous question wrong.**

To ensure that everyone receives the same content, the test selects a specific number of questions of each type. The test may call for your next question to be a relatively hard problem solving item involving arithmetic operations. But, if there are no more relatively difficult problem solving items involving arithmetic, you might be given an easier item.

Most people are not skilled at estimating item difficulty, so don't worry when taking the test or waste valuable time trying to determine the difficulty of the questions you are answering.

Because each question is presented on the basis of your answers to all previous questions, you must answer each question as it appears. You may not skip, return to, or change your responses to previous questions. Random guessing can significantly lower your scores. If you do not know the answer to a question, you should try to eliminate as many choices as possible, then select the answer you think is best. If you answer a question incorrectly by mistake—or correctly by lucky guess—your answers to subsequent questions will lead you back to questions that are at the appropriate level of difficulty for you.

Each multiple-choice question used in the GMAT® exam has been thoroughly reviewed by professional test developers. New multiple-choice questions are tested each time the exam is administered. Answers to trial questions are not counted in the scoring of your test, but the trial questions are not identified and could appear anywhere in the test. Therefore, you should try to do your best on every question.

The test includes the types of questions found in this *Guide*, but the format and presentation of the questions are different on the computer. When you take the exam:

- Only one question at a time is presented on the computer screen.

- The answer choices for the multiple-choice questions will be preceded by circles, rather than by letters.

- Different question types appear in random order in the multiple-choice sections of the test.

- You must select your answer using the computer.

- You must choose an answer and confirm your choice before moving on to the next question.

- You may not go back to change answers to previous questions.

Format of the GMAT®		
	Questions	Timing

Analytical Writing
    Analysis of an Issue
    Analysis of an Argument
	1
	1
		30 min.
		30 min.

Optional break		5 min.

Quantitative
    Problem Solving
    Data Sufficiency
	37	75 min.

Optional break		5 min.

Verbal
    Reading Comprehension
    Critical Reasoning
    Sentence Correction
	41	75 min.

	Total Time:	210–220 min.

1.3 What Is the Content of the Test Like?

It is important to recognize that the GMAT® test evaluates skills and abilities developed over a relatively long period of time. Although the sections contain questions that are basically verbal and mathematical, the complete test provides one method of measuring overall ability.

Keep in mind that although the questions in this *Guide* are arranged by question type and ordered from easy to difficult, the test is organized differently. When you take the test, you may see different types of questions in any order.

1.4 Quantitative Section

The GMAT® Quantitative section measures your ability to reason quantitatively, solve quantitative problems, and interpret graphic data.

Two types of multiple-choice questions are used in the Quantitative section:

- Problem solving
- Data sufficiency

Problem solving and data sufficiency questions are intermingled throughout the Quantitative section. Both types of questions require basic knowledge of:

- Arithmetic
- Elementary algebra
- Commonly known concepts of geometry

To review the basic mathematical concepts that will be tested in the GMAT® Quantitative questions, see the math review in chapter 3. For test-taking tips specific to the question types in the Quantitative section of the GMAT® exam, sample questions, and answer explanations, see chapters 4 and 5.

1.5 Verbal Section

The GMAT® Verbal section measures your ability to read and comprehend written material, to reason and evaluate arguments, and to correct written material to conform to standard written English. Because the Verbal section includes reading sections from several different content areas, you may be generally familiar with some of the material; however, neither the reading passages nor the questions assume detailed knowledge of the topics discussed.

Three types of multiple-choice questions are used in the Verbal section:

- Reading comprehension
- Critical reasoning
- Sentence correction

These question types are intermingled throughout the Verbal section.

1.6 What Computer Skills Will I Need?

You only need minimal computer skills to take the GMAT® Computer-Adaptive Test (CAT). You will be required to type your essays on the computer keyboard using standard word-processing keystrokes. In the multiple-choice sections, you will select your responses using either your mouse or the keyboard.

To learn more about the specific skills required to take the GMAT CAT®, download the free test-preparation software available at www.mba.com.

1.7 What Are the Test Centers Like?

The GMAT® test is administered at a test center providing the quiet and privacy of individual computer workstations. You will have the opportunity to take two five-minute breaks—one after completing the essays and another between the Quantitative and Verbal sections. An erasable notepad will be provided for your use during the test.

1.8 How Are Scores Calculated?

Your GMAT® scores are determined by:

- the number of questions you answer
- whether you answer correctly or incorrectly
- the level of difficulty and other statistical characteristics of each question

Your Verbal, Quantitative, and Total GMAT® scores are determined by a complex mathematical procedure that takes into account the difficulty of the questions that were presented to you and how you answered them. When you answer the easier questions correctly, you get a chance to answer harder questions—making it possible to earn a higher score. After you have completed all the questions on the test—or when your time is up—the computer will calculate your scores. Your scores on the Verbal and Quantitative sections are combined to produce your Total score. If you have not responded to all the questions in a section (37 Quantitative questions or 41 Verbal questions), your score is adjusted, using the proportion of questions answered.

Appendix A contains the 2007 percentile ranking tables that explain how your GMAT® scores compare with scores of other 2007 GMAT® test takers.

1.9 Analytical Writing Assessment Scores

The Analytical Writing Assessment consists of two writing tasks: Analysis of an Issue and Analysis of an Argument. The responses to each of these tasks are scored on a 6-point scale, with 6 being the highest score and 1, the lowest. A score of zero (0) is given to responses that are off-topic, are in a foreign language, merely attempt to copy the topic, consist only of keystroke characters, or are blank.

The readers who evaluate the responses are college and university faculty members from various subject matter areas, including management education. These readers read holistically—that is, they respond to the overall quality of your critical thinking and writing. (For details on how readers are qualified, visit www.mba.com.) In addition, responses may be scored by an automated scoring program designed to reflect the judgment of expert readers.

Each response is given two independent ratings. If the ratings differ by more than a point, a third reader adjudicates. (Because of ongoing training and monitoring, discrepant ratings are rare.)

Your final score is the average (rounded to the nearest half point) of the four scores independently assigned to your responses—two scores for the Analysis of an Issue and two for the Analysis of an Argument. For example, if you earned scores of 6 and 5 on the Analysis of an Issue and 4 and 4 on the Analysis of an Argument, your final score would be 5: $(6 + 5 + 4 + 4) \div 4 = 4.75$, which rounds up to 5.

Your Analytical Writing Assessment scores are computed and reported separately from the multiple-choice sections of the test and have no effect on your Verbal, Quantitative, or Total scores. The schools that you have designated to receive your scores may receive your responses to the Analytical Writing Assessment with your score report. Your own copy of your score report will not include copies of your responses.

1.10 Test Development Process

The GMAT® exam is developed by experts who use standardized procedures to ensure high-quality, widely appropriate test material. All questions are subjected to independent reviews and are revised or discarded as necessary. Multiple-choice questions are tested during GMAT® test administrations. Analytical Writing Assessment tasks are tried out on first-year business school students and then assessed for their fairness and reliability. For more information on test development, see www.mba.com.

2.0 How To Prepare

2.0 How To Prepare

2.1 How Can I Best Prepare to Take the Test?

We at the Graduate Management Admission Council® (GMAC®) firmly believe that the test-taking skills you can develop by using this book—and *The Official Guide for GMAT® Review, 11th Edition* if you want additional practice—are all you need to perform your best when you take the GMAT® test. By answering questions that have appeared on the GMAT® exam before, you will gain experience with the types of questions you may see on the test when you take it. As you practice with the *Guide*, you will develop confidence in your ability to reason through the test questions. No additional techniques or strategies are needed to do well on the standardized test if you develop a practical familiarity with the abilities it requires. Simply by practicing and understanding the concepts that are assessed on the exam, you will learn what you need to know to answer the questions correctly.

2.2 What About Practice Tests?

Because a computer-adaptive test cannot be presented in paper form, we have created GMATPrep® software to help you prepare for the exam. The software is available for download at no charge for those who have created a user profile on www.mba.com. It is also provided on a disk, by request, to anyone who has registered for the GMAT® test. The software includes two practice GMAT® tests, plus additional practice questions, information about the test, and tutorials to help you become familiar with how the GMAT® test will appear on the computer screen at the test center.

We recommend that you download the software as you start to prepare for the exam. Take one practice test to better familiarize yourself with the test and to get an idea of how you might score. After you have studied, using this book, and as your test date approaches, take the second practice test to determine whether you need to shift your focus to other areas you need to strengthen.

Myth -vs- **FACT**

M – **You need very advanced math skills to get a high GMAT® score.**

F – **The math skills tested on the GMAT® test are quite basic.**

The GMAT® exam only requires basic quantitative analytic skills. You should review the underlying math skills (algebra, geometry, basic arithmetic) presented in this book, but the required skill level is low. The difficulty of GMAT® Quantitative questions stems from the logic and analysis used to solve the problems and not the underlying math skills.

2.3 Where Can I Get Additional Practice?

If you complete all the questions in this book and would like additional practice, you may purchase *The Official Guide for GMAT® Review, 11th Edition* or *The Official Guide for GMAT® Verbal Review* at www.mba.com.

Note: There may be some overlap between this book and the review sections of the GMATPrep® software.

2.4 General Test-Taking Suggestions

Specific test-taking strategies for individual question types are presented later in this book. The following are general suggestions to help you perform your best on the test.

Use your time wisely.

Although the GMAT® exam stresses accuracy more than speed, it is important to use your time wisely. On average, you will have about 1¾ minutes for each verbal question and about 2 minutes for each quantitative question. Once you start the test, an onscreen clock will continuously count the time you have left. You can hide this display if you want, but it is a good idea to check the clock periodically to monitor your progress. The clock will automatically alert you when 5 minutes remain in the allotted time for the section you are working on.

Answer practice questions ahead of time.

After you become generally familiar with all question types, use the sample questions in this book to prepare for the actual test. It may be useful to time yourself as you answer the practice questions to get an idea of how long you will have for each question during the actual GMAT® test as well as to determine whether you are answering quickly enough to complete the test in the time allotted.

Read all test directions carefully.

The directions explain exactly what is required to answer each question type. If you read hastily, you may miss important instructions and lower your scores. To review directions during the test, click on the Help icon. But be aware that the time you spend reviewing directions will count against the time allotted for that section of the test.

Read each question carefully and thoroughly.

Before you answer a multiple-choice question, determine exactly what is being asked, then eliminate the wrong answers and select the best choice. Never skim a question or the possible answers; skimming may cause you to miss important information or nuances.

Do not spend too much time on any one question.

If you do not know the correct answer, or if the question is too time-consuming, try to eliminate choices you know are wrong, select the best of the remaining answer choices, and move on to the next question. Try not to worry about the impact on your score—guessing may lower your score, but not finishing the section will lower your score more.

Bear in mind that if you do not finish a section in the allotted time, you will still receive a score.

> *Myth* -vs- **FACT**
>
> ℳ – **It is more important to respond correctly to the test questions than it is to finish the test.**
>
> F – **There is a severe penalty for not completing the GMAT® test.**
>
> If you are stumped by a question, give it your best guess and move on. If you guess incorrectly, the computer program will likely give you an easier question, which you are likely to answer correctly, and the computer will rapidly return to giving you questions matched to your ability. If you don't finish the test, your score will be reduced greatly. Failing to answer five verbal questions, for example, could reduce a person's score from the 91st percentile to the 77th percentile. Pacing is important.

Confirm your answers ONLY when you are ready to move on.

Once you have selected your answer to a multiple-choice question, you will be asked to confirm it. Once you confirm your response, you cannot go back and change it. You may not skip questions, because the computer selects each question on the basis of your responses to preceding questions.

Plan your essay answers before you begin to write.

The best way to approach the two writing tasks comprised in the Analytical Writing Assessment section of the GMAT® exam is to read the directions carefully, take a few minutes to think about the question, and plan a response before you begin writing.

Take care to organize your ideas and develop them fully, but leave time to reread your response and make any revisions that you think would improve it.

Myth -vs- **FACT**

M – **The first 10 questions are critical and you should invest the most time on those.**

F – **All questions count.**

It is true that the computer-adaptive testing algorithm uses the first 10 questions to obtain an initial estimate of your ability; however, that is only an *initial* estimate. As you continue to answer questions, the algorithm self-corrects by computing an updated estimate on the basis of all the questions you have taken, and then administers items that are closely matched to this new estimate of your ability. Your final score is based on all your responses and considers the difficulty of all the questions you answered. Taking additional time on the first 10 questions will not game the system and can hurt your ability to finish the test.

3.0   Math Review

3.0 Math Review

Although this chapter provides a review of some of the mathematical concepts of arithmetic, algebra, and geometry, it is not intended to be a textbook. You should use this chapter to familiarize yourself with the kinds of topics that are tested in the GMAT® exam. You may wish to consult an arithmetic, algebra, or geometry book for a more detailed discussion of some of the topics.

The topics that are covered in section 3.1, "Arithmetic," include the following:

1. Properties of Integers
2. Fractions
3. Decimals
4. Real Numbers
5. Ratio and Proportion
6. Percents
7. Powers and Roots of Numbers
8. Descriptive Statistics
9. Sets
10. Counting Methods
11. Discrete Probability

The content of section 3.2, "Algebra," does not extend beyond what is usually covered in a first-year high school algebra course. The topics included are as follows:

1. Simplifying Algebraic Expressions
2. Equations
3. Solving Linear Equations with One Unknown
4. Solving Two Linear Equations with Two Unknowns
5. Solving Equations by Factoring
6. Solving Quadratic Equations
7. Exponents
8. Inequalities
9. Absolute Value
10. Functions

Section 3.3, "Geometry," is limited primarily to measurement and intuitive geometry or spatial visualization. Extensive knowledge of theorems and the ability to construct proofs, skills that are usually developed in a formal geometry course, are not tested. The topics included in this section are the following:

1. Lines
2. Intersecting Lines and Angles
3. Perpendicular Lines
4. Parallel Lines
5. Polygons (Convex)
6. Triangles
7. Quadrilaterals
8. Circles
9. Rectangular Solids and Cylinders
10. Coordinate Geometry

Section 3.4, "Word Problems," presents examples of and solutions to the following types of word problems:

1. Rate Problems
2. Work Problems
3. Mixture Problems
4. Interest Problems
5. Discount
6. Profit
7. Sets
8. Geometry Problems
9. Measurement Problems
10. Data Interpretation

3.1 Arithmetic

1. Properties of Integers

An *integer* is any number in the set {. . . –3, –2, –1, 0, 1, 2, 3, . . .}. If x and y are integers and $x \neq 0$, then x is a *divisor* (*factor*) of y provided that $y = xn$ for some integer n. In this case, y is also said to be *divisible* by x or to be a *multiple* of x. For example, 7 is a divisor or factor of 28 since 28 = (7)(4), but 8 is not a divisor of 28 since there is no integer n such that 28 = 8n.

If x and y are positive integers, there exist unique integers q and r, called the *quotient* and *remainder*, respectively, such that $y = xq + r$ and $0 \leq r < x$. For example, when 28 is divided by 8, the quotient is 3 and the remainder is 4 since 28 = (8)(3) + 4. Note that y is divisible by x if and only if the remainder r is 0; for example, 32 has a remainder of 0 when divided by 8 because 32 is divisible by 8. Also, note that when a smaller integer is divided by a larger integer, the quotient is 0 and the remainder is the smaller integer. For example, 5 divided by 7 has the quotient 0 and the remainder 5 since 5 = (7)(0) + 5.

Any integer that is divisible by 2 is an *even integer*; the set of even integers is {. . . –4, –2, 0, 2, 4, 6, 8, . . .}. Integers that are not divisible by 2 are *odd integers*; {. . . –3, –1, 1, 3, 5, . . .} is the set of odd integers.

If at least one factor of a product of integers is even, then the product is even; otherwise the product is odd. If two integers are both even or both odd, then their sum and their difference are even. Otherwise, their sum and their difference are odd.

A *prime* number is a positive integer that has exactly two different positive divisors, 1 and itself. For example, 2, 3, 5, 7, 11, and 13 are prime numbers, but 15 is not, since 15 has four different positive divisors, 1, 3, 5, and 15. The number 1 is not a prime number since it has only one positive divisor. Every integer greater than 1 either is prime or can be uniquely expressed as a product of prime factors. For example, 14 = (2)(7), 81 = (3)(3)(3)(3), and 484 = (2)(2)(11)(11).

The numbers –2, –1, 0, 1, 2, 3, 4, 5 are *consecutive integers*. Consecutive integers can be represented by n, $n + 1$, $n + 2$, $n + 3$, . . . , where n is an integer. The numbers 0, 2, 4, 6, 8 are *consecutive even integers*, and 1, 3, 5, 7, 9 are *consecutive odd integers*. Consecutive even integers can be represented by $2n$, $2n + 2$, $2n + 4$, . . . , and consecutive odd integers can be represented by $2n + 1$, $2n + 3$, $2n + 5$, . . . , where n is an integer.

Properties of the integer 1. If n is any number, then $1 \cdot n = n$, and for any number $n \neq 0$, $n \cdot \dfrac{1}{n} = 1$.

The number 1 can be expressed in many ways; for example, $\dfrac{n}{n} = 1$ for any number $n \neq 0$.

Multiplying or dividing an expression by 1, in any form, does not change the value of that expression.

Properties of the integer 0. The integer 0 is neither positive nor negative. If n is any number, then $n + 0 = n$ and $n \cdot 0 = 0$. Division by 0 is not defined.

2. Fractions

In a fraction $\frac{n}{d}$, n is the *numerator* and d is the *denominator*. The denominator of a fraction can never be 0, because division by 0 is not defined.

Two fractions are said to be *equivalent* if they represent the same number. For example, $\frac{8}{36}$ and $\frac{14}{63}$ are equivalent since they both represent the number $\frac{2}{9}$. In each case, the fraction is reduced to lowest terms by dividing both numerator and denominator by their *greatest common divisor* (gcd). The gcd of 8 and 36 is 4 and the gcd of 14 and 63 is 7.

Addition and subtraction of fractions.

Two fractions with the same denominator can be added or subtracted by performing the required operation with the numerators, leaving the denominators the same. For example, $\frac{3}{5} + \frac{4}{5} = \frac{3+4}{5} = \frac{7}{5}$, and $\frac{5}{7} - \frac{2}{7} = \frac{5-2}{7} = \frac{3}{7}$. If two fractions do not have the same denominator, express them as equivalent fractions with the same denominator. For example, to add $\frac{3}{5}$ and $\frac{4}{7}$, multiply the numerator and denominator of the first fraction by 7 and the numerator and denominator of the second fraction by 5, obtaining $\frac{21}{35}$ and $\frac{20}{35}$, respectively; $\frac{21}{35} + \frac{20}{35} = \frac{41}{35}$.

For the new denominator, choosing the *least common multiple* (lcm) of the denominators usually lessens the work. For $\frac{2}{3} + \frac{1}{6}$, the lcm of 3 and 6 is 6 (not $3 \times 6 = 18$), so

$$\frac{2}{3} + \frac{1}{6} = \frac{2}{3} \times \frac{2}{2} + \frac{1}{6} = \frac{4}{6} + \frac{1}{6} = \frac{5}{6}.$$

Multiplication and division of fractions.

To multiply two fractions, simply multiply the two numerators and multiply the two denominators. For example, $\frac{2}{3} \times \frac{4}{7} = \frac{2 \times 4}{3 \times 7} = \frac{8}{21}$.

To divide by a fraction, invert the divisor (that is, find its *reciprocal*) and multiply. For example

$$\frac{2}{3} \div \frac{4}{7} = \frac{2}{3} \times \frac{7}{4} = \frac{14}{12} = \frac{7}{6}.$$

In the problem above, the reciprocal of $\frac{4}{7}$ is $\frac{7}{4}$. In general, the reciprocal of a fraction $\frac{n}{d}$ is $\frac{d}{n}$ where n and d are not zero.

Mixed numbers.

A number that consists of a whole number and a fraction, for example, $7\frac{2}{3}$, is a mixed number: $7\frac{2}{3}$ means $7 + \frac{2}{3}$.

To change a mixed number into a fraction, multiply the whole number by the denominator of the fraction and add this number to the numerator of the fraction; then put the result over the denominator of the fraction. For example, $7\frac{2}{3} = \frac{(3 \times 7) + 2}{3} = \frac{23}{3}$.

3. Decimals

In the decimal system, the position of the period or *decimal point* determines the place value of the digits. For example, the digits in the number 7,654.321 have the following place values:

Thousands		Hundreds	Tens	Ones or units		Tenths	Hundredths	Thousandths
7	,	6	5	4	.	3	2	1

Some examples of decimals follow.

$$0.321 = \frac{3}{10} + \frac{2}{100} + \frac{1}{1,000} = \frac{321}{1,000}$$

$$0.0321 = \frac{0}{10} + \frac{3}{100} + \frac{2}{1,000} + \frac{1}{10,000} = \frac{321}{10,000}$$

$$1.56 = 1 + \frac{5}{10} + \frac{6}{100} = \frac{156}{100}$$

Sometimes decimals are expressed as the product of a number with only one digit to the left of the decimal point and a power of 10. This is called *scientific notation*. For example, 231 can be written as 2.31×10^2 and 0.0231 can be written as 2.31×10^{-2}. When a number is expressed in scientific notation, the exponent of the 10 indicates the number of places that the decimal point is to be moved in the number that is to be multiplied by a power of 10 in order to obtain the product. The decimal point is moved to the right if the exponent is positive and to the left if the exponent is negative. For example, 20.13×10^3 is equal to 20,130 and 1.91×10^{-4} is equal to 0.000191.

Addition and subtraction of decimals.

To add or subtract two decimals, the decimal points of both numbers should be lined up. If one of the numbers has fewer digits to the right of the decimal point than the other, zeros may be inserted to the right of the last digit. For example, to add 17.6512 and 653.27, set up the numbers in a column and add:

$$
\begin{array}{r}
17.6512 \\
+\ 653.2700 \\
\hline
670.9212
\end{array}
$$

Likewise for 653.27 minus 17.6512:

$$
\begin{array}{r}
653.2700 \\
-17.6512 \\
\hline
635.6188
\end{array}
$$

Multiplication of decimals.

To multiply decimals, multiply the numbers as if they were whole numbers and then insert the decimal point in the product so that the number of digits to the right of the decimal point is equal to the sum of the numbers of digits to the right of the decimal points in the numbers being multiplied. For example:

$$
\begin{array}{rl}
2.09 & \text{(2 digits to the right)} \\
\times\ 1.3 & \text{(1 digit to the right)} \\
\hline
627 & \\
209 & \\
\hline
2.717 & \text{(2+1=3 digits to the right)}
\end{array}
$$

Division of decimals.

To divide a number (the dividend) by a decimal (the divisor), move the decimal point of the divisor to the right until the divisor is a whole number. Then move the decimal point of the dividend the same number of places to the right, and divide as you would by a whole number. The decimal point in the quotient will be directly above the decimal point in the new dividend. For example, to divide 698.12 by 12.4:

$$
12.4\overline{)698.12}
$$

will be replaced by:

$$
124\overline{)6981.2}
$$

and the division would proceed as follows:

$$
\begin{array}{r}
56.3 \\
124\overline{)6981.2} \\
\underline{620} \\
781 \\
\underline{744} \\
372 \\
\underline{372} \\
0
\end{array}
$$

4. Real Numbers

All *real* numbers correspond to points on the number line and all points on the number line correspond to real numbers. All real numbers except zero are either positive or negative.

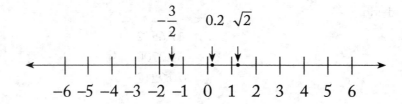

On a number line, numbers corresponding to points to the left of zero are negative and numbers corresponding to points to the right of zero are positive. For any two numbers on the number line, the number to the left is less than the number to the right; for example,

$$-4 < -3 < -\frac{3}{2} < -1, \text{ and } 1 < \sqrt{2} < 2.$$

To say that the number n is between 1 and 4 on the number line means that $n > 1$ and $n < 4$, that is, $1 < n < 4$. If n is "between 1 and 4, inclusive," then $1 \le n \le 4$.

The distance between a number and zero on the number line is called the *absolute value* of the number. Thus 3 and –3 have the same absolute value, 3, since they are both three units from zero. The absolute value of 3 is denoted $|3|$. Examples of absolute values of numbers are

$$|-5| = |5| = 5, \left|-\frac{7}{2}\right| = \frac{7}{2}, \text{ and } |0| = 0$$

Note that the absolute value of any nonzero number is positive.

Here are some properties of real numbers that are used frequently. If x, y, and z are real numbers, then

(1) $x + y = y + x$ and $xy = yx$.
    For example, $8 + 3 = 3 + 8 = 11$, and $(17)(5) = (5)(17) = 85$.

(2) $(x + y) + z = x + (y + z)$ and $(xy)z = x(yz)$.
    For example, $(7 + 5) + 2 = 7 + (5 + 2) = 7 + (7) = 14$, and $\left(5\sqrt{3}\right)\left(\sqrt{3}\right) = \left(5\sqrt{3}\ \sqrt{3}\right) = (5)(3) = 15$.

(3) $x(y + z) = xy + xz$.
    For example, $718(36) + 718(64) = 718(36 + 64) = 718(100) = 71,800$.

(4) If x and y are both positive, then $x + y$ and xy are positive.

(5) If x and y are both negative, then $x + y$ is negative and xy is positive.

(6) If x is positive and y is negative, then xy is negative.

(7) If $xy = 0$, then $x = 0$ or $y = 0$. For example, $3y = 0$ implies $y = 0$.

(8) $|x + y| \le |x| + |y|$. For example, if $x = 10$ and $y = 2$, then $|x + y| = |12| = 12 = |x| + |y|$; and if $x = 10$ and $y = -2$, then $|x + y| = |8| = 8 < 12 = |x| + |y|$.

5. Ratio and Proportion

The *ratio* of the number a to the number b ($b \neq 0$) is $\dfrac{a}{b}$.

A ratio may be expressed or represented in several ways. For example, the ratio of 2 to 3 can be written as 2 to 3, 2:3, or $\dfrac{2}{3}$. The order of the terms of a ratio is important. For example, the ratio of the number of months with exactly 30 days to the number with exactly 31 days is $\dfrac{4}{7}$, not $\dfrac{7}{4}$.

A *proportion* is a statement that two ratios are equal; for example, $\dfrac{2}{3} = \dfrac{8}{12}$ is a proportion. One way to solve a proportion involving an unknown is to cross multiply, obtaining a new equality. For example, to solve for n in the proportion $\dfrac{2}{3} = \dfrac{n}{12}$, cross multiply, obtaining $24 = 3n$; then divide both sides by 3, to get $n = 8$.

6. Percents

Percent means *per hundred* or *number out of 100*. A percent can be represented as a fraction with a denominator of 100, or as a decimal. For example, $37\% = \dfrac{37}{100} = 0.37$.

To find a certain percent of a number, multiply the number by the percent expressed as a decimal or fraction. For example:

$$20\% \text{ of } 90 = 0.2 \times 90 = 18$$
$$\text{or}$$
$$20\% \text{ of } 90 = \frac{20}{100} \times 90 = \frac{1}{5} \times 90 = 18.$$

Percents greater than 100%.

Percents greater than 100% are represented by numbers greater than 1. For example:

$$300\% = \frac{300}{100} = 3$$
$$250\% \text{ of } 80 = 2.5 \times 80 = 200.$$

Percents less than 1%.

The percent 0.5 % means $\dfrac{1}{2}$ of 1 percent. For example, 0.5 % of 12 is equal to $0.005 \times 12 = 0.06$.

Percent change.

Often a problem will ask for the percent increase or decrease from one quantity to another quantity. For example, "If the price of an item increases from \$24 to \$30, what is the percent increase in price?" To find the percent increase, first find the amount of the increase; then divide this increase by the original amount, and express this quotient as a percent. In the example above, the percent increase would be found in the following way: the amount of the increase is $(30 - 24) = 6$. Therefore, the percent increase is $\dfrac{6}{24} = 0.25 = 25\%$.

Likewise, to find the percent decrease (for example, the price of an item is reduced from \$30 to \$24), first find the amount of the decrease; then divide this decrease by the original amount, and express this quotient as a percent. In the example above, the amount of decrease is $(30 - 24) = 6$. Therefore, the percent decrease is $\dfrac{6}{30} = 0.20 = 20\%$.

Note that the percent increase from 24 to 30 is not the same as the percent decrease from 30 to 24.

In the following example, the increase is greater than 100 percent: If the cost of a certain house in 1983 was 300 percent of its cost in 1970, by what percent did the cost increase?

If n is the cost in 1970, then the percent increase is equal to $\dfrac{3n - n}{n} = \dfrac{2n}{n} = 2$, or 200%.

7. Powers and Roots of Numbers

When a number k is to be used n times as a factor in a product, it can be expressed as k^n, which means the nth power of k. For example, $2^2 = 2 \times 2 = 4$ and $2^3 = 2 \times 2 \times 2 = 8$ are powers of 2.

Squaring a number that is greater than 1, or raising it to a higher power, results in a larger number; squaring a number between 0 and 1 results in a smaller number. For example:

$$3^2 = 9 \qquad\qquad (9 > 3)$$

$$\left(\frac{1}{3}\right)^2 = \frac{1}{9} \qquad\qquad \left(\frac{1}{9} < \frac{1}{3}\right)$$

$$(0.1)^2 = 0.01 \qquad\qquad (0.01 < 0.1)$$

A *square root* of a number n is a number that, when squared, is equal to n. The square root of a negative number is not a real number. Every positive number n has two square roots, one positive and the other negative, but $\sqrt{n}$ denotes the positive number whose square is n. For example, $\sqrt{9}$ denotes 3. The two square roots of 9 are $\sqrt{9} = 3$ and $-\sqrt{9} = -3$.

Every real number r has exactly one real *cube root*, which is the number s such that $s^3 = r$. The real cube root of r is denoted by $\sqrt[3]{r}$. Since $2^3 = 8$, $\sqrt[3]{8} = 2$. Similarly, $\sqrt[3]{-8} = -2$, because $(-2)^3 = -8$.

8. Descriptive Statistics

A list of numbers, or numerical data, can be described by various statistical measures. One of the most common of these measures is the *average*, or *(arithmetic) mean*, which locates a type of "center" for the data. The average of n numbers is defined as the sum of the n numbers divided by n. For example, the average of 6, 4, 7, 10, and 4 is $\dfrac{6 + 4 + 7 + 10 + 4}{5} = \dfrac{31}{5} = 6.2$.

The *median* is another type of center for a list of numbers. To calculate the median of n numbers, first order the numbers from least to greatest; if n is odd, the median is defined as the middle number, whereas if n is even, the median is defined as the average of the two middle numbers. In the example above, the numbers, in order, are 4, 4, 6, 7, 10, and the median is 6, the middle number.

For the numbers 4, 6, 6, 8, 9, 12, the median is $\dfrac{6+8}{2} = 7$. Note that the mean of these numbers is 7.5.

The median of a set of data can be less than, equal to, or greater than the mean. Note that for a large set of data (for example, the salaries of 800 company employees), it is often true that about half of the data is less than the median and about half of the data is greater than the median; but this is not always the case, as the following data show.

3, 5, 7, 7, 7, 7, 7, 7, 8, 9, 9, 9, 9, 10, 10

Here the median is 7, but only $\dfrac{2}{15}$ of the data is less than the median.

The *mode* of a list of numbers is the number that occurs most frequently in the list. For example, the mode of 1, 3, 6, 4, 3, 5 is 3. A list of numbers may have more than one mode. For example, the list 1, 2, 3, 3, 3, 5, 7, 10, 10, 10, 20 has two modes, 3 and 10.

The degree to which numerical data are spread out or dispersed can be measured in many ways. The simplest measure of dispersion is the *range*, which is defined as the greatest value in the numerical data minus the least value. For example, the range of 11, 10, 5, 13, 21 is $21 - 5 = 16$. Note how the range depends on only two values in the data.

One of the most common measures of dispersion is the *standard deviation*. Generally speaking, the more the data are spread away from the mean, the greater the standard deviation. The standard deviation of n numbers can be calculated as follows: (1) find the arithmetic mean, (2) find the differences between the mean and each of the n numbers, (3) square each of the differences, (4) find the average of the squared differences, and (5) take the nonnegative square root of this average. Shown below is this calculation for the data 0, 7, 8, 10, 10, which have arithmetic mean 7.

x	$x - 7$	$(x - 7)^2$
0	-7	49
7	0	0
8	1	1
10	3	9
10	3	9
	Total	68

Standard deviation $\sqrt{\dfrac{68}{5}} \approx 3.7$

Notice that the standard deviation depends on every data value, although it depends most on values that are farthest from the mean. This is why a distribution with data grouped closely around the mean will have a smaller standard deviation than will data spread far from the mean. To illustrate this, compare the data 6, 6, 6.5, 7.5, 9, which also have mean 7. Note that the numbers in the second set of data seem to be grouped more closely around the mean of 7 than the numbers in the first set. This is reflected in the standard deviation, which is less for the second set (approximately 1.1) than for the first set (approximately 3.7).

There are many ways to display numerical data that show how the data are distributed. One simple way is with a *frequency distribution*, which is useful for data that have values occurring with varying frequencies. For example, the 20 numbers

$$-4 \quad 0 \quad 0 \quad -3 \quad -2 \quad -1 \quad -1 \quad 0 \quad -1 \quad -4$$
$$-1 \quad -5 \quad 0 \quad -2 \quad 0 \quad -5 \quad -2 \quad 0 \quad 0 \quad -1$$

are displayed on the next page in a frequency distribution by listing each different value x and the frequency f with which x occurs.

Data Value x	Frequency y
−5	2
−4	2
−3	1
−2	3
−1	5
0	7
Total	20

From the frequency distribution, one can readily compute descriptive statistics:

Mean: $= \dfrac{(-5)(2)+(-4)(2)+(-3)(1)+(-2)(3)+(-1)(5)+(0)(7)}{20} = -1.6$

Median: −1 (the average of the 10th and 11th numbers)
Mode: 0 (the number that occurs most frequently)
Range: 0 − (−5) = 5

Standard deviation: $\sqrt{\dfrac{(-5+1.6)^2(2)+(-4+1.6)^2(2)+...+(0+1.6)^2(7)}{20}} \approx 1$

9. Sets

In mathematics a *set* is a collection of numbers or other objects. The objects are called the *element*s of the set. If S is a set having a finite number of elements, then the number of elements is denoted by $|S|$. Such a set is often defined by listing its elements; for example, $S = \{-5,0,1\}$ is a set with $|S| = 3$. The order in which the elements are listed in a set does not matter; thus $\{-5, 0, 1\} = \{0, 1, -5\}$. If all the elements of a set S are also elements of a set T, then S is a *subset* of T; for example, $S = \{-5, 0, 1\}$ is a subset of $T = \{-5, 0, 1, 4, 10\}$.

For any two sets A and B, the *union* of A and B is the set of all elements that are in A or in B or in both. The *intersection* of A and B is the set of all elements that are both in A and in B. The union is denoted by $A \cup B$ and the intersection is denoted by $A \cap B$. As an example, if $A = \{3, 4\}$ and $B = \{4, 5, 6\}$, then $A \cup B = \{3, 4, 5, 6\}$ and $A \cap B = \{4\}$. Two sets that have no elements in common are said to be *disjoint* or *mutually exclusive*.

The relationship between sets is often illustrated with a *Venn diagram* in which sets are represented by regions in a plane. For two sets S and T that are not disjoint and neither is a subset of the other, the intersection $S \cap T$ is represented by the shaded region of the diagram below.

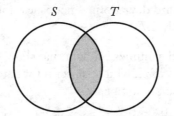

This diagram illustrates a fact about any two finite sets S and T: the number of elements in their union equals the sum of their individual numbers of elements minus the number of elements in their intersection (because the latter are counted twice in the sum); more concisely,

$$|S \cup T| = |S| + |T| - |S \cap T|.$$

This counting method is called the general addition rule for two sets. As a special case, if S and T are disjoint, then

$$|S \cup T| = |S| + |T|$$

since $|S \cap T| = 0$.

10. Counting Methods

There are some useful methods for counting objects and sets of objects without actually listing the elements to be counted. The following principle of multiplication is fundamental to these methods.

If an object is to be chosen from a set of m objects and a second object is to be chosen from a different set of n objects, then there are mn ways of choosing both objects simultaneously.

As an example, suppose the objects are items on a menu. If a meal consists of one entree and one dessert and there are 5 entrees and 3 desserts on the menu, then there are $5 \times 3 = 15$ different meals that can be ordered from the menu. As another example, each time a coin is flipped, there are two possible outcomes, heads and tails. If an experiment consists of 8 consecutive coin flips, then the experiment has 2^8 possible outcomes, where each of these outcomes is a list of heads and tails in some order.

A symbol that is often used with the multiplication principle is the *factorial*. If n is an integer greater than 1, then n factorial, denoted by the symbol $n!$, is defined as the product of all the integers from 1 to n. Therefore,

$$2! = (1)(2) = 2,$$
$$3! = (1)(2)(3) = 6,$$
$$4! = (1)(2)(3)(4) = 24, \text{ etc.}$$

Also, by definition, $0! = 1! = 1$.

The factorial is useful for counting the number of ways that a set of objects can be ordered. If a set of n objects is to be ordered from 1st to nth, then there are n choices for the 1st object, $n - 1$ choices for the 2nd object, $n - 2$ choices for the 3rd object, and so on, until there is only 1 choice for the nth object. Thus, by the multiplication principle, the number of ways of ordering the n objects is

$$n(n - 1)(n - 2) \cdots (3)(2)(1) = n!.$$

For example, the number of ways of ordering the letters A, B, and C is $3!$, or 6:

ABC, ACB, BAC, BCA, CAB, and CBA.

These orderings are called the *permutations* of the letters A, B, and C.

A permutation can be thought of as a selection process in which objects are selected one by one in a certain order. If the order of selection is not relevant and only k objects are to be selected from a larger set of n objects, a different counting method is employed. Specifically, consider a set of n

objects from which a complete selection of k objects is to be made without regard to order, where $0 \leq k \leq n$. Then the number of possible complete selections of k objects is called the number of *combinations* of n objects taken k at a time and is denoted by $\binom{n}{k}$. The value of $\binom{n}{k}$ is given by $\binom{n}{k} = \dfrac{n!}{k!(n-k)!}$.

Note that $\binom{n}{k}$ is the number of k-element subsets of a set with n elements. For example, if $S = \{A, B, C, D, E\}$, then the number of 2-element subsets of S, or the number of combinations of 5 letters taken 2 at a time, is $\binom{5}{2} = \dfrac{5!}{2!3!} = \dfrac{120}{(2)(6)} = 10.$

The subsets are $\{A, B\}$, $\{A, C\}$, $\{A, D\}$, $\{A, E\}$, $\{B, C\}$, $\{B, D\}$, $\{B, E\}$, $\{C, D\}$, $\{C, E,\}$, and $\{D, E\}$.

Note that $\binom{5}{2} = 10 = \binom{5}{3}$ because every 2-element subset chosen from a set of 5 elements corresponds to a unique 3-element subset consisting of the elements *not* chosen.

In general, $\binom{n}{k} = \binom{n}{n-k}$.

11. Discrete Probability

Many of the ideas discussed in the preceding three topics are important to the study of discrete probability. Discrete probability is concerned with *experiments* that have a finite number of *outcomes*. Given such an experiment, an *event* is a particular set of outcomes. For example, rolling a number cube with faces numbered 1 to 6 (similar to a 6-sided die) is an experiment with 6 possible outcomes: 1, 2, 3, 4, 5, or 6. One event in this experiment is that the outcome is 4, denoted $\{4\}$; another event is that the outcome is an odd number: $\{1, 3, 5\}$.

The probability than an event E occurs, denoted by $P(E)$, is a number between 0 and 1, inclusive. If E has no outcomes, then E is *impossible* and $P(E) = 0$; if E is the set of all possible outcomes of the experiment, then E is *certain* to occur and $P(E) = 1$. Otherwise, E is possible but uncertain, and $0 < P(E) < 1$. If F is a subset of E, then $P(F) \leq P(E)$. In the example above, if the probability of each of the 6 outcomes is the same, then the probability of each outcome is $\dfrac{1}{6}$, and the outcomes are said to be *equally likely*. For experiments in which all the individual outcomes are equally likely, the probability of an event E is

$$P(E) = \frac{\text{The number of outcomes in } E}{\text{The total number of possible outcomes}}.$$

In the example, the probability that the outcome is an odd number is

$$P(\{1,3,5\}) = \frac{|\{1,3,5\}|}{6} = \frac{3}{6}.$$

Given an experiment with events E and F, the following events are defined:

"*not E*" is the set of outcomes that are not outcomes in E;

"*E or F*" is the set of outcomes in E or F or both, that is, $E \cup F$;

"*E and F*" is the set of outcomes in both E and F, that is, $E \cap F$.

The probability that E does not occur is $P(\text{not } E) = 1 - P(E)$. The probability that "*E or F*" occurs is $P(E \text{ or } F) = P(E) + P(F) - P(E \text{ and } F)$, using the general addition rule at the end of section 3.1.9 ("Sets"). For the number cube, if E is the event that the outcome is an odd number, $\{1, 3, 5\}$, and F is the event that the outcome is a prime number, $\{2, 3, 5\}$, then $P(E \text{ and } F) = P(\{3,5\}) = \dfrac{2}{6}$ and so $P(E \text{ or } F) = P(E) - P(E \text{ and } F) = \dfrac{3}{6} + \dfrac{3}{6} - \dfrac{2}{6} = \dfrac{4}{6}$.

Note that the event "*E or F*" is $E \cup F = \{1,2,3,5\}$, and hence $P(E \text{ of } F) = \dfrac{|\{1,2,3,5\}|}{6} = \dfrac{4}{6}$.

If the event "*E and F*" is impossible (that is, $E \cap F$ has no outcomes), then E and F are said to be *mutually exclusive* events, and $P(E \text{ and } F) = 0$. Then the general addition rule is reduced to $P(E \text{ or } F) = P(E) + P(F)$.

This is the special addition rule for the probability of two mutually exclusive events.

Two events A and B are said to be *independent* if the occurrence of either event does not alter the probability that the other event occurs. For one roll of the number cube, let $A = \{2, 4, 6\}$ and let $B = \{5, 6\}$. Then the probability that A occurs is $P(A) = \dfrac{|A|}{6} = \dfrac{3}{6} = \dfrac{1}{2}$, while, *presuming B occurs*, the probability that A occurs is

$$\frac{|A \cap B|}{|B|} = \frac{|\{6\}|}{|\{5,6\}|} = \frac{1}{2}.$$

Similarly, the probability that B occurs is $P(B) = \dfrac{|B|}{6} = \dfrac{2}{6} = \dfrac{1}{3}$, while, *presuming A occurs*, the probability that B occurs is

$$\frac{|B \cap A|}{|A|} = \frac{|\{6\}|}{|\{2,4,6\}|} = \frac{1}{3}.$$

Thus, the occurrence of either event does not affect the probability that the other event occurs. Therefore, A and B are independent.

The following multiplication rule holds for any independent events E and F:

$P(E \text{ and } F) = P(E) P(F)$.

For the independent events A and B above, $P(A \text{ and } B) = P(A)P(B) = \left(\dfrac{1}{2}\right)\left(\dfrac{1}{3}\right) = \left(\dfrac{1}{6}\right)$.

Note that the event "*A and B*" is $A \cap B = \{6\}$, and hence $P(A \text{ and } B) = P(\{6\}) = \dfrac{1}{6}$. It follows from the general addition rule and the multiplication rule above that if E and F are independent, then

$$P(E \text{ or } F) = P(E) + P(F) - P(E) P(F).$$

For a final example of some of these rules, consider an experiment with events A, B, and C for which $P(A) = 0.23$, $P(B) = 0.40$, and $P(C) = 0.85$. Also, suppose that events A and B are mutually exclusive and events B and C are independent. Then

$$P(A \text{ or } B) = P(A) + P(B) \qquad \text{(since } A \text{ and } B \text{ are mutually exclusive)}$$

$$= 0.23 + 0.40$$

$$= 0.63$$

$$P(B \text{ or } C) = P(B) + P(C) - P(B)P(C) \qquad \text{(by independence)}$$

$$= 0.40 + 0.85 - (0.40)(0.85)$$

$$= 0.91$$

Note that $P(A \text{ or } C)$ and $P(A \text{ and } C)$ cannot be determined using the information given. But it can be determined that A and C are *not* mutually exclusive since $P(A) + P(C) = 1.08$, which is greater than 1, and therefore cannot equal $P(A \text{ or } C)$; from this it follows that $P(A \text{ and } C) \geq 0.08$. One can also deduce that $P(A \text{ and } C) \leq P(A) = 0.23$, since $A \cap C$ is a subset of A, and that $P(A \text{ and } C) \leq P(C) = 0.85$ since C is a subset of $A \cup C$. Thus, one can conclude that $0.85 \leq P(A \text{ or } C) \leq 1$ and $0.08 \leq P(A \text{ and } C) \leq 0.23$.

3.2 Algebra

Algebra is based on the operations of arithmetic and on the concept of an *unknown quantity*, or *variable*. Letters such as x or n are used to represent unknown quantities. For example, suppose Pam has 5 more pencils than Fred. If F represents the number of pencils that Fred has, then the number of pencils that Pam has is $F + 5$. As another example, if Jim's present salary S is increased by 7%, then his new salary is $1.07S$. A combination of letters and arithmetic operations, such as

$$F + 5, \quad \frac{3x^2}{2x - 5}, \text{ and } 19x^2 - 6x + 3, \text{ is called an } \textit{algebraic expression.}$$

The expression $19x^2 - 6x + 3$ consists of the *terms* $19x^2$, $-6x$, and 3, where 19 is the *coefficient* of x^2, -6 is the coefficient of x^1, and 3 is a *constant term* (or coefficient of $x^0 = 1$). Such an expression is called a *second degree* (or *quadratic*) *polynomial in* x since the highest power of x is 2. The expression $F + 5$ is a *first degree* (or *linear*) *polynomial in* F since the highest power of F is 1. The expression $\frac{3x^2}{2x - 5}$ is not a polynomial because it is not a sum of terms that are each powers of x multiplied by coefficients.

1. Simplifying Algebraic Expressions

Often when working with algebraic expressions, it is necessary to simplify them by factoring or combining *like* terms. For example, the expression $6x + 5x$ is equivalent to $(6 + 5)x$, or $11x$. In the expression $9x - 3y$, 3 is a factor common to both terms: $9x - 3y = 3(3x - y)$. In the expression $5x^2 + 6y$, there are no like terms and no common factors.

If there are common factors in the numerator and denominator of an expression, they can be divided out, provided that they are not equal to zero.

For example, if $x \neq 3$, then $\dfrac{x-3}{x-3}$ is equal to 1; therefore,

$$\frac{3xy - 9y}{x - 3} = \frac{3y(x-3)}{x-3}$$
$$= (3y)(1)$$
$$= 3y.$$

To multiply two algebraic expressions, each term of one expression is multiplied by each term of the other expression. For example:

$$(3x - 4)(9y + x) = 3x(9y + x) - 4(9y + x)$$

$$= (3x)(9y) + (3x)(x) + (-4)(9y) + (-4)(x)$$

$$= 27xy + 3x^2 - 36y - 4x$$

An algebraic expression can be evaluated by substituting values of the unknowns in the expression. For example, if $x = 3$ and $y = -2$, then $3xy - x^2 + y$ can be evaluated as

$$3(3)(-2) - (3)^2 + (-2) = -18 - 9 - 2 = -29$$

2. Equations

A major focus of algebra is to solve equations involving algebraic expressions. Some examples of such equations are

$$5x - 2 = 9 - x \quad \text{(a linear equation with one unknown)}$$
$$3x + 1 = y - 2 \quad \text{(a linear equation with two unknowns)}$$
$$5x^2 + 3x - 2 = 7x \quad \text{(a quadratic equation with one unknown)}$$
$$\frac{x(x-3)(x^2+5)}{x-4} = 0 \quad \text{(an equation that is factored on one side with } \mathbf{0} \text{ on the other)}$$

The *solutions* of an equation with one or more unknowns are those values that make the equation true, or "satisfy the equation," when they are substituted for the unknowns of the equation. An equation may have no solution or one or more solutions. If two or more equations are to be solved together, the solutions must satisfy all the equations simultaneously.

Two equations having the same solution(s) are *equivalent equations*. For example, the equations

$$2 + x = 3$$
$$4 + 2x = 6$$

each have the unique solution $x = 1$. Note that the second equation is the first equation multiplied by 2. Similarly, the equations

$$3x - y = 6$$
$$6x - 2y = 12$$

have the same solutions, although in this case each equation has infinitely many solutions. If any value is assigned to x, then $3x - 6$ is a corresponding value for y that will satisfy both equations; for example, $x = 2$ and $y = 0$ is a solution to both equations, as is $x = 5$ and $y = 9$.

3. Solving Linear Equations with One Unknown

To solve a linear equation with one unknown (that is, to find the value of the unknown that satisfies the equation), the unknown should be isolated on one side of the equation. This can be done by performing the same mathematical operations on both sides of the equation. Remember that if the same number is added to or subtracted from both sides of the equation, this does not change the equality; likewise, multiplying or dividing both sides by the same nonzero number does not change the equality. For example, to solve the equation $\frac{5x-6}{3} = 4$ for x, the variable x can be isolated using the following steps:

$$5x - 6 = 12 \quad \text{(multiplying by 3)}$$
$$5x = 12 + 6 = 18 \quad \text{(adding 6)}$$
$$x = \frac{18}{5} \quad \text{(dividing by 5)}$$

The solution, $\frac{18}{5}$, can be checked by substituting it for x in the original equation to determine whether it satisfies that equation:

$$\frac{5\left(\dfrac{18}{5}\right) - 6}{3} = \frac{18 - 6}{3} = \frac{12}{3} = 4.$$

Therefore, $x = \frac{18}{5}$ is the solution.

4. Solving Two Linear Equations with Two Unknowns

For two linear equations with two unknowns, if the equations are equivalent, then there are infinitely many solutions to the equations, as illustrated at the end of section 3.2.2 ("Equations"). If the equations are not equivalent, then they have either one unique solution or no solution. The latter case is illustrated by the two equations:

$$3x + 4y = 17$$
$$6x + 8y = 35$$

Note that $3x + 4y = 17$ implies $6x + 8y = 34$, which contradicts the second equation. Thus, no values of x and y can simultaneously satisfy both equations.

There are several methods of solving two linear equations with two unknowns. With any method, if a contradiction is reached, then the equations have no solution; if a trivial equation such as $0 = 0$ is reached, then the equations are equivalent and have infinitely many solutions. Otherwise, a unique solution can be found.

One way to solve for the two unknowns is to express one of the unknowns in terms of the other using one of the equations, and then substitute the expression into the remaining equation to obtain an equation with one unknown. This equation can be solved and the value of the unknown substituted into either of the original equations to find the value of the other unknown. For example, the following two equations can be solved for x and y.

$$(1)\ 3x + 2y = 11$$
$$(2)\quad x - y = 2$$

In equation (2), $x = 2 + y$. Substitute $2 + y$ in equation (1) for x:

$$3(2 + y) + 2y = 11$$
$$6 + 3y + 2y = 11$$
$$6 + 5y = 11$$
$$5y = 5$$
$$y = 1$$

If $y = 1$, then $x = 2 + 1 = 3$.

There is another way to solve for x and y by eliminating one of the unknowns. This can be done by making the coefficients of one of the unknowns the same (disregarding the sign) in both equations and either adding the equations or subtracting one equation from the other. For example, to solve the equations

$$(1)\ 6x + 5y = 29$$
$$(2)\ 4x - 3y = -6$$

by this method, multiply equation (1) by 3 and equation (2) by 5 to get

$$18x + 15y = 87$$
$$20x - 15y = -30$$

Adding the two equations eliminates y, yielding $38x = 57$, or $x = \dfrac{3}{2}$. Finally, substituting $\dfrac{3}{2}$ for x in one of the equations gives $y = 4$. These answers can be checked by substituting both values into both of the original equations.

5. Solving Equations by Factoring

Some equations can be solved by factoring. To do this, first add or subtract expressions to bring all the expressions to one side of the equation, with 0 on the other side. Then try to factor the nonzero side into a product of expressions. If this is possible, then using property (7) in section 3.1.4 ("Real Numbers") each of the factors can be set equal to 0, yielding several simpler equations that possibly can be solved. The solutions of the simpler equations will be solutions of the factored equation. As an example, consider the equation $x^3 - 2x^2 + x = -5(x - 1)^2$:

$$x^3 - 2x^2 + x + 5\,(x - 1)^2 = 0$$
$$x(x^2 + 2x + 1) + 5\,(x - 1)^2 = 0$$
$$x(x - 1)^2 + 5\,(x - 1)^2 = 0$$
$$(x + 5)\,(x - 1)^2 = 0$$
$$x + 5 = 0 \text{ or } (x - 1)^2 = 0$$
$$x = -5 \text{ or } x = 1.$$

For another example, consider $\dfrac{x(x - 3)(x^2 + 5)}{x - 4} = 0$. A fraction equals 0 if and only if its numerator equals 0. Thus, $x(x - 3)(x^2 + 5) = 0$:

$$x = 0 \text{ or } x{-}3 = 0 \text{ or } x^2 + 5 = 0 \text{ or}$$
$$x = 0 \text{ or } x = 3 \text{ or } x^2 + 5 = 0.$$

But $x^2 + 5 = 0$ has no real solution because $x^2 + 5 > 0$ for every real number. Thus, the solutions are 0 and 3.

The solutions of an equation are also called the *roots* of the equation. These roots can be checked by substituting them into the original equation to determine whether they satisfy the equation.

6. Solving Quadratic Equations

The standard form for a *quadratic equation* is

$$ax^2 + bx + c = 0,$$

where a, b, and c are real numbers and $a \neq 0$; for example:

$$x^2 + 6x + 5 = 0$$
$$3x^2 - 2x = 0, \text{ and}$$
$$x^2 + 4 = 0.$$

Some quadratic equations can easily be solved by factoring. For example:

(1)
$$x^2 + 6x + 5 = 0$$
$$(x + 5)(x + 1) = 0$$
$$x + 5 = 0 \quad \text{or} \quad x + 1 = 0$$
$$x = -5 \quad \text{or} \quad x = -1$$

(2)
$$3x^2 - 3 = 8x$$
$$3x^2 - 8x - 3 = 0$$
$$(3x + 1)(x - 3) = 0$$
$$3x + 1 = 0 \quad \text{or} \quad x - 3 = 0$$
$$x = -\frac{1}{3} \quad \text{or} \quad x = 3$$

A quadratic equation has at most two real roots and may have just one or even no real root. For example, the equation $x^2 - 6x + 9 = 0$ can be expressed as $(x - 3)^2 = 0$, or $(x - 3)(x - 3) = 0$; thus the only root is 3. The equation $x^2 + 4 = 0$ has no real root; since the square of any real number is greater than or equal to zero, $x^2 + 4$ must be greater than zero.

An expression of the form $a^2 - b^2$ can be factored as $(a - b)(a + b)$.

For example, the quadratic equation $9x^2 - 25 = 0$ can be solved as follows.

$$(3x - 5)(3x + 5) = 0$$
$$3x - 5 = 0 \text{ or } 3x + 5 = 0$$
$$x = \frac{5}{3} \quad \text{or} \quad x = -\frac{5}{3}$$

If a quadratic expression is not easily factored, then its roots can always be found using the *quadratic formula*: If $ax^2 + bx + c = 0$ ($a \neq 0$), then the roots are

$$x = \frac{-b + \sqrt{b^2 - 4ac}}{2a} \text{ and } x = \frac{-b - \sqrt{b^2 - 4ac}}{2a}.$$

These are two distinct real numbers unless $b^2 - 4ac \leq 0$. If $b^2 - 4ac = 0$, then these two expressions for x are equal to $-\dfrac{b}{2a}$, and the equation has only one root. If $b^2 - 4ac < 0$, then $\sqrt{b^2 - 4ac}$ is not a real number and the equation has no real roots.

7. Exponents

A positive integer exponent of a number or a variable indicates a product, and the positive integer is the number of times that the number or variable is a factor in the product. For example, x^5 means $(x)(x)(x)(x)(x)$; that is, x is a factor in the product 5 times.

Some rules about exponents follow.

Let x and y be any positive numbers, and let r and s be any positive integers.

(1) $(x^r)(x^s) = x^{(r+s)}$; for example, $(2^2)(2^3) = 2^{(2+3)} = 2^5 = 32$.

(2) $\dfrac{x^r}{x^s} = x^{(r-s)}$; for example, $\dfrac{4^5}{4^2} = 4^{5-2} = 4^3 = 64$.

(3) $(x^r)(y^r) = (xy)^r$; for example, $(3^3)(4^3) = 12^3 = 1{,}728$.

(4) $\left(\dfrac{x}{y}\right)^r = \dfrac{x^r}{y^r}$; for example, $\left(\dfrac{2}{3}\right)^3 = \dfrac{2^3}{3^3} = \dfrac{8}{27}$.

(5) $(x^r)^s = x^{rs} = (x^s)^r$; for example, $(x^3)^4 = x^{12} = (x^4)^3$.

(6) $x^{-r} = \dfrac{1}{x^r}$; for example, $3^{-2} = \dfrac{1}{3^2} = \dfrac{1}{9}$.

(7) $x^0 = 1$; for example, $6^0 = 1$.

(8) $x^{\frac{r}{s}} = \left(x^{\frac{1}{s}}\right)^r = (x^r)^{\frac{1}{s}} = \sqrt[s]{x^r}$; for example, $8^{\frac{2}{3}} = \left(8^{\frac{1}{3}}\right)^2 = (8^2)^{\frac{1}{3}} = \sqrt[3]{8^2} = \sqrt[3]{64} = 4$

and $9^{\frac{1}{2}} = \sqrt{9} = 3$.

It can be shown that rules 1–6 also apply when r and s are not integers and are not positive, that is, when r and s are any real numbers.

8. Inequalities

An *inequality* is a statement that uses one of the following symbols:

$\neq$ not equal to
$>$ greater than
$\geq$ greater than or equal to
$<$ less than
$\leq$ less than or equal to

Some examples of inequalities are $5x - 3 < 9$, $6x \geq y$, and $\dfrac{1}{2} < \dfrac{3}{4}$. Solving a linear inequality with one unknown is similar to solving an equation; the unknown is isolated on one side of the inequality. As in solving an equation, the same number can be added to or subtracted from both sides of the inequality, or both sides of an inequality can be multiplied or divided by a positive number without changing the truth of the inequality. However, multiplying or dividing an inequality by a negative number reverses the order of the inequality. For example, $6 > 2$, but $(-1)(6) < (-1)(2)$.

To solve the inequality $3x - 2 > 5$ for x, isolate x by using the following steps:

$$3x - 2 > 5$$
$$3x > 7 \quad \text{(adding 2 to both sides)}$$
$$x > \frac{7}{3} \quad \text{(dividing both sides by 3)}$$

To solve the inequality $\dfrac{5x - 1}{-2} < 3$ for x, isolate x by using the following steps:

$$\frac{5x - 1}{-2} < 3$$
$$5x - 1 > -6 \quad \text{(multiplying both sides by } -2)$$
$$5x > -5 \quad \text{(adding 1 to both sides)}$$
$$x > -1 \quad \text{(dividing both sides by 5)}$$

9. Absolute Value

The absolute value of x, denoted $|x|$, is defined to be x if $x \geq 0$ and $-x$ if $x < 0$. Note the $\sqrt{x^2}$ denotes that nonnegative square root of x^2, and so $\sqrt{x^2} = |x|$.

10. Functions

An algebraic expression in one variable can be used to define a *function* of that variable. A function is denoted by a letter such as f or g along with the variable in the expression. For example, the expression $x^3 - 5x^2 + 2$ defines a function f that can be denoted by

$$f(x) = x^3 - 5x^2 + 2.$$

The expression $\dfrac{2z + 7}{\sqrt{z + 1}}$ defines a function g that can be denoted by

$$g(z) = \frac{2z + 7}{\sqrt{z + 1}}$$

The symbols "$f(x)$" or "$g(z)$" do not represent products; each is merely the symbol for an expression, and is read "f of x" or "g of z."

Function notation provides a short way of writing the result of substituting a value for a variable. If $x = 1$ is substituted in the first expression, the result can be written $f(1) = -2$, and $f(1)$ is called the "value of f at $x = 1$." Similarly, if $z = 0$ is substituted in the second expression, then the value of g at $z = 0$ is $g(0) = 7$.

Once a function $f(x)$ is defined, it is useful to think of the variable x as an input and $f(x)$ as the corresponding output. In any function there can be no more than one output for any given input. However, more that one input can give the same output; for example, if $h(x) = |x + 3|$, then $h(-4) = 1 = h(-2)$.

The set of all allowable inputs for a function is called the *domain* of the function. For f and g defined above, the domain of f is the set of all real numbers and the domain of g is the set of all numbers greater than -1. The domain of any function can be arbitrarily specified, as in the function defined by "$h(x) = 9x - 5$ for $0 \le x \le 10$." Without such a restriction, the domain is assumed to be all values of x that result in a real number when substituted into the function.

The domain of a function can consist of only the positive integers and possibly 0. For example,

$$a(n) = n^2 + \frac{n}{5} \text{ for } n = 0, 1, 2, 3, \ldots.$$

Such a function is called a *sequence* and $a(n)$ is denoted by a_n. The value of the sequence a_n at $n = 3$ is $a_3 = 3^2 + \frac{3}{5} = 9.60$. As another example, consider the sequence defined by $b_n = (-1)^n (n!)$ for

$n = 1, 2, 3, \ldots.$ A sequence like this is often indicated by listing its values in the order $b_1, b_2, b_3, \ldots, b_n, \ldots$ as follows:
$-1, 2, -6, \ldots, (-1)^n(n!), \ldots,$ and $(-1)^n(n!)$ is called the nth term of the sequence.

3.3 Geometry

1. Lines

In geometry, the word "line" refers to a straight line that extends without end in both directions.

The line above can be referred to as line PQ or line ℓ. The part of the line from P to Q is called a *line segment*. P and Q are the *endpoints* of the segment. The notation PQ is used to denote both the segment and the length of the segment. The intention of the notation can be determined from the context.

2. Intersecting Lines and Angles

If two lines intersect, the opposite angles are called *vertical angles* and have the same measure. In the figure

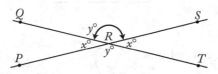

$\angle PRQ$ and $\angle SRT$ are vertical angles and $\angle QRS$ and $\angle PRT$ are vertical angles. Also, $x + y = 180$ since PRS is a straight line.

3. Perpendicular Lines

An angle that has a measure of 90° is a *right angle*. If two lines intersect at right angles, the lines are *perpendicular*. For example:

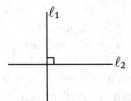

ℓ_1 and ℓ_2 above are perpendicular, denoted by $\ell_1 \perp \ell_2$. A right angle symbol in an angle of intersection indicates that the lines are perpendicular.

4. Parallel Lines

If two lines that are in the same plane do not intersect, the two lines are *parallel*. In the figure

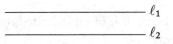

lines ℓ_1 and ℓ_2 are parallel, denoted by $\ell_1 \parallel \ell_2$. If two parallel lines are intersected by a third line, as shown below, then the angle measures are related as indicated, where $x + y = 180$.

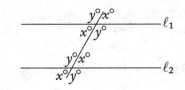

5. Polygons (Convex)

A *polygon* is a closed plane figure formed by three or more line segments, called the *sides* of the polygon. Each side intersects exactly two other sides at their endpoints. The points of intersection of the sides are *vertices*. The term "polygon" will be used to mean a convex polygon, that is, a polygon in which each interior angle has a measure of less than 180°.

The following figures are polygons:

The following figures are not polygons:

A polygon with three sides is a *triangle*; with four sides, a *quadrilateral*; with five sides, a *pentagon*; and with six sides, a *hexagon*.

The sum of the interior angle measures of a triangle is 180°. In general, the sum of the interior angle measures of a polygon with n sides is equal to $(n - 2)180°$. For example, this sum for a pentagon is $(5 - 2)180 = (3)180 = 540$ degrees.

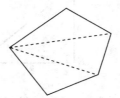

Note that a pentagon can be partitioned into three triangles and therefore the sum of the angle measures can be found by adding the sum of the angle measures of three triangles.

The *perimeter* of a polygon is the sum of the lengths of its sides.

The commonly used phrase "area of a triangle" (or any other plane figure) is used to mean the area of the region enclosed by that figure.

6. Triangles

There are several special types of triangles with important properties. But one property that all triangles share is that the sum of the lengths of any two of the sides is greater than the length of the third side, as illustrated below.

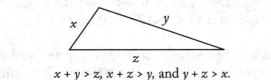

$x + y > z$, $x + z > y$, and $y + z > x$.

An *equilateral* triangle has all sides of equal length. All angles of an equilateral triangle have equal measure. An *isosceles* triangle has at least two sides of the same length. If two sides of a triangle have the same length, then the two angles opposite those sides have the same measure. Conversely, if two angles of a triangle have the same measure, then the sides opposite those angles have the same length. In isosceles triangle PQR below, $x = y$ since $PQ = QR$.

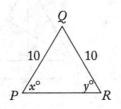

A triangle that has a right angle is a *right* triangle. In a right triangle, the side opposite the right angle is the *hypotenuse*, and the other two sides are the *legs*. An important theorem concerning right triangles is the *Pythagorean theorem*, which states: In a right triangle, the square of the length of the hypotenuse is equal to the sum of the squares of the lengths of the legs.

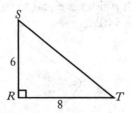

In the figure above, $\triangle RST$ is a right triangle, so $(RS)^2 + (RT)^2 = (ST)^2$. Here, $RS = 6$ and $RT = 8$, so $ST = 10$, since $6^2 + 8^2 = 36 + 64 = 100 = (ST)^2$ and $ST = \sqrt{100}$. Any triangle in which the lengths of the sides are in the ratio 3:4:5 is a right triangle. In general, if a, b, and c are the lengths of the sides of a triangle and $a^2 + b^2 = c^2$, then the triangle is a right triangle.

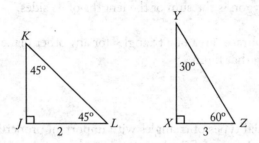

In $45°$ –$45°$ –$90°$ triangles, the lengths of the sides are in the ratio $1:1:\sqrt{2}$. For example, in $\triangle JKL$, if $JL = 2$, then $JK = 2$ and $KL = 2\sqrt{2}$. In $30°$ –$60°$ –$90°$ triangles, the lengths of the sides are in the ratio $1:\sqrt{3}: 2$. For example, in $\triangle XYZ$, if $XZ = 3$, then $XY = 3\sqrt{3}$ and $YZ = 6$.

The *altitude* of a triangle is the segment drawn from a vertex perpendicular to the side opposite that vertex. Relative to that vertex and altitude, the opposite side is called the *base*.

The area of a triangle is equal to:

$$\frac{\text{(the length of the altitude)} \times \text{(the length of the base)}}{2}$$

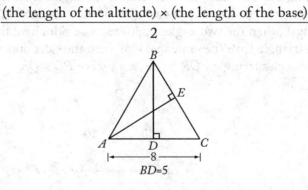

In $\triangle ABC$, BD is the altitude to base AC and AE is the altitude to base BC. The area of $\triangle ABC$ is equal to

$$\frac{BD \times AC}{2} = \frac{5 \times 8}{2} = 20.$$

The area is also equal to $\dfrac{AE \times BC}{2}$. If $\triangle ABC$ above is isosceles and $AB = BC$, then altitude BD bisects the base; that is, $AD = DC = 4$. Similarly, any altitude of an equilateral triangle bisects the side to which it is drawn.

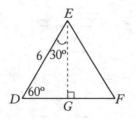

In equilateral triangle DEF, if $DE = 6$, then $DG = 3$ and $EG = 3\sqrt{3}$. The area of $\triangle DEF$ is equal to $\dfrac{3\sqrt{3} \times 6}{2} = 9\sqrt{3}$.

7. Quadrilaterals

A polygon with four sides is a *quadrilateral*. A quadrilateral in which both pairs of opposite sides are parallel is a *parallelogram*. The opposite sides of a parallelogram also have equal length.

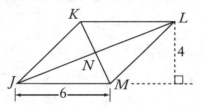

In parallelogram $JKLM$, $JK \parallel LM$ and $JK = LM$; $KL \parallel JM$ and $KL = JM$.

The diagonals of a parallelogram bisect each other (that is, $KN = NM$ and $JN = NL$).

The area of a parallelogram is equal to

(the length of the altitude) × (the length of the base).

The area of $JKLM$ is equal to $4 \times 6 = 24$.

A parallelogram with right angles is a *rectangle*, and a rectangle with all sides of equal length is a *square*.

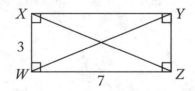

The perimeter of $WXYZ = 2(3) + 2(7) = 20$ and the area of $WXYZ$ is equal to $3 \times 7 = 21$.

The diagonals of a rectangle are equal; therefore $WY = XZ = \sqrt{9 + 49} = \sqrt{58}$.

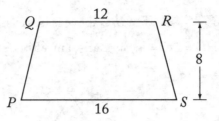

A quadrilateral with two sides that are parallel, as shown above, is a *trapezoid*. The area of trapezoid *PQRS* may be calculated as follows:

$$\frac{1}{2} \text{ (sum of bases)(height)} = \frac{1}{2} (QR + PS)(8) = \frac{1}{2} (28 \times 8) = 112.$$

8. Circles

A *circle* is a set of points in a plane that are all located the same distance from a fixed point (the *center* of the circle).

A *chord* of a circle is a line segment that has its endpoints on the circle. A chord that passes through the center of the circle is a *diameter* of the circle. A *radius* of a circle is a segment from the center of the circle to a point on the circle. The words "diameter" and "radius" are also used to refer to the lengths of these segments.

The *circumference* of a circle is the distance around the circle. If r is the radius of the circle, then the circumference is equal to $2\pi r$, where π is approximately $\frac{22}{7}$ or 3.14. The *area* of a circle of radius r is equal to πr^2.

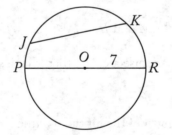

In the circle above, O is the center of the circle and JK and PR are chords. PR is a diameter and OR is a radius. If $OR = 7$, then the circumference of the circle is $2\pi(7) = 14\pi$ and the area of the circle is $\pi(7)2 = 49\pi$.

The number of degrees of arc in a circle (or the number of degrees in a complete revolution) is 360.

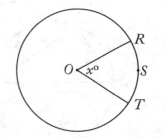

In the circle with center O above, the length of arc RST is $\dfrac{x}{360}$ of the circumference of the circle; for example, if $x = 60$, then arc RST has length $\dfrac{1}{6}$ of the circumference of the circle.

A line that has exactly one point in common with a circle is said to be *tangent* to the circle, and that common point is called the *point of tangency*. A radius or diameter with an endpoint at the point of tangency is perpendicular to the tangent line, and, conversely, a line that is perpendicular to a diameter at one of its endpoints is tangent to the circle at that endpoint.

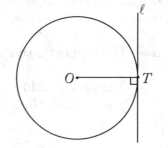

The line ℓ above is tangent to the circle and radius OT is perpendicular to ℓ.

If each vertex of a polygon lies on a circle, then the polygon is *inscribed* in the circle and the circle is *circumscribed* about the polygon. If each side of a polygon is tangent to a circle, then the polygon is *circumscribed* about the circle and the circle is *inscribed* in the polygon.

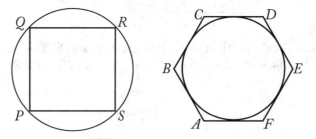

In the figure above, quadrilateral $PQRS$ is inscribed in a circle and hexagon $ABCDEF$ is circumscribed about a circle.

If a triangle is inscribed in a circle so that one of its sides is a diameter of the circle, then the triangle is a right triangle.

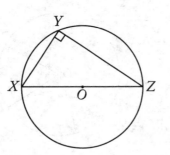

In the circle above, XZ is a diameter and the measure of $\angle XYZ$ is 90°.

9. Rectangular Solids and Cylinders

A *rectangular solid* is a three-dimensional figure formed by six rectangular surfaces, as shown below. Each rectangular surface is a *face*. Each solid or dotted line segment is an *edge*, and each point at which the edges meet is a *vertex*. A rectangular solid has six faces, twelve edges, and eight vertices. Opposite faces are parallel rectangles that have the same dimensions. A rectangular solid in which all edges are of equal length is a *cube*.

The *surface area* of a rectangular solid is equal to the sum of the areas of all the faces. The *volume* is equal to

$$(\text{length}) \times (\text{width}) \times (\text{height});$$

in other words, $(\text{area of base}) \times (\text{height}).$

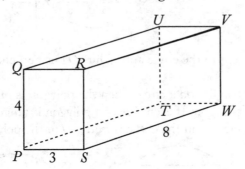

In the rectangular solid above, the dimensions are 3, 4, and 8. The surface area is equal to $2(3 \times 4) + 2(3 \times 8) + 2(4 \times 8) = 136$. The volume is equal to $3 \times 4 \times 8 = 96$.

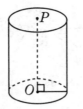

The figure above is a right circular *cylinder*. The two bases are circles of the same size with centers O and P, respectively, and altitude (height) OP is perpendicular to the bases. The surface area of a right circular cylinder with a base of radius r and height h is equal to $2(\pi r^2) + 2\pi rh$ (the sum of the areas of the two bases plus the area of the curved surface).

The volume of a cylinder is equal to $\pi r^2 h$, that is,

$$(\text{area of base}) \times (\text{height}).$$

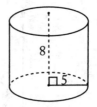

In the cylinder above, the surface area is equal to

$$2(25\pi) + 2\pi(5)(8) = 130\pi,$$

and the volume is equal to

$$25\pi(8) = 200\pi.$$

10. Coordinate Geometry

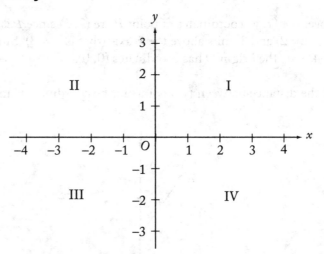

The figure above shows the (rectangular) *coordinate plane*. The horizontal line is called the *x-axis* and the perpendicular vertical line is called the *y-axis*. The point at which these two axes intersect, designated *O*, is called the *origin*. The axes divide the plane into four quadrants, I, II, III, and IV, as shown.

Each point in the plane has an *x-coordinate* and a *y-coordinate*. A point is identified by an ordered pair (x, y) of numbers in which the *x*-coordinate is the first number and the *y*-coordinate is the second number.

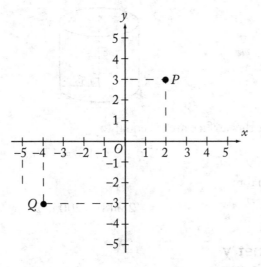

In the graph above, the (x, y) coordinates of point P are $(2, 3)$ since P is 2 units to the right of the y-axis (that is, $x = 2$) and 3 units above the x-axis (that is, $y = 3$). Similarly, the (x, y) coordinates of point Q are $(-4, -3)$. The origin O has coordinates $(0, 0)$.

One way to find the distance between two points in the coordinate plane is to use the Pythagorean theorem.

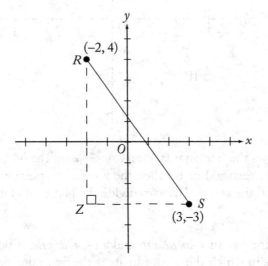

To find the distance between points R and S using the Pythagorean theorem, draw the triangle as shown. Note that Z has (x, y) coordinates $(-2, -3)$, $RZ = 7$, and $ZS = 5$. Therefore, the distance between R and S is equal to

$$\sqrt{7^2 + 5^2} = \sqrt{74}$$

For a line in the coordinate plane, the coordinates of each point on the line satisfy a linear equation of the form $y = mx + b$ (or the form $x = a$ if the line is vertical). For example, each point on the line on the next page satisfies the equation $y = -\frac{1}{2}x + 1$. One can verify this for the points $(-2, 2)$, $(2, 0)$, and $(0, 1)$ by substituting the respective coordinates for x and y in the equation.

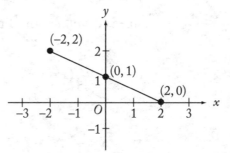

In the equation $y = mx + b$ of a line, the coefficient m is the *slope* of the line and the constant term b is the *y-intercept* of the line. For any two points on the line, the slope is defined to be the ratio of the difference in the y-coordinates to the difference in the x-coordinates. Using $(-2, 2)$ and $(2, 0)$ above, the slope is

$$\frac{\text{The difference in the } y\text{-coordinates}}{\text{The difference in the } x\text{-coordinates}} = \frac{0-2}{2-(-2)} = \frac{-2}{4} = \frac{1}{2}.$$

The y-intercept is the y-coordinate of the point at which the line intersects the y-axis. For the line above, the y-intercept is 1, and this is the resulting value of y when x is set equal to 0 in the equation $y = -\frac{1}{2}x = 1$. The *x-intercept* is the x-coordinate of the point at which the line intersects the x-axis. The x-intercept can be found by setting $y = 0$ and solving for x. For the line $y = -\frac{1}{2}x + 1$, this gives

$$-\frac{1}{2}x + 1 = 0$$

$$-\frac{1}{2}x = -1$$

$$x = 2$$

Thus, the x-intercept is 2.

Given any two points (x_1, y_1) and (x_2, y_2) with $x_1 \neq x_2$, the equation of the line passing through these points can be found by applying the definition of slope. Since the slope is $m = \frac{y_2 - y_1}{x_2 - x_1}$, then using a point known to be on the line, say (x_1, y_1), any point (x, y) on the line must satisfy $\frac{y - y_1}{x - x_1} = m$, or $y - y_1 = m(x - x_1)$. (Using (x_2, y_2) as the known point would yield an equivalent equation.) For example, consider the points $(-2, 4)$ and $(3, -3)$ on the line below.

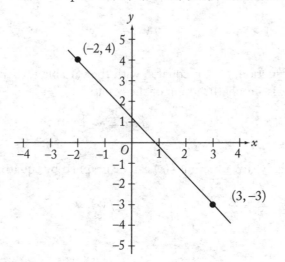

The slope of this line is $\dfrac{-3-4}{3-(-2)} = \dfrac{-7}{5}$, so an equation of this line can be found using the point $(3, -3)$ as follows:

$$y - (-3) = \frac{7}{5}(x - 3)$$

$$y + 3 = -\frac{7}{5}x + \frac{21}{5}$$

$$y = -\frac{7}{5}x + \frac{6}{5}.$$

The y-intercept is $\dfrac{6}{5}$. The *x-intercept* can be found as follows:

$$0 = -\frac{7}{5}x + \frac{6}{5}$$

$$\frac{7}{5}x = \frac{6}{5}$$

$$x = \frac{6}{7}$$

Both of these intercepts can be seen on the graph.

If the slope of a line is negative, the line slants downward from left to right; if the slope is positive, the line slants upward. If the slope is 0, the line is horizontal; the equation of such a line is of the form $y = b$ since $m = 0$. For a vertical line, slope is not defined, and the equation is of the form $x = a$, where a is the x-intercept.

There is a connection between graphs of lines in the coordinate plane and solutions of two linear equations with two unknowns. If two linear equations with unknowns x and y have a unique solution, then the graphs of the equations are two lines that intersect in one point, which is the solution. If the equations are equivalent, then they represent the same line with infinitely many points or solutions. If the equations have no solution, then they represent parallel lines, which do not intersect.

There is also a connection between functions (see section 3.2.10) and the coordinate plane. If a function is graphed in the coordinate plane, the function can be understood in different and useful ways. Consider the function defined by

$$f(x) = -\frac{7}{5}x + \frac{6}{5}.$$

If the value of the function, $f(x)$, is equated with the variable y, then the graph of the function in the xy-coordinate plane is simply the graph of the equation

$$y = -\frac{7}{5}x + \frac{6}{5}$$

shown above. Similarly, any function $f(x)$ can be graphed by equating y with the value of the function:

$$y = f(x).$$

So for any x in the domain of the function f, the point with coordinates $(x, f(x))$ is on the graph of f, and the graph consists entirely of these points.

As another example, consider a quadratic polynomial function defined by $f(x) = x^2 - 1$. One can plot several points $(x, f(x))$ on the graph to understand the connection between a function and its graph:

x	$f(x)$
−2	3
−1	0
0	−1
1	0
2	3

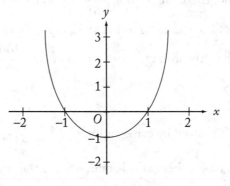

If all the points were graphed for $-2 \le x \le 2$, then the graph would appear as follows.

The graph of a quadratic function is called a *parabola* and always has the shape of the curve above, although it may be upside down or have a greater or lesser width. Note that the roots of the equation $f(x) = x^2 - 1 = 0$ are $x = 1$ and $x = -1$; these coincide with the x-intercepts since x-intercepts are found by setting $y = 0$ and solving for x. Also, the y-intercept is $f(0) = -1$ because this is the value of y corresponding to $x = 0$. For any function f, the x-intercepts are the solutions of the equation $f(x)=0$ and the y-intercept is the value $f(0)$.

3.4 Word Problems

Many of the principles discussed in this chapter are used to solve word problems. The following discussion of word problems illustrates some of the techniques and concepts used in solving such problems.

1. Rate Problems

The distance that an object travels is equal to the product of the average speed at which it travels and the amount of time it takes to travel that distance, that is,

$$\text{Rate} \times \text{Time} = \text{Distance}.$$

Example 1: If a car travels at an average speed of 70 kilometers per hour for 4 hours, how many kilometers does it travel?

Solution: Since rate × time = distance, simply multiply 70 km/hour × 4 hours. Thus, the car travels 280 kilometers in 4 hours.

To determine the average rate at which an object travels, divide the total distance traveled by the total amount of traveling time.

Example 2: On a 400-mile trip, car X traveled half the distance at 40 miles per hour (mph) and the other half at 50 mph. What was the average speed of car X?

Solution: First it is necessary to determine the amount of traveling time. During the first 200 miles, the car traveled at 40 mph; therefore, it took $\dfrac{200}{40} = 5$ hours to travel the first 200 miles. During the second 200 miles, the car traveled at 50 mph; therefore, it took $\dfrac{200}{50} = 4$ hours to travel the second 200 miles. Thus, the average speed of car X was $\dfrac{400}{9} = 44\dfrac{4}{9}$ mph. Note that the average speed is *not* $\dfrac{40 + 50}{2} = 45$.

Some rate problems can be solved by using ratios.

Example 3: If 5 shirts cost $44, then, at this rate, what is the cost of 8 shirts?

Solution: If c is the cost of the 8 shirts, then $\dfrac{5}{44} = \dfrac{8}{c}$. Cross multiplication results in the equation

$$5c = 8 \times 44 = 352$$

$$c = \dfrac{352}{5} = 70.40$$

The 8 shirts cost $70.40.

2. Work Problems

In a work problem, the rates at which certain persons or machines work alone are usually given, and it is necessary to compute the rate at which they work together (or vice versa).

The basic formula for solving work problems is $\dfrac{1}{r} + \dfrac{1}{s} = \dfrac{1}{h}$, where r and s are, for example, the number of hours it takes Rae and Sam, respectively, to complete a job when working alone, and h is the number of hours it takes Rae and Sam to do the job when working together. The reasoning is that in 1 hour Rae does $\dfrac{1}{r}$ of the job, Sam does $\dfrac{1}{s}$ of the job, and Rae and Sam together do $\dfrac{1}{h}$ of the job.

Example 1: If machine X can produce 1,000 bolts in 4 hours and machine Y can produce 1,000 bolts in 5 hours, in how many hours can machines X and Y, working together at these constant rates, produce 1,000 bolts?

Solution:

$$\frac{1}{4} + \frac{1}{5} = \frac{1}{h}$$

$$\frac{5}{20} + \frac{4}{20} = \frac{1}{h}$$

$$\frac{9}{20} = \frac{1}{h}$$

$$9h = 20$$

$$h = \frac{20}{9} = 2\frac{2}{9}$$

Working together, machines X and Y can produce 1,000 bolts in $2\dfrac{2}{9}$ hours.

Example 2: If Art and Rita can do a job in 4 hours when working together at their respective constant rates and Art can do the job alone in 6 hours, in how many hours can Rita do the job alone?

Solution:

$$\frac{1}{6} + \frac{1}{R} = \frac{1}{4}$$

$$\frac{R+6}{6R} = \frac{1}{4}$$

$$4R + 24 = 6R$$

$$24 = 2R$$

$$12 = R$$

Working alone, Rita can do the job in 12 hours.

3. Mixture Problems

In mixture problems, substances with different characteristics are combined, and it is necessary to determine the characteristics of the resulting mixture.

Example 1: If 6 pounds of nuts that cost $1.20 per pound are mixed with 2 pounds of nuts that cost $1.60 per pound, what is the cost per pound of the mixture?

Solution: The total cost of the 8 pounds of nuts is

$$6(\$1.20) + 2(\$1.60) = \$10.40.$$

The cost per pound is $\dfrac{\$10.40}{8} = \$1.30.$

Example 2: How many liters of a solution that is 15 percent salt must be added to 5 liters of a solution that is 8 percent salt so that the resulting solution is 10 percent salt?

Solution: Let n represent the number of liters of the 15% solution. The amount of salt in the 15% solution [$0.15n$] plus the amount of salt in the 8% solution [$(0.08)(5)$] must be equal to the amount of salt in the 10% mixture [$0.10 (n + 5)$]. Therefore,

$$0.15n + 0.08(5) = 0.10(n + 5)$$
$$15n + 40 = 10n + 50$$
$$5n = 10$$
$$n = 2 \text{ liters}$$

Two liters of the 15% salt solution must be added to the 8% solution to obtain the 10% solution.

4. Interest Problems

Interest can be computed in two basic ways. With simple annual interest, the interest is computed on the principal only and is equal to (principal) × (interest rate) × (time). If interest is compounded, then interest is computed on the principal as well as on any interest already earned.

Example 1: If $8,000 is invested at 6 percent simple annual interest, how much interest is earned after 3 months?

Solution: Since the annual interest rate is 6%, the interest for 1 year is

$$(0.06)(\$8,000) = \$480.$$

The interest earned in 3 months is $\dfrac{3}{12}(\$480) = \$120.$

Example 2: If $10,000 is invested at 10 percent annual interest, compounded semiannually, what is the balance after 1 year?

Solution: The balance after the first 6 months would be

$$10,000 + (10,000)(0.05) = \$10,500.$$

The balance after one year would be $\quad 10,500 + (10,500)(0.05) = \$11,025.$

Note that the interest rate for each 6-month period is 5%, which is half of the 10% annual rate. The balance after one year can also be expressed as

$$10,000\left(1+\frac{0.10}{2}\right)^2 \text{ dollars.}$$

5. Discount

If a price is discounted by n percent, then the price becomes $(100 - n)$ percent of the original price.

Example 1: A certain customer paid $24 for a dress. If that price represented a 25 percent discount on the original price of the dress, what was the original price of the dress?

Solution: If p is the original price of the dress, then $0.75p$ is the discounted price and $0.75p = \$24$, or $p = \$32$. The original price of the dress was $32.

Example 2: The price of an item is discounted by 20 percent and then this reduced price is discounted by an additional 30 percent. These two discounts are equal to an overall discount of what percent?

Solution: If p is the original price of the item, then $0.8p$ is the price after the first discount. The price after the second discount is $(0.7)(0.8)p = 0.56p$. This represents an overall discount of 44 percent $(100\% - 56\%)$.

6. Profit

Gross profit is equal to revenues minus expenses, or selling price minus cost.

Example: A certain appliance costs a merchant $30. At what price should the merchant sell the appliance in order to make a gross profit of 50 percent of the cost of the appliance?

Solution: If s is the selling price of the appliance, then $s - 30 = (0.5)(30)$, or $s = \$45$. The merchant should sell the appliance for $45.

7. Sets

If S is the set of numbers 1, 2, 3, and 4, you can write $S = \{1,2,3,4\}$. Sets can also be represented by Venn diagrams. That is, the relationship among the members of sets can be represented by circles.

Example 1: Each of 25 people is enrolled in history, mathematics, or both. If 20 are enrolled in history and 18 are enrolled in mathematics, how many are enrolled in both history and mathematics?

Solution: The 25 people can be divided into three sets: those who study history only, those who study mathematics only, and those who study history and mathematics. Thus a Venn diagram may be drawn as follows, where n is the number of people enrolled in both courses, $20 - n$ is the number enrolled in history only, and $18 - n$ is the number enrolled in mathematics only.

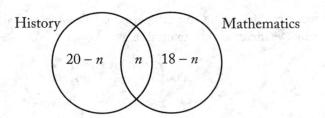

History   Mathematics

$20 - n$ n $18 - n$

Since there is a total of 25 people, $(20 - n) + n + (18 - n) = 25$, or $n = 13$. Thirteen people are enrolled in both history and mathematics. Note that $20 + 18 - 13 = 25$, which is the general addition rule for two sets (see section 3.1.9).

Example 2: In a certain production lot, 40 percent of the toys are red and the remaining toys are green. Half of the toys are small and half are large. If 10 percent of the toys are red and small, and 40 toys are green and large, how many of the toys are red and large?

Solution: For this kind of problem, it is helpful to organize the information in a table:

	Red	Green	Total
Small	10%		50%
Large			50%
Total	40%	60%	100%

The numbers in the table are the percents given. The following percents can be computed on the basis of what is given:

	Red	Green	Total
Small	10%	40%	50%
Large	30%	20%	50%
Total	40%	60%	100%

Since 20% of the number of toys (n) are green and large, $0.20n = 40$ (40 toys are green and large), or $n = 200$. Therefore, 30% of the 200 toys, or $(0.3)(200) = 60$, are red and large.

8. Geometry Problems

The following is an example of a word problem involving geometry.
Example:

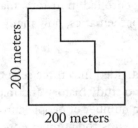

200 meters

200 meters

The figure above shows an aerial view of a piece of land. If all angles shown are right angles, what is the perimeter of the piece of land?

Solution: For reference, label the figure as

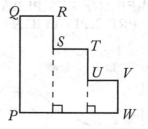

If all the angles are right angles, then $QR + ST + UV = PW$, and $RS + TU + VW = PQ$. Hence, the perimeter of the land is $2PW + 2PQ = 2 \times 200 + 2 \times 200 = 800$ meters.

9. Measurement Problems

Some questions on the GMAT® involve metric units of measure, whereas others involve English units of measure. However, except for units of time, if a question requires conversion from one unit of measure to another, the relationship between those units will be given.

Example: A train travels at a constant rate of 25 meters per second. How many kilometers does it travel in 5 minutes? (1 kilometer = 1,000 meters)

Solution: In 1 minute the train travels $(25)(60) = 1,500$ meters, so in 5 minutes it travels 7,500 meters. Since 1 kilometer = 1,000 meters, it follows that 7,500 meters equals $\dfrac{7,500}{1,000}$, or 7.5 kilometers.

10. Data Interpretation

Occasionally a question or set of questions will be based on data provided in a table or graph. Some examples of tables and graphs are given below.

Example 1:

Population by Age Group (in thousands)	
Age	Population
17 years and under	63,376
18–44 years	86,738
45–64 years	43,845
65 years and over	24,054

How many people are 44 years old or younger?

Solution: The figures in the table are given in thousands. The answer in thousands can be obtained by adding 63,376 thousand and 86,738 thousand. The result is 150,114 thousand, which is 150,114,000.

Example 2:

AVERAGE TEMPERATURE AND PRECIPITATION IN CITY X

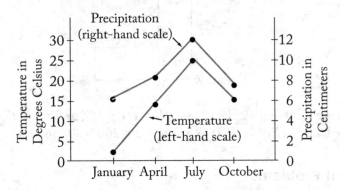

What are the average temperature and precipitation in City X during April?

Solution: Note that the scale on the left applies to the temperature line graph and the one on the right applies to the precipitation line graph. According to the graph, during April the average temperature is approximately 14° Celsius and the average precipitation is 8 centimeters.

Example 3:

DISTRIBUTION OF AL'S WEEKLY NET SALARY

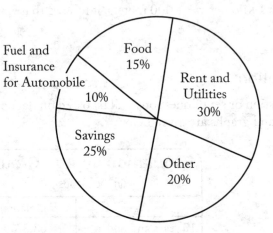

To how many of the categories listed was at least $80 of Al's weekly net salary allocated?

Solution: In the circle graph, the relative sizes of the sectors are proportional to their corresponding values and the sum of the percents given is 100%. Note that $\frac{80}{350}$ is approximately 23%, so at least $80 was allocated to each of 2 categories—Rent and Utilities, and Savings—since their allocations are each greater than 23%.

To register for the GMAT® test go to www.mba.com

4.0   Problem Solving

4.0 Problem Solving

The Quantitative section of the GMAT® test uses problem solving and data sufficiency questions to gauge your skill level. This chapter focuses on problem solving questions. Remember that quantitative questions require knowledge of—

- Arithmetic
- Elementary algebra
- Commonly known concepts of geometry

Problem solving questions are designed to test your basic mathematical skills and understanding of elementary mathematical concepts, as well as your ability to reason quantitatively, solve quantitative problems, and interpret graphic data. The mathematics knowledge required to answer the questions is no more advanced than what is generally taught in a secondary school (or high school) mathematics classes.

In these questions, you are asked to solve each problem and select the best of the five answer choices given. Begin by reading the question thoroughly to determine exactly what information is given and to make sure you understand what is being asked. Scan the answer choices to understand your options. If the problem seems simple, take a few moments to see if you can determine the answer. Then check your answer against the choices provided.

If you do not see your answer among the choices, or if the problem is complicated, take a closer look at the answer choices and think again about what the problem is asking. See if you can eliminate some of the answer choices and narrow down your options. If you are still unable to narrow the answer down to a single choice, reread the question. Keep in mind that the answer will be based solely on the information provided in the question—don't allow your own experience and assumptions to interfere with your ability to find the correct answer to the question.

If you find yourself stuck on a question or unable to select the single correct answer, keep in mind that you have about 2 minutes to answer each quantitative question. You may run out of time if you take too long to answer any one question, so you may simply need to pick the answer that seems to make the most sense. Although guessing is generally not the best way to achieve a high GMAT® score, making an educated guess is a good strategy for answering questions you are unsure of. Even if your answer to a particular question is incorrect, your answers to other questions will allow the test to accurately gauge your ability level.

The following pages include the directions that will precede questions of this type, test-taking strategies, sample questions, and explanations for all the problems. These explanations present problem solving strategies that could be helpful in answering the questions.

4.1 Test-Taking Strategies for Problem Solving Questions

1. **Pace yourself.**

   Consult the on-screen timer periodically. Work as carefully as possible, but do not spend valuable time checking answers or pondering problems that you find difficult.

2. **Use the erasable notepad provided.**

   Working a problem out may help you avoid errors in solving the problem. If diagrams or figures are not presented, it may help if you draw your own.

3. **Read each question carefully to determine what is being asked.**

   For word problems, take one step at a time, reading each sentence carefully and translating the information into equations or other useful mathematical representations.

4. **Scan the answer choices before attempting to answer a question.**

   Scanning the answers can prevent you from putting answers in a form that is not given (e.g., finding the answer in decimal form, such as 0.25, when the choices are given in fractional form, such as 1/4). Also, if the question requires approximations, a shortcut could serve well (e.g., you may be able to approximate 48 percent of a number by using half).

5. **Don't waste time trying to solve a problem that is too difficult for you.**

   Make your best guess and move on to the next question.

4.2 The Directions

These directions are very similar to those you will see for problem solving questions when you take the GMAT® test. If you read them carefully and understand them clearly before sitting for the GMAT® exam, you will not need to spend too much time reviewing them once the test begins.

Solve the problem and indicate the best of the answer choices given.

Numbers: All numbers used are real numbers.

Figures: A figure accompanying a problem solving question is intended to provide information useful in solving the problem. Figures are drawn as accurately as possible EXCEPT when it is stated in a specific problem that its figure is not drawn to scale. Straight lines may sometimes appear jagged. All figures lie in a plane unless otherwise indicated.

4.3 Problem Solving Sample Questions

Solve the problem and indicate the best of the answer choices given.

Numbers: All numbers used are real numbers.

Figures: All figures accompanying a problem solving question are intended to provide information useful in solving the problem. Figures are drawn as accurately as possible EXCEPT when a specific problem states that its figure is not drawn to scale. Straight lines may sometimes appear jagged. All figures lie in a plane unless otherwise indicated.

1. If Mario was 32 years old 8 years ago, how old was he x years ago?

   (A) $x - 40$
   (B) $x - 24$
   (C) $40 - x$
   (D) $24 - x$
   (E) $24 + x$

2. If k is an integer and 0.0010101×10^k is greater than 1,000, what is the least possible value of k?

   (A)   2
   (B)   3
   (C)   4
   (D)   5
   (E)   6

3. If $(b - 3)\left(4 + \dfrac{2}{b}\right) = 0$ and $b \neq 3$, then $b =$

   (A) -8

   (B) -2

   (C) $-\dfrac{1}{2}$

   (D) $\dfrac{1}{2}$

   (E)   2

4. The number $2 - 0.5$ is how many times the number $1 - 0.5$?

   (A)   2
   (B)   2.5
   (C)   3
   (D)   3.5
   (E)   4

5. In which of the following pairs are the two numbers reciprocals of each other?

   I.   3 and $\dfrac{1}{3}$

   II. $\dfrac{1}{17}$ and $\dfrac{-1}{17}$

   III. $\sqrt{3}$ and $\dfrac{\sqrt{3}}{3}$

   (A)   I only
   (B)   II only
   (C)   I and II
   (D)   I and III
   (E)   II and III

6. The price of a certain television set is discounted by 10 percent, and the reduced price is then discounted by 10 percent. This series of successive discounts is equivalent to a single discount of

   (A)   20%
   (B)   19%
   (C)   18%
   (D)   11%
   (E)   10%

7. Which of the following equations is NOT equivalent to $25x^2 = y^2 - 4$?

   (A) $25x^2 + 4 = y^2$
   (B) $75x^2 = 3y^2 - 12$
   (C) $25x^2 = (y + 2)(y - 2)$
   (D) $5x = y - 2$
   (E) $x^2 = \dfrac{y^2 - 4}{25}$

8. If there are 664,579 prime numbers among the first 10 million positive integers, approximately what percent of the first 10 million positive integers are prime numbers?

   (A)   0.0066%
   (B)   0.066%
   (C)   0.66%
   (D)   6.6%
   (E)   66%

9. How many multiples of 4 are there between 12 and 96, inclusive?

   (A)   21
   (B)   22
   (C)   23
   (D)   24
   (E)   25

10. In Country X a returning tourist may import goods with a total value of $500 or less tax free, but must pay an 8 percent tax on the portion of the total value in excess of $500. What tax must be paid by a returning tourist who imports goods with a total value of $730?

    (A) $58.40
    (B) $40.00
    (C) $24.60
    (D) $18.40
    (E) $16.00

11. Which of the following is greater than $\frac{2}{3}$?

    (A) $\frac{33}{50}$

    (B) $\frac{8}{11}$

    (C) $\frac{3}{5}$

    (D) $\frac{13}{27}$

    (E) $\frac{5}{8}$

12. If 60 percent of a rectangular floor is covered by a rectangular rug that is 9 feet by 12 feet, what is the area, in square feet, of the floor?

    (A)   65
    (B)   108
    (C)   180
    (D)   270
    (E)   300

13. If "basis points" are defined so that 1 percent is equal to 100 basis points, then 82.5 percent is how many basis points greater than 62.5 percent?

    (A)   0.02
    (B)   0.2
    (C)   20
    (D)   200
    (E)   2,000

14. Three machines, individually, can do a certain job in 4, 5, and 6 hours, respectively. What is the greatest part of the job that can be done in one hour by two of the machines working together at their respective rates?

    (A) $\frac{11}{30}$

    (B) $\frac{9}{20}$

    (C) $\frac{3}{5}$

    (D) $\frac{11}{15}$

    (E) $\frac{5}{6}$

15. The value of $-3-(-10)$ is how much greater than the value of $-10-(-3)$?

    (A)   0
    (B)   6
    (C)   7
    (D)   14
    (E)   26

16. If X and Y are sets of integers, X Δ Y denotes the set of integers that belong to set X or set Y, but not both. If X consists of 10 integers, Y consists of 18 integers, and 6 of the integers are in both X and Y, then X Δ Y consists of how many integers?

(A)   6
(B)   16
(C)   22
(D)   30
(E)   174

17.   In the figure above, the sum of the three numbers in the horizontal row equals the product of the three numbers in the vertical column. What is the value of xy?

(A)   6
(B)   15
(C)   35
(D)   75
(E)   90

18. $(1+\sqrt{5})(1-\sqrt{5}) =$

(A)   −4
(B)   2
(C)   6
(D) $-4-2\sqrt{5}$
(E) $6-2\sqrt{5}$

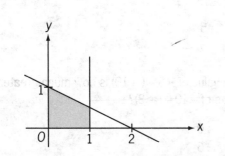

19.   In the rectangular coordinate system above, the shaded region is bounded by straight lines. Which of the following is NOT an equation of one of the boundary lines?

(A) $x = 0$
(B) $y = 0$
(C) $x = 1$
(D) $x - y = 0$
(E) $x + 2y = 2$

20.   A certain population of bacteria doubles every 10 minutes. If the number of bacteria in the population initially was 10^4, what was the number in the population 1 hour later?

(A) $2(10^4)$
(B) $6(10^4)$
(C) $(2^6)(10^4)$
(D) $(10^6)(10^4)$
(E) $(10^4)^6$

21.   How many minutes does it take to travel 120 miles at 400 miles per hour?

(A)   3
(B) $3\dfrac{1}{3}$
(C) $8\dfrac{2}{3}$
(D)   12
(E)   18

22.   If the perimeter of a rectangular garden plot is 34 feet and its area is 60 square feet, what is the length of each of the longer sides?

(A)   5 ft
(B)   6 ft
(C)   10 ft
(D)   12 ft
(E)   15 ft

23.   A certain manufacturer produces items for which the production costs consist of annual fixed costs totaling $130,000 and variable costs averaging $8 per item. If the manufacturer's selling price per item is $15, how many items must the manufacturer produce and sell to earn an annual profit of $150,000?

(A)   2,858
(B)   18,667
(C)   21,429
(D)   35,000
(E)   40,000

24. In a poll of 66,000 physicians, only 20 percent responded; of these, 10 percent disclosed their preference for pain reliever X. How many of the physicians who responded did not disclose a preference for pain reliever X?

    (A)   1,320
    (B)   5,280
    (C)   6,600
    (D)   10,560
    (E)   11,880

25. $\dfrac{3}{100} + \dfrac{5}{1,000} + \dfrac{7}{100,000} =$

    (A)   0.357
    (B)   0.3507
    (C)   0.35007
    (D)   0.0357
    (E)   0.03507

26. If the number n of calculators sold per week varies with the price p in dollars according to the equation $n = 300 - 20p$, what would be the total weekly revenue from the sale of $10 calculators?

    (A) $ 100
    (B) $ 300
    (C) $1,000
    (D) $2,800
    (E) $3,000

27. Which of the following fractions is equal to the decimal 0.0625?

    (A) $\dfrac{5}{8}$

    (B) $\dfrac{3}{8}$

    (C) $\dfrac{1}{16}$

    (D) $\dfrac{1}{18}$

    (E) $\dfrac{3}{80}$

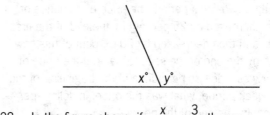

28. In the figure above, if $\dfrac{x}{x+y} = \dfrac{3}{8}$, then $x =$

    (A)   60
    (B)   67.5
    (C)   72
    (D)   108
    (E)   112.5

29. If positive integers x and y are not both odd, which of the following must be even?

    (A) xy
    (B) $x + y$
    (C) $x - y$
    (D) $x + y - 1$
    (E) $2(x + y) - 1$

30. On 3 sales John has received commissions of $240, $80, and $110, and he has 1 additional sale pending. If John is to receive an average (arithmetic mean) commission of exactly $150 on the 4 sales, then the 4th commission must be

    (A) $164
    (B) $170
    (C) $175
    (D) $182
    (E) $185

31. The annual budget of a certain college is to be shown on a circle graph. If the size of each sector of the graph is to be proportional to the amount of the budget it represents, how many degrees of the circle should be used to represent an item that is 15 percent of the budget?

    (A)   15°
    (B)   36°
    (C)   54°
    (D)   90°
    (E)   150°

32. During a two-week period, the price of an ounce of silver increased by 25 percent by the end of the first week and then decreased by 20 percent of this new price by the end of the second week. If the price of silver was x dollars per ounce at the beginning of the two-week period, what was the price, in dollars per ounce, by the end of the period?

    (A)   0.8x
    (B)   0.95x
    (C)   x
    (D)   1.05x
    (E)   1.25x

33. In a certain pond, 50 fish were caught, tagged, and returned to the pond. A few days later, 50 fish were caught again, of which 2 were found to have been tagged. If the percent of tagged fish in the second catch approximates the percent of tagged fish in the pond, what is the approximate number of fish in the pond?

    (A)   400
    (B)   625
    (C)   1,250
    (D)   2,500
    (E)   10,000

34. $\sqrt{16+16} =$

    (A) $4\sqrt{2}$
    (B) $8\sqrt{2}$
    (C) $16\sqrt{2}$
    (D)   8
    (E)   16

35. An automobile's gasoline mileage varies, depending on the speed of the automobile, between 18.0 and 22.4 miles per gallon, inclusive. What is the maximum distance, in miles, that the automobile could be driven on 15 gallons of gasoline?

    (A)   336
    (B)   320
    (C)   303
    (D)   284
    (E)   270

36. The organizers of a fair projected a 25 percent increase in attendance this year over that of last year, but attendance this year actually decreased by 20 percent. What percent of the projected attendance was the actual attendance?

    (A)   45%
    (B)   56%
    (C)   64%
    (D)   75%
    (E)   80%

37. What is the ratio of $\frac{3}{4}$ to the product $4\left(\frac{3}{4}\right)$?

    (A) $\frac{1}{4}$

    (B) $\frac{1}{3}$

    (C) $\frac{4}{9}$

    (D) $\frac{9}{4}$

    (E)   4

38. If $3 - x = 2x - 3$, then $4x =$

    (A)   −24
    (B)   − 8
    (C)   0
    (D)   8
    (E)   24

39. If $x > 3,000$, then the value of $\frac{x}{2x + 1}$ is closest to

    (A) $\frac{1}{6}$

    (B) $\frac{1}{3}$

    (C) $\frac{10}{21}$

    (D) $\frac{1}{2}$

    (E) $\frac{3}{2}$

40. If 18 is 15 percent of 30 percent of a certain number, what is the number?

(A)   9
(B)   36
(C)   40
(D)   81
(E)   400

41. If $x = (0.08)^2$, $y = \dfrac{1}{(0.08)^2}$, and

$z = (1 - 0.08)^2 - 1$, which of the following is true?

(A) $x = y = z$
(B) $y < z < x$
(C) $z < x < y$
(D) $y <$ and $x = z$
(E) $x < y$ and $x = z$

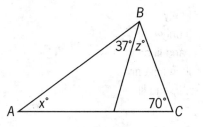

42. In $\triangle ABC$ above, what is x in terms of z?

(A) $z + 73$
(B) $z - 73$
(C) $70 - z$
(D) $z - 70$
(E) $73 - z$

43. $\dfrac{(3)(0.072)}{0.54} =$

(A)   0.04
(B)   0.3
(C)   0.4
(D)   0.8
(E)   4.0

44. What is the maximum number of $1\frac{1}{4}$ foot pieces of wire that can be cut from a wire that is 24 feet long?

(A)   11
(B)   18
(C)   19
(D)   20
(E)   30

$$\frac{61.24 \times (0.998)^2}{\sqrt{403}}$$

45. The expression above is approximately equal to

(A)   1
(B)   3
(C)   4
(D)   5
(E)   6

46. If the numbers $\dfrac{17}{24}$, $\dfrac{1}{2}$, $\dfrac{3}{8}$, $\dfrac{3}{4}$, and $\dfrac{9}{16}$ were ordered from greatest to least, the middle number of the resulting sequence would be

(A) $\dfrac{17}{24}$

(B) $\dfrac{1}{2}$

(C) $\dfrac{3}{8}$

(D) $\dfrac{3}{4}$

(E) $\dfrac{9}{16}$

47. Last year if 97 percent of the revenues of a company came from domestic sources and the remaining revenues, totaling $450,000, came from foreign sources, what was the total of the company's revenues?

(A) $ 1,350,000
(B) $ 1,500,000
(C) $ 4,500,000
(D) $ 15,000,000
(E) $150,000,000

48. $\dfrac{2 + 2\sqrt{6}}{2} =$

(A) $\sqrt{6}$
(B) $2\sqrt{6}$
(C) $1 + \sqrt{6}$
(D) $1 + 2\sqrt{6}$
(E) $2 + \sqrt{6}$

49. A certain fishing boat is chartered by 6 people who are to contribute equally to the total charter cost of $480. If each person contributes equally to a $150 down payment, how much of the charter cost will each person still owe?

    (A) $80
    (B) $66
    (C) $55
    (D) $50
    (E) $45

50. Craig sells major appliances. For each appliance he sells, Craig receives a commission of $50 plus 10 percent of the selling price. During one particular week Craig sold 6 appliances for selling prices totaling $3,620. What was the total of Craig's commissions for that week?

    (A) $412
    (B) $526
    (C) $585
    (D) $605
    (E) $662

51. What number when multiplied by $\frac{4}{7}$ yields $\frac{6}{7}$ as the result?

    (A) $\frac{2}{7}$

    (B) $\frac{3}{3}$

    (C) $\frac{3}{2}$

    (D) $\frac{24}{7}$

    (E) $\frac{7}{2}$

52. If 3 pounds of dried apricots that cost x dollars per pound are mixed with 2 pounds of prunes that cost y dollars per pound, what is the cost, in dollars, per pound of the mixture?

    (A) $\dfrac{3x + 2y}{5}$

    (B) $\dfrac{3x + 2y}{x + y}$

    (C) $\dfrac{3x + 2y}{xy}$

    (D) $5(3x + 2y)$

    (E) $3x + 2y$

53. Which of the following must be equal to zero for all real numbers x?

    I. $-\dfrac{1}{x}$

    II. $x + (-x)$

    III. x^0

    (A) I only
    (B) II only
    (C) I and III only
    (D) II and III only
    (E) I, II, and III

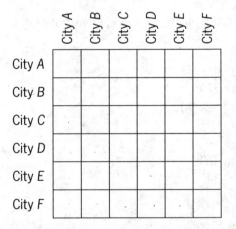

54. In the table above, what is the least number of table entries that are needed to show the mileage between each city and each of the other five cities?

    (A) 15
    (B) 1
    (C) 5
    (D) 0
    (E) 6

55. If $(t - 8)$ is a factor of $t^2 - kt - 48$, then $k =$

    (A)   16
    (B)   12
    (C)   2
    (D)   6
    (E)   14

56. $\dfrac{31}{125} =$

    (A)   0.248
    (B)   0.252
    (C)   0.284
    (D)   0.312
    (E)   0.320

57. Members of a social club met to address 280 newsletters. If they addressed $\dfrac{1}{4}$ of the newsletters during the first hour and $\dfrac{2}{5}$ of the remaining newsletters during the second hour, how many newsletters did they address during the second hour?

    (A)   28
    (B)   42
    (C)   63
    (D)   84
    (E)   112

58. $\left(\sqrt{3} + 2\right)\left(\sqrt{3} - 2\right) =$

    (A) $\sqrt{3} - 4$
    (B) $\sqrt{6} - 4$
    (C) -1
    (D) 1
    (E) 2

59. The arithmetic mean and standard deviation of a certain normal distribution are 13.5 and 1.5, respectively. What value is exactly 2 standard deviations less than the mean?

    (A)   10.5
    (B)   11.0
    (C)   11.5
    (D)   12.0
    (E)   12.5

60. When N is divided by T, the quotient is S and the remainder is V. Which of the following expressions is equal to N?

    (A) ST
    (B) $S + V$
    (C) $ST + V$
    (D) $T(S + V)$
    (E) $T(S - V)$

    38, 69, 22, 73, 31, 47, 13, 82

61. Which of the following numbers is greater than three-fourths of the numbers but less than one-fourth of the numbers in the list above?

    (A)   56
    (B)   68
    (C)   69
    (D)   71
    (E)   73

62. The cost of picture frame M is $10.00 less than 3 times the cost of picture frame N. If the cost of frame M is $50.00, what is the cost of frame N?

    (A) $13.33
    (B) $16.66
    (C) $20.00
    (D) $26.66
    (E) $40.00

63. If $S = \{0, 4, 5, 2, 11, 8\}$, how much greater than the median of the numbers in S is the mean of the numbers in S?

    (A)   0.5
    (B)   1.0
    (C)   1.5
    (D)   2.0
    (E)   2.5

64. The value of $\sqrt[3]{-89}$ is

    (A)   between -9 and -10
    (B)   between -8 and -9
    (C)   between -4 and -5
    (D)   between -3 and -4
    (E)   undefined

65. Of the following, which is least?

(A) $\dfrac{1}{0.2}$

(B) $(0.2)^2$

(C) 0.02

(D) $\dfrac{0.2}{2}$

(E) 0.2

66. If $d = 2.0453$ and d^* is the decimal obtained by rounding d to the nearest hundredth, what is the value of $d^* - d$?

(A) −0.0053
(B) −0.0003
(C) 0.0007
(D) 0.0047
(E) 0.0153

67. Company K's earnings were $12 million last year. If this year's earnings are projected to be 150 percent greater than last year's earnings, what are Company K's projected earnings this year?

(A) $13.5 million
(B) $15 million
(C) $18 million
(D) $27 million
(E) $30 million

68. If −3 is 6 more than x, what is the value of $\dfrac{x}{3}$?

(A) −9
(B) −6
(C) −3
(D) −1
(E) 1

69. An athlete runs R miles in H hours, then rides a bicycle Q miles in the same number of hours. Which of the following represents the athlete's average speed, in miles per hour, for these two activities combined?

(A) $\dfrac{R - Q}{H}$

(B) $\dfrac{R - Q}{2H}$

(C) $\dfrac{2(R + Q)}{H}$

(D) $\dfrac{2(R + Q)}{2H}$

(E) $\dfrac{R + Q}{2H}$

70. If a certain sample of data has a mean of 20.0 and a standard deviation of 3.0, which of the following values is more than 2.5 standard deviations from the mean?

(A) 12.0
(B) 13.5
(C) 17.0
(D) 23.5
(E) 26.5

County	Amount Recycled	Amount Disposed of
A	16,700	142,800
B	8,800	48,000
C	13,000	51,400
D	3,900	20,300
E	3,300	16,200

71. The table above shows the amount of waste material, in tons, recycled by each of five counties in a single year and the amount of waste material, also in tons, that was disposed of in landfills by the five counties in that year. Which county had the lowest ratio of waste material disposed of to waste material recycled in the year reported in the table?

(A) A
(B) B
(C) C
(D) D
(E) E

72. If $a = 7$ and $b = -7$, what is the value of $2a - 2b + b^2$?

    (A) -49
    (B) 21
    (C) 49
    (D) 63
    (E) 77

73. Equal amounts of water were poured into two empty jars of different capacities, which made one jar $\frac{1}{4}$ full and the other jar $\frac{1}{3}$ full. If the water in the jar with the lesser capacity is then poured into the jar with the greater capacity, what fraction of the larger jar will be filled with water?

    (A) $\frac{1}{7}$

    (B) $\frac{2}{7}$

    (C) $\frac{1}{2}$

    (D) $\frac{7}{12}$

    (E) $\frac{2}{3}$

74. If Mel saved more than $10 by purchasing a sweater at a 15 percent discount, what is the smallest amount the original price of the sweater could be, to the nearest dollar?

    (A) 45
    (B) 67
    (C) 75
    (D) 83
    (E) 150

75. If $x = -1$, then $-(x^4 + x^3 + x^2 + x) =$

    (A) -10
    (B) -4
    (C) 0
    (D) 4
    (E) 10

76. Today Rose is twice as old as Sam and Sam is 3 years younger than Tina. If Rose, Sam, and Tina are all alive 4 years from today, which of the following must be true on that day?

    I.   Rose is twice as old as Sam.
    II.   Sam is 3 years younger than Tina.
    III. Rose is older than Tina.

    (A)   I only
    (B)   II only
    (C)   III only
    (D)   I and II
    (E)   II and III

77. If a square region has area x, what is the length of its diagonal in terms of x?

    (A) $\sqrt{x}$
    (B) $\sqrt{2x}$
    (C) $2\sqrt{x}$
    (D) $x\sqrt{2}$
    (E) $2x$

78. The temperature in degrees Celsius (C) can be converted to temperature in degrees Fahrenheit (F) by the formula $F = \frac{9}{5}C + 32$. What is the temperature at which $F = C$?

    (A) $20°$
    (B) $\left(\frac{32}{5}\right)°$
    (C) $0°$
    (D) $-20°$
    (E) $-40°$

79. During a car trip, Maria stopped to rest after she traveled $\frac{1}{2}$ of the total distance to her destination. She stopped again after she traveled $\frac{1}{4}$ of the distance remaining between her first stop and her destination, and then she drove the remaining 120 miles to her destination. What was the total distance, in miles, from Maria's starting point to her destination?

    (A) 280
    (B) 320
    (C) 360
    (D) 420
    (E) 480

80. If x is to be chosen at random from the set $\{1, 2, 3, 4\}$ and y is to be chosen at random from the set $\{5, 6, 7\}$, what is the probability that xy will be even?

    (A) $\dfrac{1}{6}$

    (B) $\dfrac{1}{3}$

    (C) $\dfrac{1}{2}$

    (D) $\dfrac{2}{3}$

    (E) $\dfrac{5}{6}$

81. Which of the following is equal to x^{18} for all positive values of x?

    (A) $x^9 + x^9$

    (B) $(x^2)^9$

    (C) $(x^9)^9$

    (D) $(x^3)^{15}$

    (E) $\dfrac{x^4}{x^{22}}$

82. Three business partners, Q, R, and S, agree to divide their total profit for a certain year in the ratios $2 : 5 : 8$, respectively. If Q's share was $4,000, what was the total profit of the business partners for the year?

    (A) $ 26,000
    (B) $ 30,000
    (C) $ 52,000
    (D) $ 60,000
    (E) $300,000

83. If $u > t$, $r > q$, $s > t$, and $t > r$, which of the following must be true?

    I. $u > s$
    II. $s > q$
    III. $u > r$

    (A) I only
    (B) II only
    (C) III only
    (D) I and II
    (E) II and III

84. The average (arithmetic mean) of 6 numbers is 8.5. When one number is discarded, the average of the remaining numbers becomes 7.2. What is the discarded number?

    (A) 7.8
    (B) 9.8
    (C) 10.0
    (D) 12.4
    (E) 15.0

85. In the rectangular coordinate system above, the area of $\triangle RST$ is

    (A) $\dfrac{bc}{2}$

    (B) $\dfrac{b(c-1)}{2}$

    (C) $\dfrac{c(b-1)}{2}$

    (D) $\dfrac{a(c-1)}{2}$

    (E) $\dfrac{c(a-1)}{2}$

86. Which of the following equations has a root in common with $x^2 - 6x + 5 = 0$?

    (A) $x^2 + 1 = 0$
    (B) $x^2 - x - 2 = 0$
    (C) $x^2 - 10x - 5 = 0$
    (D) $2x^2 - 2 = 0$
    (E) $x^2 - 2x - 3 = 0$

87. One inlet pipe fills an empty tank in 5 hours. A second inlet pipe fills the same tank in 3 hours. If both pipes are used together, how long will it take to fill $\frac{2}{3}$ of the tank?

    (A) $\frac{8}{15}$ hr

    (B) $\frac{3}{4}$ hr

    (C) $\frac{5}{4}$ hr

    (D) $\frac{15}{8}$ hr

    (E) $\frac{8}{3}$ hr

88. $\left(\frac{1}{5}\right)^2 - \left(\frac{1}{5}\right)\left(\frac{1}{4}\right) =$

    (A) $-\frac{1}{20}$

    (B) $-\frac{1}{100}$

    (C) $\frac{1}{100}$

    (D) $\frac{1}{20}$

    (E) $\frac{1}{5}$

89. If the length and width of a rectangular garden plot were each increased by 20 percent, what would be the percent increase in the area of the plot?

    (A) 20%
    (B) 24%
    (C) 36%
    (D) 40%
    (E) 44%

90. The population of a bacteria culture doubles every 2 minutes. Approximately how many minutes will it take for the population to grow from 1,000 to 500,000 bacteria?

    (A) 10
    (B) 12
    (C) 14
    (D) 16
    (E) 18

91. For a light that has an intensity of 60 candles at its source, the intensity in candles, S, of the light at a point d feet from the source is given by the formula $S = \frac{60k}{d^2}$, where k is a constant. If the intensity of the light is 30 candles at a distance of 2 feet from the source, what is the intensity of the light at a distance of 20 feet from the source?

    (A) $\frac{3}{10}$ candle

    (B) $\frac{1}{2}$ candle

    (C) 1 candle

    (D) 2 candles

    (E) 3 candles

92. If $b < 2$ and $2x - 3b = 0$, which of the following must be true?

    (A) $x > -3$
    (B) $x < 2$
    (C) $x = 3$
    (D) $x < 3$
    (E) $x > 3$

93. $\dfrac{(-1.5)(1.2) - (4.5)(0.4)}{30} =$

    (A) -1.2
    (B) -0.12
    (C)   0
    (D)   0.12
    (E)   1.2

94. René earns $8.50 per hour on days other than Sundays and twice that rate on Sundays. Last week she worked a total of 40 hours, including 8 hours on Sunday. What were her earnings for the week?

    (A) $272
    (B) $340
    (C) $398
    (D) $408
    (E) $476

95. In a shipment of 120 machine parts, 5 percent were defective. In a shipment of 80 machine parts, 10 percent were defective. For the two shipments combined, what percent of the machine parts were defective?

    (A)   6.5%
    (B)   7.0%
    (C)   7.5%
    (D)   8.0%
    (E)   8.5%

96. If $8^{2x+3} = 2^{3x+6}$, then $x =$

    (A) -3
    (B) -1
    (C)   0
    (D)   1
    (E)   3

97. Of the following, the closest approximation to $\sqrt{\dfrac{5.98(601.5)}{15.79}}$ is

    (A)   5
    (B)   15
    (C)   20
    (D)   25
    (E)   225

98. Which of the following CANNOT be the greatest common divisor of two positive integers x and y?

    (A)   1
    (B) x
    (C) y
    (D) $x - y$
    (E) $x + y$

99. If a, b, and c are nonzero numbers and $a + b = c$, which of the following is equal to 1?

    (A) $\dfrac{a - b}{c}$

    (B) $\dfrac{a - c}{b}$

    (C) $\dfrac{b - c}{a}$

    (D) $\dfrac{b - a}{c}$

    (E) $\dfrac{c - b}{a}$

100. Last year Carlos saved 10 percent of his annual earnings. This year he earned 5 percent more than last year and he saved 12 percent of his annual earnings. The amount saved this year was what percent of the amount saved last year?

    (A)   122%
    (B)   124%
    (C)   126%
    (D)   128%
    (E)   130%

101. A corporation that had $115.19 billion in profits for the year paid out $230.10 million in employee benefits. Approximately what percent of the profits were the employee benefits? (1 billion = 10^9)

    (A)   50%
    (B)   20%
    (C)   5%
    (D)   2%
    (E)   0.2%

Questions 102–103 refer to the following definition.

For any positive integer n, $n > 1$, the "length" of n is the number of positive primes (not necessarily distinct) whose product is n. For example, the length of 50 is 3 since $50 = (2)(5)(5)$.

102. Which of the following integers has length 3?

(A) 3
(B) 15
(C) 60
(D) 64
(E) 105

103. What is the greatest possible length of a positive integer less than 1,000?

(A) 10
(B) 9
(C) 8
(D) 7
(E) 6

104. If $x + y = 8z$, then which of the following represents the average (arithmetic mean) of x, y, and z, in terms of z?

(A) $2z + 1$
(B) $3z$
(C) $5z$
(D) $\dfrac{z}{3}$
(E) $\dfrac{3z}{2}$

105. On the number line, if $r < s$, if p is halfway between r and s, and if t is halfway between p and r, then $\dfrac{s - t}{t - r} =$

(A) $\dfrac{1}{4}$
(B) $\dfrac{1}{3}$
(C) $\dfrac{4}{3}$
(D) 3
(E) 4

106. If x and y are different integers and $x^2 = xy$, which of the following must be true?

I. $x = 0$
II. $y = 0$
III. $x = -y$

(A) I only
(B) II only
(C) III only
(D) I and III only
(E) I, II, and III

107. If $\dfrac{3}{x} = 2$ and $\dfrac{y}{4} = 3$, then $\dfrac{3 + y}{x + 4} =$

(A) $\dfrac{10}{9}$
(B) $\dfrac{3}{2}$
(C) $\dfrac{20}{11}$
(D) $\dfrac{30}{11}$
(E) 5

108. Which of the following fractions has the greatest value?

(A) $\dfrac{6}{(2^2)(5^2)}$
(B) $\dfrac{1}{(2^3)(5^2)}$
(C) $\dfrac{28}{(2^2)(5^3)}$
(D) $\dfrac{62}{(2^3)(5^3)}$
(E) $\dfrac{122}{(2^4)(5^3)}$

109. Which of the following CANNOT yield an integer when divided by 10?

    (A) The sum of two odd integers
    (B) An integer less than 10
    (C) The product of two primes
    (D) The sum of three consecutive integers
    (E) An odd integer

110. A certain clock marks every hour by striking a number of times equal to the hour, and the time required for a stroke is exactly equal to the time interval between strokes. At 6:00 the time lapse between the beginning of the first stroke and the end of the last stroke is 22 seconds. At 12:00, how many seconds elapse between the beginning of the first stroke and the end of the last stroke?

    (A) 72
    (B) 50
    (C) 48
    (D) 46
    (E) 44

111. If $k \neq 0$ and $k - \dfrac{3 - 2k^2}{k} = \dfrac{x}{k}$, then $x =$

    (A) $-3 - k^2$
    (B) $k^2 - 3$
    (C) $3k^2 - 3$
    (D) $k - 3 - 2k^2$
    (E) $k - 3 + 2k^2$

112. $\dfrac{\frac{1}{2} + \frac{1}{3}}{\frac{1}{4}} =$

    (A) $\dfrac{1}{12}$
    (B) $\dfrac{5}{24}$
    (C) $\dfrac{2}{3}$
    (D) $\dfrac{9}{4}$
    (E) $\dfrac{10}{3}$

113. For all numbers s and t, the operation $*$ is defined by $s * t = (s - 1)(t + 1)$. If $(-2) * x = -12$, then $x =$

    (A) 2
    (B) 3
    (C) 5
    (D) 6
    (E) 11

114. Salesperson A's compensation for any week is $360 plus 6 percent of the portion of A's total sales above $1,000 for that week. Salesperson B's compensation for any week is 8 percent of B's total sales for that week. For what amount of total weekly sales would both salespeople earn the same compensation?

    (A) $21,000
    (B) $18,000
    (C) $15,000
    (D) $ 4,500
    (E) $ 4,000

115. The sum of the ages of Doris and Fred is y years. If Doris is 12 years older than Fred, how many years old will Fred be y years from now, in terms of y?

    (A) $y - 6$
    (B) $2y - 6$
    (C) $\dfrac{y}{2} - 6$
    (D) $\dfrac{3y}{2} - 6$
    (E) $\dfrac{5y}{2} - 6$

116. If a basketball team scores an average (arithmetic mean) of x points per game for n games and then scores y points in its next game, what is the team's average score for the $n + 1$ games?

    (A) $\dfrac{nx + y}{n + 1}$
    (B) $x + \dfrac{y}{n + 1}$
    (C) $x + \dfrac{y}{n}$
    (D) $\dfrac{n(x + y)}{n + 1}$
    (E) $\dfrac{x + ny}{n + 1}$

117. Of the following numbers, which one is third greatest?

    (A) $2\sqrt{2} - 1$

    (B) $\sqrt{2} + 1$

    (C) $1 - \sqrt{2}$

    (D) $\sqrt{2} - 1$

    (E) $\sqrt{2}$

118. At a certain pizzeria, $\frac{1}{8}$ of the pizzas sold in one week were mushroom and $\frac{1}{3}$ of the <u>remaining</u> pizzas sold were pepperoni. If n of the pizzas sold were pepperoni, how many were mushroom?

    (A) $\frac{3}{8}n$

    (B) $\frac{3}{7}n$

    (C) $\frac{7}{16}n$

    (D) $\frac{7}{8}n$

    (E) $3n$

119. Two trains, X and Y, started simultaneously from opposite ends of a 100-mile route and traveled toward each other on parallel tracks. Train X, traveling at a constant rate, completed the 100-mile trip in 5 hours; train Y, traveling at a constant rate, completed the 100 mile trip in 3 hours. How many miles had train X traveled when it met train Y?

    (A) 37.5

    (B) 40.0

    (C) 60.0

    (D) 62.5

    (E) 77.5

120. One week a certain truck rental lot had a total of 20 trucks, all of which were on the lot Monday morning. If 50 percent of the trucks that were rented out during the week were returned to the lot on or before Saturday morning of that week, and if there were at least 12 trucks on the lot that Saturday morning, what is the greatest number of different trucks that could have been rented out during the week?

    (A) 18

    (B) 16

    (C) 12

    (D) 8

    (E) 4

121. What is the value of $2x^2 - 2.4x - 1.7$ for $x = 0.7$?

    (A) -0.72

    (B) -1.42

    (C) -1.98

    (D) -2.40

    (E) -2.89

122. If s, u, and v are positive integers and $2s = 2u + 2v$, which of the following must be true?

    I. $s = u$

    II. $u \neq v$

    III. $s > v$

    (A) None

    (B) I only

    (C) II only

    (D) III only

    (E) II and III

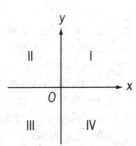

123. In the rectangular coordinate system shown above, which quadrant, if any, contains no point (x, y) that satisfies the inequality $2x - 3y \leq -6$?

    (A) None

    (B) I

    (C) II

    (D) III

    (E) IV

124. The cost to rent a small bus for a trip is x dollars, which is to be shared equally among the people taking the trip. If 10 people take the trip rather than 16, how many more dollars, in terms of x, will it cost per person?

(A) $\dfrac{x}{6}$

(B) $\dfrac{x}{10}$

(C) $\dfrac{x}{16}$

(D) $\dfrac{3x}{40}$

(E) $\dfrac{3x}{80}$

125. If x is an integer and y = 3x + 2, which of the following CANNOT be a divisor of y?

(A) 4
(B) 5
(C) 6
(D) 7
(E) 8

126. A certain electronic component is sold in boxes of 54 for $16.20 and in boxes of 27 for $13.20. A customer who needed only 54 components for a project had to buy 2 boxes of 27 because boxes of 54 were unavailable. Approximately how much more did the customer pay for each component due to the unavailability of the larger boxes?

(A) $0.33
(B) $0.19
(C) $0.11
(D) $0.06
(E) $0.03

127. As a salesperson, Phyllis can choose one of two methods of annual payment: either an annual salary of $35,000 with no commission or an annual salary of $10,000 plus a 20 percent commission on her total annual sales. What must her total annual sales be to give her the same annual pay with either method?

(A) $100,000
(B) $120,000
(C) $125,000
(D) $130,000
(E) $132,000

128. If $\dfrac{x+y}{xy} = 1$, then y =

(A) $\dfrac{x}{x-1}$

(B) $\dfrac{x}{x+1}$

(C) $\dfrac{x-1}{x}$

(D) $\dfrac{x+1}{x}$

(E) x

129. Last year Department Store X had a sales total for December that was 4 times the average (arithmetic mean) of the monthly sales totals for January through November. The sales total for December was what fraction of the sales total for the year?

(A) $\dfrac{1}{4}$

(B) $\dfrac{4}{15}$

(C) $\dfrac{1}{3}$

(D) $\dfrac{4}{11}$

(E) $\dfrac{4}{5}$

130. Working alone, printers X, Y, and Z can do a certain printing job, consisting of a large number of pages, in 12, 15, and 18 hours, respectively. What is the ratio of the time it takes printer X to do the job, working alone at its rate, to the time it takes printers Y and Z to do the job, working together at their individual rates?

(A) $\dfrac{4}{11}$

(B) $\dfrac{1}{2}$

(C) $\dfrac{15}{22}$

(D) $\dfrac{22}{15}$

(E) $\dfrac{11}{4}$

131. A rabbit on a controlled diet is fed daily 300 grams of a mixture of two foods, food X and food Y. Food X contains 10 percent protein and food Y contains 15 percent protein. If the rabbit's diet provides exactly 38 grams of protein daily, how many grams of food X are in the mixture?

   (A) 100
   (B) 140
   (C) 150
   (D) 160
   (E) 200

132. A company that ships boxes to a total of 12 distribution centers uses color coding to identify each center. If either a single color or a pair of two different colors is chosen to represent each center and if each center is uniquely represented by that choice of one or two colors, what is the minimum number of colors needed for the coding? (Assume that the order of the colors in a pair does not matter.)

   (A) 4
   (B) 5
   (C) 6
   (D) 12
   (E) 24

133. If $x \neq 2$, then $\dfrac{3x^2(x-2) - x + 2}{x - 2} =$

   (A) $3x^2 - x + 2$
   (B) $3x^2 + 1$
   (C) $3x^2$
   (D) $3x^2 - 1$
   (E) $3x^2 - 2$

134. If $d > 0$ and $0 < 1 - \dfrac{c}{d} < 1$, which of the following must be true?

  I. $c > 0$

  II. $\dfrac{c}{d} < 1$

  III. $c^2 + d^2 > 1$

   (A) I only
   (B) II only
   (C) I and II only
   (D) II and III only
   (E) I, II, and III

135. $\dfrac{\frac{1}{2}}{\frac{1}{4} + \frac{1}{6}} =$

   (A) $\dfrac{6}{5}$

   (B) $\dfrac{5}{6}$

   (C) $\dfrac{5}{24}$

   (D) $\dfrac{1}{5}$

   (E) $\dfrac{1}{12}$

136. A train travels from New York City to Chicago, a distance of approximately 840 miles, at an average rate of 60 miles per hour and arrives in Chicago at 6:00 in the evening, Chicago time. At what hour in the morning, New York City time, did the train depart for Chicago? (Note: Chicago time is one hour earlier than New York City time.)

   (A) 4:00
   (B) 5:00
   (C) 6:00
   (D) 7:00
   (E) 8:00

137. Last year Manfred received 26 paychecks. Each of his first 6 paychecks was $750; each of his remaining paychecks was $30 more than each of his first 6 paychecks. To the nearest dollar, what was the average (arithmetic mean) amount of his paychecks for the year?

(A) $752
(B) $755
(C) $765
(D) $773
(E) $775

138. If 25 percent of p is equal to 10 percent of q, and $pq \neq 0$, then p is what percent of q?

(A) 2.5%
(B) 15%
(C) 20%
(D) 35%
(E) 40%

139. If the length of an edge of cube X is twice the length of an edge of cube Y, what is the ratio of the volume of cube Y to the volume of cube X?

(A) $\dfrac{1}{2}$

(B) $\dfrac{1}{4}$

(C) $\dfrac{1}{6}$

(D) $\dfrac{1}{8}$

(E) $\dfrac{1}{27}$

140. Machines A and B always operate independently and at their respective constant rates. When working alone, machine A can fill a production lot in 5 hours, and machine B can fill the same lot in x hours. When the two machines operate simultaneously to fill the production lot, it takes them 2 hours to complete the job. What is the value of x?

(A) $3\dfrac{1}{3}$

(B) 3

(C) $2\dfrac{1}{2}$

(D) $2\dfrac{1}{3}$

(E) $1\dfrac{1}{2}$

141. An artist wishes to paint a circular region on a square poster that is 2 feet on a side. If the area of the circular region is to be $\dfrac{1}{2}$ the area of the poster, what must be the radius of the circular region in feet?

(A) $\dfrac{1}{\pi}$

(B) $\sqrt{\dfrac{2}{\pi}}$

(C) 1

(D) $\dfrac{2}{\sqrt{\pi}}$

(E) $\dfrac{\pi}{1}$

142. If a is a positive integer, and if the units' digit of a^2 is 9 and the units' digit of $(a + 1)^2$ is 4, what is the units' digit of $(a + 2)^2$?

(A) 1
(B) 3
(C) 5
(D) 6
(E) 14

143. A $500 investment and a $1,500 investment have a combined yearly return of 8.5 percent of the total of the two investments. If the $500 investment has a yearly return of 7 percent, what percent yearly return does the $1,500 investment have?

(A)   9%

(B)   10%

(C) $10\frac{5}{8}\%$

(D)   11%

(E)   12%

144. For any integer n greater than 1, $\lfloor n$ denotes the product of all the integers from 1 to n, inclusive. How many prime numbers are there between $\lfloor 6 + 2$ and $\lfloor 6 + 6$, inclusive?

(A)   None

(B)   One

(C)   Two

(D)   Three

(E)   Four

145. If $\left(7^{\frac{3}{4}}\right)^n = 7$, what is the value of n?

(A) $\dfrac{1}{3}$

(B) $\dfrac{2}{3}$

(C) $\dfrac{4}{3}$

(D) $\dfrac{5}{3}$

(E) s

146. Which of the following is equal to the average (arithmetic mean) of $(x + 2)^2$ and $(x - 2)^2$?

(A) x^2

(B) $x^2 + 2$

(C) $x^2 + 4$

(D) $x^2 + 2x$

(E) $x^2 + 4x$

147. If $x^4 + y^4 = 100$ then the greatest possible value of x is between

(A)   0 and 3

(B)   3 and 6

(C)   6 and 9

(D)   9 and 12

(E)   12 and 15

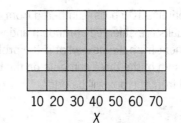

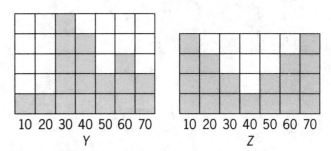

148. If the variables, X, Y, and Z take on only the values 10, 20, 30, 40, 50, 60, or 70 with frequencies indicated by the shaded regions above, for which of the frequency distributions is the mean equal to the median?

(A) X only

(B) Y only

(C) Z only

(D) X and Y

(E) X and Z

149. For how many integers n is $2^n = n^2$?

(A)   None

(B)   One

(C)   Two

(D)   Three

(E)   More than three

150. If r and s are integers and $rs + r$ is odd, which of the following must be even?

(A) r

(B) s

(C) $r + s$

(D) $rs - r$

(E) $r^2 + s$

151. A box contains 100 balls, numbered from 1 to 100. If three balls are selected at random and with replacement from the box, what is the probability that the sum of the three numbers on the balls selected from the box will be odd?

    (A) $\dfrac{1}{4}$

    (B) $\dfrac{3}{8}$

    (C) $\dfrac{1}{2}$

    (D) $\dfrac{5}{8}$

    (E) $\dfrac{3}{4}$

152. If $0 < x < 1$, which of the following inequalities must be true?

    I. $x^5 < x^3$

    II. $x^4 + x^5 < x^3 + x^2$

    III. $x^4 - x^5 < x^2 - x^3$

    (A)   None
    (B)   I only
    (C)   II only
    (D)   I and II only
    (E)   I, II, and III

153. If $(2^x)(2^y) = 8$ and $(9^x)(3^y) = 81$, then $(x, y) =$

    (A)   (1, 2)
    (B)   (2, 1)
    (C)   (1, 1)
    (D)   (2, 2)
    (E)   (1, 3)

154. If $a = 1$ and $\dfrac{a - b}{c} = 1$, which of the following is NOT a possible value of b?

    (A)   −2
    (B)   −1
    (C)   0
    (D)   1
    (E)   2

155. If $\dfrac{x}{y} = \dfrac{2}{3}$, then $\dfrac{x - y}{x} =$

    (A) $-\dfrac{1}{2}$

    (B) $-\dfrac{1}{3}$

    (C) $\dfrac{1}{3}$

    (D) $\dfrac{1}{2}$

    (E) $\dfrac{5}{2}$

156. The contents of a certain box consist of 14 apples and 23 oranges. How many oranges must be removed from the box so that 70 percent of the pieces of fruit in the box will be apples?

    (A)   3
    (B)   6
    (C)   14
    (D)   17
    (E)   20

157. Last year, a certain public transportation system sold an average (arithmetic mean) of 41,000 tickets per day on weekdays (Monday through Friday) and an average of 18,000 tickets per day on Saturday and Sunday. Which of the following is closest to the total number of tickets sold last year?

    (A)   1 million
    (B)   1.25 million
    (C)   10 million
    (D)   12.5 million
    (E)   125 million

District	Number of Votes	Percent of Votes for Candidate P	Percent of Votes for Candidate Q
1	800	60	40
2	1,000	50	50
3	1,500	50	50
4	1,800	40	60
5	1,200	30	70

158. The table above shows the results of a recent school board election in which the candidate with the higher total number of votes from the five districts was declared the winner. Which district had the greatest number of votes for the winner?

    (A) 1
    (B) 2
    (C) 3
    (D) 4
    (E) 5

159. A group of store managers must assemble 280 displays for an upcoming sale. If they assemble 25 percent of the displays during the first hour and 40 percent of the remaining displays during the second hour, how many of the displays will not have been assembled by the end of the second hour?

    (A) 70
    (B) 98
    (C) 126
    (D) 168
    (E) 182

1	2	3	4	5	6	7
-2	-4	-6	-8	-10	-12	-14
3	6	9	12	15	18	21
-4	-8	-12	-16	-20	-24	-28
5	10	15	20	25	30	35
-6	-12	-18	-24	-30	-36	-42
7	14	21	28	35	42	49

160. What is the sum of the integers in the table above?

    (A) 28
    (B) 112
    (C) 336
    (D) 448
    (E) 784

3, k, 2, 8, m, 3

161. The arithmetic mean of the list of numbers above is 4. If k and m are integers and $k \neq m$, what is the median of the list?

    (A) 2
    (B) 2.5
    (C) 3
    (D) 3.5
    (E) 4

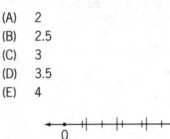

162. On the number line above, the segment from 0 to 1 has been divided into fifths, as indicated by the large tick marks, and also into sevenths, as indicated by the small tick marks. What is the least possible distance between any two of the tick marks?

    (A) $\dfrac{1}{70}$

    (B) $\dfrac{1}{35}$

    (C) $\dfrac{2}{35}$

    (D) $\dfrac{1}{12}$

    (E) $\dfrac{1}{7}$

163. $\dfrac{(8^2)(3^3)(2^4)}{96^2} =$

    (A) 3
    (B) 6
    (C) 2
    (D) 12
    (E) 18

164. When 10 is divided by the positive integer n, the remainder is $n - 4$. Which of the following could be the value of n?

    (A) 3
    (B) 4
    (C) 7
    (D) 8
    (E) 12

165. If $\frac{1}{2}$ of the money in a certain trust fund was invested in stocks, $\frac{1}{4}$ in bonds, $\frac{1}{5}$ in a mutual fund, and the remaining $10,000 in a government certificate, what was the total amount of the trust fund?

(A) $ 100,000
(B) $ 150,000
(C) $ 200,000
(D) $ 500,000
(E) $2,000,000

166. If m is an integer such that $(-2)^{2m} = 2^{9-m}$, then $m =$

(A) 1
(B) 2
(C) 3
(D) 4
(E) 6

167. In a mayoral election, Candidate X received $\frac{1}{3}$ more votes than Candidate Y, and Candidate Y received $\frac{1}{4}$ fewer votes than Candidate Z. If Candidate Z received 24,000 votes, how many votes did Candidate X receive?

(A) 18,000
(B) 22,000
(C) 24,000
(D) 26,000
(E) 32,000

168. An airline passenger is planning a trip that involves three connecting flights that leave from Airports A, B, and C, respectively. The first flight leaves Airport A every hour, beginning at 8:00 a.m., and arrives at Airport B $2\frac{1}{2}$ hours later. The second flight leaves Airport B every 20 minutes, beginning at 8:00 a.m., and arrives at Airport C $1\frac{1}{6}$ hours later. The third flight leaves Airport C every hour, beginning at 8:45 a.m. What is the least total amount of time the passenger must spend between flights if all flights keep to their schedules?

(A) 25 min
(B) 1 hr 5 min
(C) 1 hr 15 min
(D) 2 hr 20 min
(E) 3 hr 40 min

169. If n is a positive integer and n^2 is divisible by 72, then the largest positive integer that must divide n is

(A) 6
(B) 12
(C) 24
(D) 36
(E) 48

170. If n is a positive integer and $k + 2 = 3^n$, which of the following could NOT be a value of k?

(A) 1
(B) 4
(C) 7
(D) 25
(E) 79

171. A certain grocery purchased x pounds of produce for p dollars per pound. If y pounds of the produce had to be discarded due to spoilage and the grocery sold the rest for s dollars per pound, which of the following represents the gross profit on the sale of the produce?

(A) $(x - y)\,s - xp$
(B) $(x - y)\,p - ys$
(C) $(s - p)\,y - xp$
(D) $xp - ys$
(E) $(x - y)\,(s - p)$

172. If x, y, and z are positive integers such that x is a factor of y, and x is a multiple of z, which of the following is NOT necessarily an integer?

(A) $\dfrac{x+z}{z}$

(B) $\dfrac{y+z}{x}$

(C) $\dfrac{x+y}{z}$

(D) $\dfrac{xy}{z}$

(E) $\dfrac{yz}{x}$

173. If $\dfrac{a}{b} = \dfrac{2}{3}$, which of the following is NOT true?

(A) $\dfrac{a+b}{b} = \dfrac{5}{3}$

(B) $\dfrac{b}{b-a} = 3$

(C) $\dfrac{a-b}{b} = \dfrac{1}{3}$

(D) $\dfrac{2a}{3b} = \dfrac{4}{9}$

(E) $\dfrac{a+3b}{a} = \dfrac{11}{2}$

$$\begin{array}{r} \square\,\triangle \\ \times\ \ \triangle\,\square \\ \hline \end{array}$$

174. The product of the two-digit numbers above is the three-digit number $\square\,\Diamond\,\square$, where $\square$, $\triangle$, and $\Diamond$, are three different nonzero digits. If $\square \times \triangle < 10$, what is the two-digit number $\square\,\triangle$?

(A) 11
(B) 12
(C) 13
(D) 21
(E) 31

175. A square countertop has a square tile inlay in the center, leaving an untiled strip of uniform width around the tile. If the ratio of the tiled area to the untiled area is 25 to 39, which of the following could be the width, in inches, of the strip?

I. 1
II. 3
III. 4

(A) I only
(B) II only
(C) I and II only
(D) I and III only
(E) I, II, and III

176. $\dfrac{2\frac{3}{5} - 1\frac{2}{3}}{\frac{2}{3} - \frac{3}{5}}$

(A) 16
(B) 14
(C) 3
(D) 1
(E) −1

4.4 Problem Solving Answer Key

1.	C	36.	C	71.	C	106.	A	141.	B
2.	E	37.	A	72.	E	107.	D	142.	A
3.	C	38.	D	73.	C	108.	D	143.	A
4.	C	39.	D	74.	B	109.	E	144.	A
5.	D	40.	E	75.	C	110.	D	145.	C
6.	B	41.	C	76.	B	111.	C	146.	C
7.	D	42.	E	77.	B	112.	E	147.	B
8.	D	43.	C	78.	E	113.	B	148.	E
9.	B	44.	C	79.	B	114.	C	149.	C
10.	D	45.	B	80.	D	115.	D	150.	B
11.	B	46.	E	81.	B	116.	A	151.	C
12.	C	47.	D	82.	B	117.	E	152.	E
13.	E	48.	C	83.	E	118.	B	153.	A
14.	B	49.	C	84.	E	119.	A	154.	D
15.	D	50.	E	85.	B	120.	B	155.	A
16.	B	51.	C	86.	D	121.	D	156.	D
17.	A	52.	A	87.	C	122.	D	157.	D
18.	A	53.	B	88.	B	123.	E	158.	D
19.	D	54.	A	89.	E	124.	E	159.	C
20.	C	55.	C	90.	E	125.	C	160.	B
21.	E	56.	A	91.	A	126.	B	161.	C
22.	D	57.	D	92.	D	127.	C	162.	B
23.	E	58.	C	93.	B	128.	A	163.	A
24.	E	59.	A	94.	D	129.	B	164.	C
25.	E	60.	C	95.	B	130.	D	165.	C
26.	C	61.	D	96.	B	131.	B	166.	C
27.	C	62.	C	97.	B	132.	B	167.	C
28.	B	63.	A	98.	E	133.	D	168.	B
29.	A	64.	C	99.	E	134.	C	169.	B
30.	B	65.	C	100.	C	135.	A	170.	B
31.	C	66.	D	101.	E	136.	B	171.	A
32.	C	67.	E	102.	E	137.	D	172.	B
33.	C	68.	C	103.	B	138.	E	173.	C
34.	A	69.	E	104.	B	139.	D	174.	D
35.	A	70.	A	105.	D	140.	A	175.	E
								176.	B

4.5 Problem Solving Answer Explanations

The following discussion is intended to familiarize you with the most efficient and effective approaches to the kinds of problems common to problem solving questions. The particular questions in this chapter are generally representative of the kinds of problem solving questions you will encounter on the GMAT®. Remember that it is the problem solving strategy that is important, not the specific details of a particular question.

1. If Mario was 32 years old 8 years ago, how old was he x years ago?

    (A) $x - 40$
    (B) $x - 24$
    (C) $40 - x$
    (D) $24 - x$
    (E) $24 + x$

    Arithmetic Operations on rational numbers

    Since Mario was 32 years old 8 years ago, his age now is 32 + 8 = 40 years old. Therefore, x years ago Mario was $40 - x$ years old.

    The correct answer is C.

2. If k is an integer and 0.0010101×10^k is greater than 1,000, what is the least possible value of k?

    (A) 2
    (B) 3
    (C) 4
    (D) 5
    (E) 6

    Arithmetic Operations on rational numbers

    Any number multiplied by 10^k, where k is a positive integer, will move the decimal point of the number to the right k places. 0.0010101 needs to have the decimal point moved to the right at least 6 places to have a value greater than 1,000.

    The correct answer is E.

3. If $(b-3)\left(4+\dfrac{2}{b}\right) = 0$ and $b \neq 3$, then $b =$

    (A) -8
    (B) -2
    (C) $-\dfrac{1}{2}$
    (D) $\dfrac{1}{2}$
    (E) 2

    Algebra Second-degree equations

    When the product of two multiplied values is 0, one of the values must be 0.

    $$(b-3)\left(4+\frac{2}{b}\right) = 0$$

    $b - 3 = 0 \qquad 4 + \dfrac{2}{b} = 0 \qquad$ set each factor equal to 0

    $b = 3 \qquad\quad \dfrac{2}{b} = -4 \qquad$ solve each factor for b

    $\qquad\qquad\quad 2 = -4b$

    $\qquad\qquad\quad -\dfrac{1}{2} = b$

    Since it is given that $b \neq 3$, then $b = -\dfrac{1}{2}$.

    The correct answer is C.

4. The number 2 – 0.5 is how many times the number 1 – 0.5?

    (A) 2
    (B) 2.5
    (C) 3
    (D) 3.5
    (E) 4

Arithmetic Operations on rational numbers

Set up an equation in the order given in the problem, and solve for x.

$(2 - 0.5) = (1 - 0.5)x$

$1.5 = 0.5x$

$3 = x$

The correct answer is C.

5. In which of the following pairs are the two numbers reciprocals of each other?

   I. $\quad 3$ and $\dfrac{1}{3}$

   II. $\quad \dfrac{1}{17}$ and $\dfrac{-1}{17}$

   III. $\quad \sqrt{3}$ and $\dfrac{\sqrt{3}}{3}$

   (A) I only
   (B) II only
   (C) I and II
   (D) I and III
   (E) II and III

Arithmetic Properties of numbers (reciprocals)

Two numbers are reciprocals of each other if and only if their product is 1.

I. $\quad 3(1/3) = 1 \qquad\qquad$ reciprocals

II. $\quad (1/17)(-1/17) = -1/289 \quad$ not reciprocals

III. $\left(\sqrt{3}\right)\left(\dfrac{\sqrt{3}}{3}\right) = \dfrac{3}{3} = 1 \qquad$ reciprocals

The correct answer is D.

6. The price of a certain television set is discounted by 10 percent, and the reduced price is then discounted by 10 percent. This series of successive discounts is equivalent to a single discount of

(A) 20%
(B) 19%
(C) 18%
(D) 11%
(E) 10%

Arithmetic Percent

Discounts are calculated by computing the cost and then analyzing the result. Thus, a 10% discount means a cost of 90%. Since this 10% discounting is done twice, the final cost on an item with original cost P is $(0.9)(0.9P) = 0.81P$. Thus, the original price is discounted by $100\% - 81\% = 19\%$.

The correct answer is B.

7. Which of the following equations is NOT equivalent to $25x^2 = y^2 - 4$?

   (A) $\quad 25x^2 + 4 = y^2$
   (B) $\quad 75x^2 = 3y^2 - 12$
   (C) $\quad 25x^2 = (y + 2)(y - 2)$
   (D) $\quad 5x = y - 2$
   (E) $\quad x^2 = \dfrac{y^2 - 4}{25}$

Algebra Second-degree equations

A   adds 4 to both sides of the original equation
    EQUIVALENT

B   multiplies both sides of the original equation by 3
    EQUIVALENT

C   correctly factors $y^2 - 4$ into $(y + 2)(y - 2)$
    EQUIVALENT

D   incorrectly calculates the square root of $y^2 - 4$
    NOT equivalent

E   divides both sides of the original equation by 25
    EQUIVALENT

The correct answer is D.

8. If there are 664,579 prime numbers among the first 10 million positive integers, approximately what percent of the first 10 million positive integers are prime numbers?

(A)   0.0066%
(B)   0.066%
(C)   0.66%
(D)   6.6%
(E)   66%

Arithmetic Percents

The ratio of 664,579 to 10 million is approximately 660,000 to 10,000,000 or

$$\frac{66}{1,000} = 0.066 = 6.6\%.$$

The correct answer is D.

9. How many multiples of 4 are there between 12 and 96, inclusive?

(A)   21
(B)   22
(C)   23
(D)   24
(E)   25

Arithmetic Properties of numbers

Since 12 is the 3rd multiple of 4 (12 = 3 × 4) and 96 is the 24th multiple of 4 (96 = 24 × 4), the number of multiples of 4 between 12 and 96, inclusive, is the same as the number of integers between 3 and 24, inclusive, namely, 24 − 3 + 1 = 22.

The correct answer is B.

10. In Country X a returning tourist may import goods with a total value of $500 or less tax free, but must pay an 8 percent tax on the portion of the total value in excess of $500. What tax must be paid by a returning tourist who imports goods with a total value of $730?

(A) $58.40
(B) $40.00
(C) $24.60
(D) $18.40
(E) $16.00

Arithmetic Percents

The tourist must pay tax on $730 − $500 = $230. The amount of the tax is 0.08($230) = $18.40.

The correct answer is D.

11. Which of the following is greater than $\frac{2}{3}$?

(A) $\frac{33}{50}$

(B) $\frac{8}{11}$

(C) $\frac{3}{5}$

(D) $\frac{13}{27}$

(E) $\frac{5}{8}$

Arithmetic Properties of numbers

Convert the fractions to decimal values and compare them.

$$\frac{2}{3} = 0.666666 \ldots$$

A $\frac{33}{50} = 0.66$

B $\frac{8}{11} = 0.727272 \ldots$

C $\frac{3}{5} = 0.6$

D $\frac{13}{27} = 0.481481 \ldots$

E $\frac{5}{8} = 0.625$

The correct answer is B.

12. If 60 percent of a rectangular floor is covered by a rectangular rug that is 9 feet by 12 feet, what is the area, in square feet, of the floor?

(A)   65
(B)   108
(C)   180
(D)   270
(E)   300

Geometry + Arithmetic Area + Percents

First, calculate the area of the rug. Using the formula for area = (width)(length), the area of the rug is thus 9(12) = 108 square feet.

Then, letting x = the area of the floor in square feet, build an equation to express the given information that the rug's area is equal to 60% of the floor area, and work the problem.

108 = 0.6x solve for x

180 = x

The correct answer is C.

13. If "basis points" are defined so that 1 percent is equal to 100 basis points, then 82.5 percent is how many basis points greater than 62.5 percent?

(A) 0.02
(B) 0.2
(C) 20
(D) 200
(E) 2,000

Arithmetic Operations on rational numbers

The difference in the percents is 82.5 – 62.5 = 20 percent. Since 1 percent equals 100 basis points, then 20 percent equals 20(100) or 2,000 basis points.

The correct answer is E.

14. Three machines, individually, can do a certain job in 4, 5, and 6 hours, respectively. What is the greatest part of the job that can be done in one hour by two of the machines working together at their respective rates?

(A) $\dfrac{11}{30}$

(B) $\dfrac{9}{20}$

(C) $\dfrac{3}{5}$

(D) $\dfrac{11}{15}$

(E) $\dfrac{5}{6}$

Arithmetic Operations on rational numbers

In one hour these machines can do $\dfrac{1}{4}$, $\dfrac{1}{5}$, and $\dfrac{1}{6}$ of the job, respectively. To get the greatest part of the job done, use the fastest machines. Since the third machine does the smallest part of the job in one hour and only two machines are to be used, the third machine should be eliminated. Therefore, using the first two machines will complete $\dfrac{1}{4} + \dfrac{1}{5} = \dfrac{5}{20} + \dfrac{4}{20} = \dfrac{9}{20}$ of the job in one hour.

The correct answer is B.

15. The value of – 3 – (– 10) is how much greater than the value of – 10 – (– 3)?

(A) 0
(B) 6
(C) 7
(D) 14
(E) 26

Arithmetic Operations on rational numbers

Work the problem.

–3 – (–10) = 7

–10 – (–3) = –7

7 – (–7) = 14

The correct answer is D.

16. If X and Y are sets of integers, $X \triangle Y$ denotes the set of integers that belong to set X or set Y, but not both. If X consists of 10 integers, Y consists of 18 integers, and 6 of the integers are in both X and Y, then $X \triangle Y$ consists of how many integers?

(A) 6
(B) 16
(C) 22
(D) 30
(E) 174

Arithmetic Properties of numbers

Since $X \Delta Y$ denotes the set of integers that belong to the set X or the set Y, but not both, the number of integers in $X \Delta Y$ is the number in the union of X and Y, minus the number in the intersection. First, calculate the number of integers in the union of X and Y; the number of integers in the union is the number in X plus the number in Y, minus their overlap (the number in the intersection), which is $10 + 18 - 6 = 22$. Then, subtracting the number in the intersection from the number in the union, the number of integers in $X \Delta Y$ is determined to be $22 - 6 = 16$.

Another way of solving this is to understand that $X \Delta Y$ consists of those integers just in X together with those just in Y. Of the 10 integers in X, 6 are also in Y, leaving 4 integers just in X. Of the 18 integers in Y, 6 are also in X, leaving 12 integers just in Y. Thus, the number of integers in $X \Delta Y$ is $4 + 12 = 16$. The Venn diagram below demonstrates this.

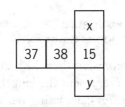

The correct answer is B.

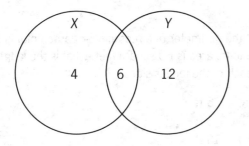

17. In the figure above, the sum of the three numbers in the horizontal row equals the product of the three numbers in the vertical column. What is the value of xy?

(A)   6
(B)   15
(C)   35
(D)   75
(E)   90

Arithmetic Operations on rational numbers

The sum of the three numbers in the horizontal row is $37 + 38 + 15$, or 90. The product of the three numbers in the vertical column is $15xy$. Thus, $15xy = 90$, or the value of $xy = 6$.

The correct answer is A.

18. $\left(1 + \sqrt{5}\right)\left(1 - \sqrt{5}\right) =$

(A) -4
(B)   2
(C)   6
(D) $-4 - 2\sqrt{5}$
(E) $6 - 2\sqrt{5}$

Arithmetic Operations on radical expressions

Work the problem.

$$\left(1 + \sqrt{5}\right)\left(1 - \sqrt{5}\right) = 1^2 + \sqrt{5} - \sqrt{5} - \left(\sqrt{5}\right)^2 =$$
$$1 - \left(\sqrt{5}\right)^2 = 1 - 5 = -4$$

The correct answer is A.

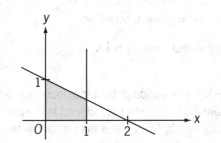

19. In the rectangular coordinate system above, the shaded region is bounded by straight lines. Which of the following is NOT an equation of one of the boundary lines?

(A) $x = 0$
(B) $y = 0$
(C) $x = 1$
(D) $x - y = 0$
(E) $x + 2y = 2$

Geometry Simple coordinate geometry

Test the answer choices to determine which one is NOT an equation of one of the boundary lines.

A   The equation of the y-axis is $x = 0$, and so this IS an equation of a boundary line.

B   The equation of the x-axis is $y = 0$, and so this IS an equation of a boundary line.

C   The equation of the line one unit to the right of the y-axis is $x = 1$, and so this IS an equation of a boundary line.

It is given that the top boundary line passes through the point $(2, 0)$. To lie on a certain line, the point must satisfy the equation of that line. Substitute the point $(2, 0)$ in the remaining equations to determine whether or not it satisfies the equation of the top boundary line.

D   Substitution in $x - y = 0$ gives $2 - 0 = 0$, which is NOT a true statement, and so this point does NOT satisfy the equation of the top boundary line.

E   Substitution in $x + 2y = 2$ gives $2 + 2(0) = 2$ or $2 + 0 = 2$, which IS a true statement, and so this point DOES satisfy the equation of the top boundary line.

The correct answer is D.

20.   A certain population of bacteria doubles every 10 minutes. If the number of bacteria in the population initially was 10^4, what was the number in the population 1 hour later?

(A) $2(10^4)$
(B) $6(10^4)$
(C) $(2^6)(10^4)$
(D) $(10^6)(10^4)$
(E) $(10^4)^6$

Arithmetic Operations on rational numbers

If the population of bacteria doubles every 10 minutes, it doubles 6 times in one hour. This doubling action can be expressed as $(2)(2)(2)(2)(2)(2)$ or 2^6. Thus, if the initial population in 10^4, the population will be $(2^6)(10^4)$ after one hour.

The correct answer is C.

21.   How many minutes does it take to travel 120 miles at 400 miles per hour?

(A)   3
(B) $3\dfrac{1}{3}$
(C) $8\dfrac{2}{3}$
(D)   12
(E)   18

Arithmetic Operations on rational numbers

Work the problem.

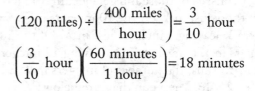

$$(120 \text{ miles}) \div \left(\frac{400 \text{ miles}}{\text{hour}} \right) = \frac{3}{10} \text{ hour}$$

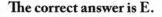

$$\left(\frac{3}{10} \text{ hour} \right)\left(\frac{60 \text{ minutes}}{1 \text{ hour}} \right) = 18 \text{ minutes}$$

The correct answer is E.

22.   If the perimeter of a rectangular garden plot is 34 feet and its area is 60 square feet, what is the length of each of the longer sides?

(A)   5 ft
(B)   6 ft
(C)   10 ft
(D)   12 ft
(E)   15 ft

Geometry + Algebra Perimeter + Area + Simultaneous equations

Letting w represent the width of the rectangular garden and l represent the length of the garden in the formulas for calculating perimeter and area, the given information can be expressed as:

$2w + 2l = 34$	Perimeter = 2(width) + 2(length)
$lw = 60$	Area = (length)(width)

First, solve for the value of l in the equation for the perimeter:

$2w + 2l = 34$	
$w + l = 17$	divide all terms by 2
$l = 17 - w$	subtract w from both sides

This reduces the problem to finding two numbers whose product is 60 and whose sum is 17. It can be seen by inspection that the two numbers are 5 and 12, so $l = 12$, and the length of the longer sides of the garden is 12 ft.

It is also possible to substitute the value of $l = 17 - w$ in the equation for the area and solve for w:

$lw = 60$

$(17 - w)w = 60$	substitution
$17w - w^2 = 60$	distribute the 17
$0 = w^2 - 17w + 60$	move all terms to one side
$0 = (w - 12)(w - 5)$	factor the quadratic
$w = 12, w = 5$	solve for w

Thus, the length of the longer sides of the garden must be $l = 17 - 5 = 12$.

The correct answer is D.

23. A certain manufacturer produces items for which the production costs consist of annual fixed costs totaling $130,000 and variable costs averaging $8 per item. If the manufacturer's selling price per item is $15, how many items must the manufacturer produce and sell to earn an annual profit of $150,000?

   (A)   2,858
   (B)   18,667
   (C)   21,429
   (D)   35,000
   (E)   40,000

Algebra Applied problems

First, profit (P) is defined as revenue (R) minus cost (C), or $P = R - C$. Further, the cost (C) is the sum of the variable costs plus the fixed costs. Thus, letting x represent the number of items produced, $P(x) = R(x) - C(x)$.

The given information can be expressed as:

$P(x) = 150,000$	profit
$R(x) = 15x$	revenue
$C(x) = 8x + 130,000$	cost = variable costs + fixed costs

Substitute these values in the equation and solve for x:

$P(x) = R(x) - C(x)$

$150,000 = 15x - (8x + 130,000)$

$150,000 = 7x - 130,000$

$280,000 = 7x$

$40,000 = x$

The correct answer is E.

24. In a poll of 66,000 physicians, only 20 percent responded; of these, 10 percent disclosed their preference for pain reliever X. How many of the physicians who responded did <u>not</u> disclose a preference for pain reliever X?

   (A)   1,320
   (B)   5,280
   (C)   6,600
   (D)   10,560
   (E)   11,880

Arithmetic Percent

The number of physicians who responded to the poll was 0.2(66,000) = 13,200. If 10 percent of the respondents disclosed a preference for X, then 90 percent did not disclose a preference for X. Thus, the number of respondents who did not disclose a preference is 0.9(13,200) = 11,880.

The correct answer is E.

25. $\dfrac{3}{100} + \dfrac{5}{1,000} + \dfrac{7}{100,000} =$

   (A)   0.357
   (B)   0.3507
   (C)   0.35007
   (D)   0.0357
   (E)   0.03507

Arithmetic Operations on rational numbers

If each fraction is written in decimal form, the sum to be found is

$$
\begin{array}{r}
0.03 \\
0.005 \\
+\ 0.00007 \\
\hline
0.03507
\end{array}
$$

The correct answer is E.

26. If the number n of calculators sold per week varies with the price p in dollars according to the equation $n = 300 - 20p$, what would be the total weekly revenue from the sale of \$10 calculators?

   (A) \$ 100
   (B) \$ 300
   (C) \$1,000
   (D) \$2,800
   (E) \$3,000

Algebra First-degree equations

Using the given equation, substitute 10 for p and solve for n to determine the number of calculators sold.

$n = 300 - 20\,p$

$n = 300 - 20(10)$

$n = 300 - 200$

$n = 100$

Then, the revenue from the sale of n calculators = $(10)(100) = 1,000$.

The correct answer is C.

27. Which of the following fractions is equal to the decimal 0.0625?

   (A) $\dfrac{5}{8}$

   (B) $\dfrac{3}{8}$

   (C) $\dfrac{1}{16}$

   (D) $\dfrac{1}{18}$

   (E) $\dfrac{3}{80}$

Arithmetic Operations on rational numbers

Work the problem.

$$0.0625 = \frac{625}{10,000} = \frac{1}{16}$$

The correct answer is C.

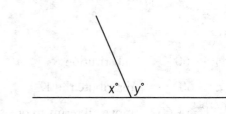

28. In the figure above, if $\dfrac{x}{x+y} = \dfrac{3}{8}$, then $x =$

   (A) 60
   (B) 67.5
   (C) 72
   (D) 108
   (E) 112.5

Geometry + Algebra Angle measures + Simultaneous equations

Since the angles x and y form a straight line, $x + y = 180$. Work the problem by substituting 180 for $x + y$ and then solving for x.

$\dfrac{x}{x+y} = \dfrac{3}{8}$

$\dfrac{x}{180} = \dfrac{3}{8}$ \qquad substitution

$8x = 540$ \qquad cross multiply

$x = 67.5$ \qquad divide both sides by 8

The correct answer is B.

29. If positive integers x and y are not both odd, which of the following must be even?

   (A) xy
   (B) $x + y$
   (C) $x - y$
   (D) $x + y - 1$
   (E) $2(x + y) - 1$

Arithmetic Properties of numbers

Since it is given that x and y are NOT both odd, either both of them are even or one is even and one is odd. Using these two alternatives, test the outcome of each answer choice to determine when both MUST be even.

A (even)(even) = even; (even)(odd) = even
   MUST be even

B even + even = even; even + odd = odd
   Need NOT be even

C even − even = even; even − odd = odd;
   odd − even = odd
   Need NOT be even

D even + even + 1 = odd; even + odd + 1 = even
   Need NOT be even

E 2(even + even) − 1 = odd;
   2(even + odd) − 1 = odd
   Need NOT be even

The correct answer is A.

30. On 3 sales John has received commissions of $240, $80, and $110, and he has 1 additional sale pending. If John is to receive an average (arithmetic mean) commission of exactly $150 on the 4 sales, then the 4th commission must be

(A) $164
(B) $170
(C) $175
(D) $182
(E) $185

Arithmetic Statistics

Letting x equal the value of John's fourth commission, and using the formula
$$\text{average} = \frac{\text{sum of values}}{\text{number of values}},$$ the given information can be expressed in the following equation, which can then be solved for x:

$\dfrac{240 + 80 + 110 + x}{4} = 150$

$430 + x = 600$ simplify numerator; multiply both sides by 4

$x = 170$ subtract 430 from both sides

The correct answer is B.

31. The annual budget of a certain college is to be shown on a circle graph. If the size of each sector of the graph is to be proportional to the amount of the budget it represents, how many degrees of the circle should be used to represent an item that is 15 percent of the budget?

(A) 15°
(B) 36°
(C) 54°
(D) 90°
(E) 150°

Arithmetic Percent + Interpretation of graphs

Since there are 360 degrees in a circle, the measure of the central angle in the circle should be 0.15(360°) = 54°.

The correct answer is C.

32. During a two-week period, the price of an ounce of silver increased by 25 percent by the end of the first week and then decreased by 20 percent of this new price by the end of the second week. If the price of silver was x dollars per ounce at the beginning of the two-week period, what was the price, in dollars per ounce, by the end of the period?

(A) 0.8x
(B) 0.95x
(C) x
(D) 1.05x
(E) 1.25x

Arithmetic Percents

At the end of the first week the price of an ounce of silver was 1.25x. At the end of the second week, the price was 20 percent less than this, or 80 percent of 1.25x, which is (0.80)(1.25)x, which is in turn equal to x.

The correct answer is C.

33. In a certain pond, 50 fish were caught, tagged, and returned to the pond. A few days later, 50 fish were caught again, of which 2 were found to have been tagged. If the percent of tagged fish in the second catch approximates the percent of tagged fish in the pond, what is the approximate number of fish in the pond?

    (A) 400
    (B) 625
    (C) 1,250
    (D) 2,500
    (E) 10,000

Algebra Applied problems

To solve this problem, it is necessary to determine two fractions: the fraction of fish tagged and the fraction of fish then caught that were already tagged. These two fractions can then set equal in a proportion, and the problem can be solved.

Letting N be the approximate total number of fish in the pond, then $\dfrac{50}{N}$ is the fraction of fish in the pond that were tagged in the first catch. Then, the fraction of tagged fish in the sample of 50 that were caught in the second catch can be expressed as $\dfrac{2}{50}$, or $\dfrac{1}{25}$. Therefore, $\dfrac{50}{N} = \dfrac{1}{25}$, or $N = (50)(25) = 1,250$.

The correct answer is C.

34. $\sqrt{16+16} =$

    (A) $4\sqrt{2}$
    (B) $8\sqrt{2}$
    (C) $16\sqrt{2}$
    (D) 8
    (E) 16

Arithmetic Operations on radical expressions

Working this problem gives

$$\sqrt{16+16} = \sqrt{(16)(2)} = \left(\sqrt{16}\right)\left(\sqrt{2}\right) = 4\sqrt{2}.$$

The correct answer is A.

35. An automobile's gasoline mileage varies, depending on the speed of the automobile, between 18.0 and 22.4 miles per gallon, inclusive. What is the maximum distance, in miles, that the automobile could be driven on 15 gallons of gasoline?

    (A) 336
    (B) 320
    (C) 303
    (D) 284
    (E) 270

Arithmetic Operations on rational numbers

The maximum distance would occur at the maximum mileage per gallon. Thus, the maximum distance would be (22.4 miles per gallon) × (15 gallons) = 336 miles.

The correct answer is A.

36. The organizers of a fair projected a 25 percent increase in attendance this year over that of last year, but attendance this year actually decreased by 20 percent. What percent of the projected attendance was the actual attendance?

    (A) 45%
    (B) 56%
    (C) 64%
    (D) 75%
    (E) 80%

Arithmetic Percents

Letting A be last year's attendance, set up the given information, and work the problem.

$$\frac{\text{Actual Attendance}}{\text{Projected Attendance}} = \frac{0.80A}{1.25A} = 0.64 = 64\%$$

The correct answer is C.

37. What is the ratio of $\frac{3}{4}$ to the product $4\left(\frac{3}{4}\right)$?

    (A) $\frac{1}{4}$

    (B) $\frac{1}{3}$

    (C) $\frac{4}{9}$

    (D) $\frac{9}{4}$

    (E) 4

    Arithmetic Operations on rational numbers

    Work the problem.

    $$\frac{\frac{3}{4}}{4\left(\frac{3}{4}\right)} = \frac{\frac{3}{4}}{\frac{12}{4}} = \frac{\frac{3}{4}}{3} = \frac{3}{4} \times \frac{1}{3} = \frac{1}{4}$$

    The correct answer is **A.**

38. If $3 - x = 2x - 3$, then $4x =$

    (A) -24
    (B) -8
    (C) 0
    (D) 8
    (E) 24

    Algebra First-degree equations

    Work the problem.

    $3 - x = 2x - 3$

    $6 = 3x$ add three to both sides; add x to both sides

    $2 = x$ divide both sides by 3

    Therefore, $4x = 4(2) = 8$.

    The correct answer is **D.**

39. If $x > 3{,}000$, then the value of $\frac{x}{2x + 1}$ is closest to

    (A) $\frac{1}{6}$

    (B) $\frac{1}{3}$

    (C) $\frac{10}{21}$

    (D) $\frac{1}{2}$

    (E) $\frac{3}{2}$

    Algebra Simplifying algebraic expressions

    For all large values of x, the value of $\frac{x}{2x + 1}$ is going to be very close to the value of $\frac{x}{2x}$, which is equal to $\frac{1}{2}$.

    The correct answer is **D.**

40. If 18 is 15 percent of 30 percent of a certain number, what is the number?

    (A) 9
    (B) 36
    (C) 40
    (D) 81
    (E) 400

    Arithmetic Percents

    Letting n be the number, the given information can be expressed as $18 = 0.15(0.30n)$. Solve this equation for n.

    $18 = 0.15(0.30n)$

    $18 = 0.045n$

    $400 = n$

    The correct answer is **E.**

41. If $x = (0.08)^2$, $y = \dfrac{1}{(0.08)^2}$, and

    $z = (1 - 0.08)^2 - 1$, which of the following is true?

    (A) $x = y = z$
    (B) $y < z < x$
    (C) $z < x < y$
    (D) $y <$ and $x = z$
    (E) $x < y$ and $x = z$

Arithmetic Operations on rational numbers

Note that y is the reciprocal of x. Since x is plainly less than 1, its reciprocal y must be greater than 1. Clearly x is also greater than 0. Further, since $1 - 0.08$ is less than 1, z's value of $(1 - 0.08)^2 - 1$, or $(1 - 0.08) \times (1 - 0.08)$ minus one, must be less than 0. Thus, the three relationships of $0 < x < 1$, $y > 1$, and $z < 0$ yield a sequence of $z < 0 < x < 1 < y$, or $z < x < y$.

The correct answer is C.

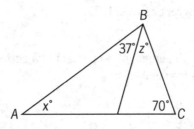

42. In $\triangle ABC$ above, what is x in terms of z?

    (A) $z + 73$
    (B) $z - 73$
    (C) $70 - z$
    (D) $z - 70$
    (E) $73 - z$

Geometry Angle measure in degrees

Since the sum of the angles in a triangle = 180°, this can be expressed as $x + 37 + z + 70 = 180$. Solve this equation for x.

$x + 37 + z + 70 = 180$ sum of angles in a triangle = 180°

$x + z + 107 = 180$ solve for x

$x = 73 - z$

The correct answer is E.

43. $\dfrac{(3)(0.072)}{0.54} =$

    (A) 0.04
    (B) 0.3
    (C) 0.4
    (D) 0.8
    (E) 4.0

Arithmetic Operations on rational numbers

Simplify the expression.

$$\frac{(3)(0.072)}{0.54} \times \frac{100}{100} = \frac{3(7.2)}{54} = \frac{21.6}{54} = 0.4$$

or

$$\frac{(3)(0.072)}{0.54} = \frac{0.216}{0.54} = 0.4$$

The correct answer is C.

44. What is the maximum number of $1\frac{1}{4}$ foot pieces of wire that can be cut from a wire that is 24 feet long?

    (A) 11
    (B) 18
    (C) 19
    (D) 20
    (E) 30

Arithmetic Operations on rational numbers

In working the problem, $24 \div 1\frac{1}{4} = \frac{24}{1.25} = 19.2$.

Since full $1\frac{1}{4}$ foot pieces of wire are needed, 19 pieces can be cut.

The correct answer is C.

$$\frac{61.24 \times (0.998)^2}{\sqrt{403}}$$

45. The expression above is approximately equal to

    (A) 1
    (B) 3
    (C) 4
    (D) 5
    (E) 6

Arithmetic Operations on radical expressions

Simplify the expression using approximations.

$$\frac{61.24 \times (0.998)^2}{\sqrt{403}} \approx \frac{60 \times 1^2}{\sqrt{400}} = \frac{60}{20} = 3$$

The correct answer is B.

46. If the numbers $\frac{17}{24}$, $\frac{1}{2}$, $\frac{3}{8}$, $\frac{3}{4}$, and $\frac{9}{16}$ were ordered from greatest to least, the middle number of the resulting sequence would be

(A) $\frac{17}{24}$

(B) $\frac{1}{2}$

(C) $\frac{3}{8}$

(D) $\frac{3}{4}$

(E) $\frac{9}{16}$

Arithmetic Operations on rational numbers

The least common denominator for all the fractions in the problem is 48. Work out their equivalencies to see clearly their relative values:

$$\frac{17}{24} = \frac{34}{48}, \frac{1}{2} = \frac{24}{48}, \frac{3}{8} = \frac{18}{48}, \frac{3}{4} = \frac{36}{48}, \frac{9}{16} = \frac{27}{48}$$

In descending order, they are

$$\frac{36}{48}, \frac{34}{48}, \frac{27}{48}, \frac{24}{48}, \frac{18}{48}, \text{ and the middle}$$

number is $\frac{27}{24} = \frac{9}{16}$.

The correct answer is E.

47. Last year if 97 percent of the revenues of a company came from domestic sources and the remaining revenues, totaling $450,000, came from foreign sources, what was the total of the company's revenues?

(A) $ 1,350,000
(B) $ 1,500,000
(C) $ 4,500,000
(D) $ 15,000,000
(E) $150,000,000

Arithmetic Percents

If 97 percent of the revenues came from domestic sources, then the remaining 3 percent, totaling $450,000, came from foreign sources. Letting x represent the total revenue, this information can be expressed as $0.03x = 450,000$, and thus

$$x = \frac{450,000}{.03} = \frac{45,000,000}{3} = 15,000,000.$$

The correct answer is D.

48. $\frac{2 + 2\sqrt{6}}{2} =$

(A) $\sqrt{6}$
(B) $2\sqrt{6}$
(C) $1 + \sqrt{6}$
(D) $1 + 2\sqrt{6}$
(E) $2 + \sqrt{6}$

Arithmetic Operations on radical expressions

Simplify the expression.

$$\frac{2 + 2\sqrt{6}}{2} = \frac{2(1 + \sqrt{6})}{2} = 1 + \sqrt{6}$$

or

$$\frac{2 + 2\sqrt{6}}{2} = \frac{2}{2} + \frac{2\sqrt{6}}{2} = 1 + \sqrt{6}$$

The correct answer is C.

49. A certain fishing boat is chartered by 6 people who are to contribute equally to the total charter cost of $480. If each person contributes equally to a $150 down payment, how much of the charter cost will each person still owe?

(A) $80
(B) $66
(C) $55
(D) $50
(E) $45

Arithmetic Operations on rational numbers

Since each of the 6 individuals contributes equally to the $150 down payment, and since it is given that the total cost of the chartered boat is $480, each person still owes $\frac{\$480 - \$150}{6} = \$55$.

The correct answer is C.

50. Craig sells major appliances. For each appliance he sells, Craig receives a commission of $50 plus 10 percent of the selling price. During one particular week Craig sold 6 appliances for selling prices totaling $3,620. What was the total of Craig's commissions for that week?

    (A) $412
    (B) $526
    (C) $585
    (D) $605
    (E) $662

Arithmetic Percent

Since Craig receives a commission of $50 on each appliance plus a 10 percent commission on total sales, his commission for that week was 6($50) + (0.1)($3,620) = $662.

The correct answer is E.

51. What number when multiplied by $\frac{4}{7}$ yields $\frac{6}{7}$ as the result?

    (A) $\frac{2}{7}$

    (B) $\frac{3}{3}$

    (C) $\frac{3}{2}$

    (D) $\frac{24}{7}$

    (E) $\frac{7}{2}$

Algebra Applied problems

Letting n represent the number, this problem can be expressed as $\frac{4}{7}n = \frac{6}{7}$, which can be solved for n by multiplying both sides by $\frac{7}{4}$:

$$\frac{4}{7}n = \frac{6}{7}$$

$$n = \frac{42}{28} \qquad \text{multiply both sides by } \frac{7}{4}$$

$$n = \frac{3}{2} \qquad \text{reduce the fraction}$$

The correct answer is C.

52. If 3 pounds of dried apricots that cost x dollars per pound are mixed with 2 pounds of prunes that cost y dollars per pound, what is the cost, in dollars, per pound of the mixture?

    (A) $\frac{3x + 2y}{5}$

    (B) $\frac{3x + 2y}{x + y}$

    (C) $\frac{3x + 2y}{xy}$

    (D) $5(3x + 2y)$

    (E) $3x + 2y$

Algebra Applied problems + Simplifying algebraic expressions

The total number of pounds in the mixture is 3 + 2 = 5 pounds, and the total cost of the mixture is $3x + 2y$ dollars. Therefore, the cost per pound of the mixture is $\frac{3x + 2y}{5}$ dollars.

The correct answer is A.

53. Which of the following must be equal to zero for all real numbers x?

    I. $-\dfrac{1}{x}$

    II. $x + (-x)$

    III. x^0

    (A)   I only
    (B)   II only
    (C)   I and III only
    (D)   II and III only
    (E)   I, II, and III

Arithmetic Properties of numbers

Consider the numeric properties of each answer choice.

I. $-\dfrac{1}{x}$ 1 divided by a number can never be zero: CANNOT equal zero

II. $x + (-x) = 0$ for all real numbers x MUST equal zero

III. $x^0 = 1$ for all nonzero real numbers x NEED NOT equal zero

The correct answer is B.

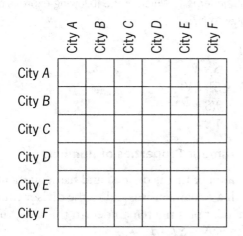

	City A	City B	City C	City D	City E	City F
City A						
City B						
City C						
City D						
City E						
City F						

54. In the table above, what is the least number of table entries that are needed to show the mileage between each city and each of the other five cities?

    (A)   15
    (B)   1
    (C)   5
    (D)   0
    (E)   6

Arithmetic Interpretation of tables

Since there is no mileage between a city and itself, and since the mileage for each pair of cities needs to be completed only once, only those boxes below (or above) the diagonal from the upper left to the lower right need to be counted. This gives $1 + 2 + 3 + 4 + 5 = 15$ distances.

The correct answer is A.

55. If $(t - 8)$ is a factor of $t^2 - kt - 48$, then $k =$

    (A)   16
    (B)   12
    (C)   2
    (D)   6
    (E)   14

Algebra Second-degree equations

If $(t - 8)$ is a factor of the expression $t^2 - kt - 48$, then the expression can be written as the product $(t - 8)(t + a)$.

$(t - 8)(t + a)$

$t^2 - 8t + at - 8a$ multiply the binomials

$t^2 - (8 - a)t - 8a$ combine the t terms

Comparing this expression to the original expression sets $-8a = -48$, or $a = 6$. Then, by substituting this value of a into the product $(t - 8)(t + a)$:

$(t - 8)(t + a)$

$(t - 8)(t + 6)$

$t^2 - 8t + 6t - 48$

$t^2 - 2t - 48$

Therefore, $k = 2$

The correct answer is C.

56. $\dfrac{31}{125} =$

    (A)   0.248
    (B)   0.252
    (C)   0.284
    (D)   0.312
    (E)   0.320

Arithmetic Operations on rational numbers

Work the problem.

$\dfrac{31}{125} = 0.248$

The correct answer is A.

57. Members of a social club met to address 280 newsletters. If they addressed $\dfrac{1}{4}$ of the newsletters during the first hour and $\dfrac{2}{5}$ of the remaining newsletters during the second hour, how many newsletters did they address during the second hour?

    (A)   28
    (B)   42
    (C)   63
    (D)   84
    (E)   112

Arithmetic Operations on rational numbers

Since $\dfrac{1}{4}$ of the newsletters were addressed during the first hour, $\dfrac{3}{4}(280) = 210$ newsletters were NOT addressed during the first hour and remained to be done in the second hour. Therefore, $\dfrac{2}{5}(210) = 84$ newsletters were addressed during the second hour.

The correct answer is D.

58. $(\sqrt{3}+2)(\sqrt{3}-2) =$

    (A) $\sqrt{3}-4$
    (B) $\sqrt{6}-4$
    (C) -1
    (D)   1
    (E)   2

Arithmetic Operations on radical expressions

Simplify the expression.

$(\sqrt{3}+2)(\sqrt{3}-2) = (\sqrt{3})^2 + 2\sqrt{3} - 2\sqrt{3} + 2(-2) = 3 - 4 = -1$

The correct answer is C.

59. The arithmetic mean and standard deviation of a certain normal distribution are 13.5 and 1.5, respectively. What value is exactly 2 standard deviations less than the mean?

    (A)   10.5
    (B)   11.0
    (C)   11.5
    (D)   12.0
    (E)   12.5

Arithmetic Statistics

Since the arithmetic mean is 13.5 and one standard deviation is 1.5, two standard deviations less than the mean is $13.5 - 2(1.5) = 10.5$.

The correct answer is A.

60. When N is divided by T, the quotient is S and the remainder is V. Which of the following expressions is equal to N?

    (A) ST
    (B) $S + V$
    (C) $ST + V$
    (D) $T(S + V)$
    (E) $T(S - V)$

Arithmetic Properties of numbers

A number that is divided and has a quotient with a remainder is equal to the divisor times the quotient plus the remainder. In this case, that means $N = ST + V$.

It can be helpful to look at this with long division:

$$\begin{array}{r} S \\ T{\overline{)\,N}} \\ -ST \\ \hline V \end{array}$$

reverse the operations from the bottom up to see that $V + ST = N$

The correct answer is C.

38, 69, 22, 73, 31, 47, 13, 82

61. Which of the following numbers is greater than three-fourths of the numbers but less than one-fourth of the numbers in the list above?

(A)   56
(B)   68
(C)   69
(D)   71
(E)   73

Arithmetic Operations on rational numbers

The numbers in the given list reordered from least to greatest are:

13, 22, 31, 38, 47, 69, 73, 82

Since there are 8 numbers in the list, $\frac{3}{4}(8) = 6$ and $\frac{1}{4}(8) = 2$. Therefore, the number must be greater than the first 6 numbers in the reordered list, or greater than 69, and be less than the last 2 numbers in the reordered list, or less than 73.

The correct answer is D.

62. The cost of picture frame M is $10.00 less than 3 times the cost of picture frame N. If the cost of frame M is $50.00, what is the cost of frame N?

(A) $13.33
(B) $16.66
(C) $20.00
(D) $26.66
(E) $40.00

Algebra Applied problems

Letting m be the cost, in dollars, of frame M, and letting n be the cost, in dollars, of frame N, the given information can be expressed as $m = 3n - 10$. Since $m = 50$, substitute 50 for m in the equation, and then solve for n.

$m = 3n - 10$

$50 = 3n - 10$ substitute 50 for m

$60 = 3n$ solve for n

$20 = n$

The correct answer is C.

63. If $S = \{0, 4, 5, 2, 11, 8\}$, how much greater than the median of the numbers in S is the mean of the numbers in S?

(A)   0.5
(B)   1.0
(C)   1.5
(D)   2.0
(E)   2.5

Arithmetic + Algebra Statistics + Concepts of sets

The median of S is found by ordering the values according to size (0, 2, 4, 5, 8, 11) and taking the average of the two middle numbers: $\frac{4+5}{2} = 4.5$.

The mean is $\frac{\text{sum of } n \text{ values}}{n} =$

$\frac{0+4+5+2+11+8}{6} = 5$

The difference between the mean and the median is $5 - 4.5 = 0.5$.

The correct answer is A.

64. The value of $\sqrt[3]{-89}$ is

(A)   between −9 and −10
(B)   between −8 and −9
(C)   between −4 and −5
(D)   between −3 and −4
(E)   undefined

Arithmetic Operations on radical expressions

The cube root of −89, or $\sqrt[3]{-89}$ is a number x such that $x^3 = -89$.

Since $(-4)^3 = -4 \times -4 \times -4 = -64$ and $(-5)^3 = -5 \times -5 \times -5 = -125$, the cube root of −89 must be a number between −4 and −5.

The correct answer is C.

65. Of the following, which is least?

(A) $\dfrac{1}{0.2}$

(B) $(0.2)^2$

(C) 0.02

(D) $\dfrac{0.2}{2}$

(E) 0.2

Arithmetic Operations on rational numbers

Simplify each expression to be able to compare values readily.

A $\dfrac{1}{0.2} = 5$

B $(0.2)^2 = 0.04$

C 0.02

D $\dfrac{0.2}{2} = 0.1$

E 0.2

The correct answer is C.

66. If d = 2.0453 and d^* is the decimal obtained by rounding d to the nearest hundredth, what is the value of $d^* - d$?

(A) −0.0053
(B) −0.0003
(C) 0.0007
(D) 0.0047
(E) 0.0153

Arithmetic Operations on rational numbers

Since d = 2.0453 rounded to the nearest hundredth is 2.05, d^* = 2.05; therefore, $d^* - d$ = 2.05 − 2.0453 = 0.0047.

The correct answer is D.

67. Company K's earnings were $12 million last year. If this year's earnings are projected to be 150 percent greater than last year's earnings, what are Company K's projected earnings this year?

(A) $13.5 million
(B) $15 million
(C) $18 million
(D) $27 million
(E) $30 million

Arithmetic Percents

Since this year's earnings are a percentage greater than last year's earnings, the amount that earnings increased over last year will need to be added to last year's earnings. The 150 percent increase in earnings over last year can be expressed as 1.50(12,000,000). The earnings for this year are then calculated as follows:

1.50(12,000,000) + 12,000,000 = 2.50(12,000,000) = $30,000,000.

The correct answer is E.

68. If −3 is 6 more than x, what is the value of $\dfrac{x}{3}$?

(A) −9
(B) −6
(C) −3
(D) −1
(E) 1

Algebra First-degree equations

From this, −3 = x + 6, which can be solved for x, and the answer to the problem can then be found by substitution as shown.

$-3 = x + 6$

$-9 = x$

$\dfrac{x}{3} = \dfrac{-9}{3} = -3$

The correct answer is C.

69. An athlete runs R miles in H hours, then rides a bicycle Q miles in the same number of hours. Which of the following represents the athlete's average speed, in miles per hour, for these two activities combined?

(A) $\dfrac{R - Q}{H}$

(B) $\dfrac{R - Q}{2H}$

(C) $\dfrac{2(R + Q)}{H}$

(D) $\dfrac{2(R + Q)}{2H}$

(E) $\dfrac{R + Q}{2H}$

Algebra Simplifying algebraic expressions

The athlete's average speed for the two activities can be expressed by the formula average speed = $\dfrac{\text{total distance}}{\text{total time}}$. Since the athlete's total distance in miles is $R + Q$ and the total time in hours is $H + H$, the average speed is represented by $\dfrac{R + Q}{H + H}$, and thus $\dfrac{R + Q}{2H}$.

The correct answer is E.

70. If a certain sample of data has a mean of 20.0 and a standard deviation of 3.0, which of the following values is more than 2.5 standard deviations from the mean?

(A) 12.0
(B) 13.5
(C) 17.0
(D) 23.5
(E) 26.5

Arithmetic Statistics

The value must be more than 2.5 standard deviations above the mean or below the mean. Calculate the possible range of values, and consider each answer choice.

2.5(3) = 7.5

20 + 7.5 = 27.5

20 − 7.5 = 12.5

The only value outside the range of 12.5 to 27.5 is 12.0.

The correct answer is A.

County	Amount Recycled	Amount Disposed of
A	16,700	142,800
B	8,800	48,000
C	13,000	51,400
D	3,900	20,300
E	3,300	16,200

71. The table above shows the amount of waste material, in tons, recycled by each of five counties in a single year and the amount of waste material, also in tons, that was disposed of in landfills by the five counties in that year. Which county had the lowest ratio of waste material disposed of to waste material recycled in the year reported in the table?

(A) A
(B) B
(C) C
(D) D
(E) E

Arithmetic Operations on rational numbers + Interpretation of tables

Using the data from the table, consider the ratio $\dfrac{\text{amount disposed of}}{\text{amount recycled}}$ for each county, and find the lowest overall.

A $\quad \dfrac{142,800}{16,700} = 8.55$

B $\quad \dfrac{48,000}{8,800} = 5.45$

C $\quad \dfrac{51,400}{13,000} = 3.95$

D $\quad \dfrac{20,300}{3,900} = 5.21$

E $\quad \dfrac{16,200}{3,300} = 4.91$

The correct answer is C.

72. If $a = 7$ and $b = -7$, what is the value of $2a - 2b + b^2$?

    (A) −49
    (B) 21
    (C) 49
    (D) 63
    (E) 77

Arithmetic Operations on rational numbers

Substitute the given values and simplify the expression:

$2a - 2b + b^2 = 2(7) - 2(-7) + (-7)^2 =$
$14 + 14 + 49 = 77$

The correct answer is E.

73. Equal amounts of water were poured into two empty jars of different capacities, which made one jar $\frac{1}{4}$ full and the other jar $\frac{1}{3}$ full. If the water in the jar with the lesser capacity is then poured into the jar with the greater capacity, what fraction of the larger jar will be filled with water?

    (A) $\frac{1}{7}$

    (B) $\frac{2}{7}$

    (C) $\frac{1}{2}$

    (D) $\frac{7}{12}$

    (E) $\frac{2}{3}$

Arithmetic Operations on rational numbers

It is given that the amounts of water in the two jars are equal; the jar with the greater capacity is $\frac{1}{4}$ full, and the jar with the lesser capacity is $\frac{1}{3}$ full. Therefore, when the water in the smaller jar (which has been $\frac{1}{3}$ full) is poured into the larger jar (which has been $\frac{1}{4}$ full), the addition of an equal amount of water will double the amount in the larger jar, which will then be $2 \times \frac{1}{4} = \frac{1}{2}$ full.

The correct answer is C.

74. If Mel saved more than $10 by purchasing a sweater at a 15 percent discount, what is the smallest amount the original price of the sweater could be, to the nearest dollar?

    (A) 45
    (B) 67
    (C) 75
    (D) 83
    (E) 150

Arithmetic + Algebra Percents + Inequalities + Applied problems

Letting P be the original price of the sweater in dollars, the given information can be expressed as $(0.15)P > 10$, and solved for P:

$(0.15)P > 10$

$P > \dfrac{10}{0.15}$

$P > 66.67$

The correct answer is B.

75. If $x = -1$, then $-(x^4 + x^3 + x^2 + x) =$

    (A) −10
    (B) − 4
    (C) 0
    (D) 4
    (E) 10

Arithmetic Operations on rational numbers

Substituting −1 for x throughout the expression, work the problem:

$- (x^4 + x^3 + x^2 + x)$

$-((-1)^4 + (-1)^3 + (-1)^2 + (-1))$ substitute $x = -1$

$-(1 - 1 + 1 - 1)$ simplify

-0

0

The correct answer is C.

76. Today Rose is twice as old as Sam and Sam is 3 years younger than Tina. If Rose, Sam, and Tina are all alive 4 years from today, which of the following must be true on that day?

    I.   Rose is twice as old as Sam.
    II.   Sam is 3 years younger than Tina.
    III. Rose is older than Tina.

    (A) I only
    (B) II only
    (C) III only
    (D) I and II
    (E) II and III

Algebra Applied problems

Build equations to express the relative ages of the individuals today. Let R = Rose's age today, S = Sam's age today, and T = Tina's age today:

$$R = 2S$$

$$S = T - 3$$

When deciding if something must be true, test the case with values known to be true. It takes only one counterexample to prove it false.

I.   Counterexample: if today $R = 6$, then $S = 3$. In four years:

$$R + 4 = 6 + 4 = 10$$

$$S + 4 = 3 + 4 = 7$$

$10 \neq 2(7)$ NOT TRUE that $R = 2S$

II. $S + 4 = T - 3 + 4$, and thus $S = T - 3$ MUST BE TRUE

(If two people are aged 3 years apart, they will remain so their entire lives.)

III. If $R = 2S$ and $S = T - 3$, then $R = 2(T - 3)$. By substitution, therefore:

$R > T$ if and only if $2(T - 3) > T$

Compute the value of T to determine when $R > T$ is true:

$2(T - 3) > T$ solve for T

$2T - 6 > T$

$T > 6$

Thus, $R > T$ only for $T > 6$.
NEED NOT BE TRUE that $R > T$

Thus, II must be true, but I and III need not be true.

The correct answer is B.

77. If a square region has area x, what is the length of its diagonal in terms of x?

    (A) $\sqrt{x}$
    (B) $\sqrt{2x}$
    (C) $2\sqrt{x}$
    (D) $x\sqrt{2}$
    (E) $2x$

Geometry Area

Letting s equal the length of a side of the square, the relationship of the length of a side of the square and the area x of the square can be expressed as $s^2 = x$, or $s = \sqrt{x}$. The diagonal of a square creates a right triangle as shown below, with d as that triangle's hypotenuse. The value of the hypotenuse of a right triangle can be determined through the application of the Pythagorean theorem, which states that the square of the length of the hypotenuse is equal to the sum of the squares of the lengths of the legs.

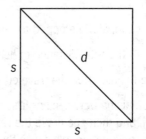

Thus, by the Pythagorean theorem:

$$d^2 = s^2 + s^2$$

$$d^2 = \left(\sqrt{x}\right)^2 + \left(\sqrt{x}\right)^2$$

$$d^2 = x + x$$

$$d^2 = 2x$$

$$d = \sqrt{2x}$$

The correct answer is B.

78. The temperature in degrees Celsius (*C*) can be converted to temperature in degrees Fahrenheit (*F*) by the formula $F = \frac{9}{5}C + 32$. What is the temperature at which $F = C$?

    (A) 20°

    (B) $\left(\frac{32}{5}\right)°$

    (C) 0°

    (D) −20°

    (E) −40°

Algebra First-degree equations

For $F = C$, substitute F for C in the formula, and solve for F.

$$F = \frac{9}{5}C + 32$$

$$F = \frac{9}{5}F + 32 \qquad \text{substitution}$$

$$-\frac{4}{5}F = 32 \qquad \text{subtract } \frac{9}{5}F \text{ from both sides}$$

$$F = -40 \qquad \text{divide both sides by } -\frac{4}{5}$$

The correct answer is E.

79. During a car trip, Maria stopped to rest after she traveled $\frac{1}{2}$ of the total distance to her destination. She stopped again after she traveled $\frac{1}{4}$ of the distance remaining between her first stop and her destination, and then she drove the remaining 120 miles to her destination. What was the total distance, in miles, from Maria's starting point to her destination?

    (A) 280

    (B) 320

    (C) 360

    (D) 420

    (E) 480

Algebra Applied problems

Let D be the total distance, in miles, from the starting point to the destination. The part of the trip before the first stop can be expressed as $\frac{1}{2}D$, and the part of the trip before the second stop can then be expressed as $\frac{1}{4}\left(\frac{1}{2}D\right)$. The information that the total distance of the trip minus the first two parts of the trip is equal to 120 miles can be expressed in the following equation, which can be solved for D.

$$D - \frac{1}{2}D - \frac{1}{4}\left(\frac{1}{2}D\right) = 120$$

$$\frac{1}{2}D - \frac{1}{8}D = 120$$

$$\frac{3}{8}D = 120$$

$$D = 320$$

The correct answer is B.

80. If *x* is to be chosen at random from the set {1, 2, 3, 4} and *y* is to be chosen at random from the set {5, 6, 7}, what is the probability that *xy* will be even?

    (A) $\frac{1}{6}$

    (B) $\frac{1}{3}$

    (C) $\frac{1}{2}$

    (D) $\frac{2}{3}$

    (E) $\frac{5}{6}$

Arithmetic + Algebra Probability + Concepts of sets

For xy to be even, either one or both of x and y need to be even.

If x is even, any of the 3 values of y will yield an even result. Since there are 2 even values for x, there are $2(3) = 6$ values for xy that are even when x is even.

If x is odd, then y needs to be even for xy to be even. Since there are 2 odd values for x and 1 even value for y, there are $2(1) = 2$ values for xy that are even when x is odd.

The total number of values for xy is $(4)(3) = 12$. Thus, the probability of xy being even is

$$\frac{6+2}{12} = \frac{8}{12} = \frac{2}{3}.$$

The correct answer is D.

81. Which of the following is equal to x^{18} for all positive values of x?

(A) $x^9 + x^9$

(B) $(x^2)^9$

(C) $(x^9)^9$

(D) $(x^3)^{15}$

(E) $\dfrac{x^4}{x^{22}}$

Algebra Simplifying algebraic expressions

Simplify each of the expressions to determine which satisfies the condition of the problem.

A $\quad x^9 + x^9 = 2x^9$

B $\quad \left(x^2\right)^9 = x^{18}$

C $\quad \left(x^9\right)^9 = x^{81}$

D $\quad \left(x^3\right)^{15} = x^{45}$

E $\quad \dfrac{x^4}{x^{22}} = x^{4-22} = x^{-18}$

The correct answer is B.

82. Three business partners, Q, R, and S, agree to divide their total profit for a certain year in the ratios $2 : 5 : 8$, respectively. If Q's share was \$4,000, what was the total profit of the business partners for the year?

(A) $ \$ 26,000$

(B) $ \$ 30,000$

(C) $ \$ 52,000$

(D) $ \$ 60,000$

(E) $\$300,000$

Algebra Applied problems

According to the ratios, Q gets $\dfrac{2}{2+5+8} = \dfrac{2}{15}$ of the total profit (T). Since Q's share is \$4,000, the following equation can be used to solve for T.

$$\frac{2}{15}T = 4,000$$

$$T = 30,000$$

The correct answer is B.

83. If $u > t$, $r > q$, $s > t$, and $t > r$, which of the following must be true?

I. $\quad u > s$

II. $\quad s > q$

III. $\quad u > r$

(A) I only

(B) II only

(C) III only

(D) I and II

(E) II and III

Arithmetic Properties of Numbers

First reorganize the given information: since $u > t$, $t > r$, and $r > q$, then it is known that $u > t > r > q$. While it is given that $s > t$, it is not known whether s is between t and u or greater than u. The number line below shows this relationship.

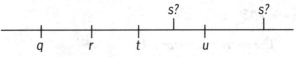

When deciding if something must be true, test the supposition with values known to be true. It takes only one counterexample to prove it false.

I. It is known that $u > t$ and $s > t$. Select a value for u that is greater than t; select a value for s that is greater than t. If it is true that $t = 2$, $u = 3$, and $s = 4$, then $s > u$. NOT TRUE that $u > s$

II. Since $s > t$, $t > r$, and $r > q$, it follows that $s > q$. MUST BE TRUE

III. Since $u > t$ and $t > r$, it follows that $u > r$. MUST BE TRUE

Thus, I is not true, but II and III are both true.

The correct answer is E.

84. The average (arithmetic mean) of 6 numbers is 8.5. When one number is discarded, the average of the remaining numbers becomes 7.2. What is the discarded number?

    (A) 7.8
    (B) 9.8
    (C) 10.0
    (D) 12.4
    (E) 15.0

Arithmetic Statistics

An average, or arithmetic mean, always equals the sum of the values divided by the number of values: Average = $\dfrac{\text{sum of } v \text{ values}}{v}$.

In the original case, $8.5 = \dfrac{\text{sum of 6 values}}{6}$, and thus the sum of the 6 values $= 51.0$.

Build an equation for the new average, now with 5 values and x as the value of the discarded number:

$7.2 = \dfrac{51 - x}{5}$ new total for 5 values; value x subtracted from the original sum

$36 = 51 - x$ solve for x

$x = 15$

The correct answer is E.

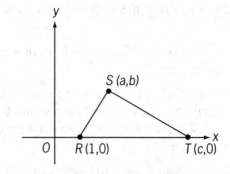

S (a,b)

O R (1,0)   T (c,0)

85. In the rectangular coordinate system above, the area of $\triangle RST$ is

    (A) $\dfrac{bc}{2}$

    (B) $\dfrac{b(c - 1)}{2}$

    (C) $\dfrac{c(b - 1)}{2}$

    (D) $\dfrac{a(c - 1)}{2}$

    (E) $\dfrac{c(a - 1)}{2}$

Geometry Simple-coordinate geometry

Since the RT segment of the triangle is horizontal and on the x-axis, the calculation of the triangle's base and height is straightforward. The farthest left x value (R) is 1, and the farthest right x value (T) is c. Thus, the length of the base of the triangle, or the distance between point R and point T, is $c - 1$. The triangle's highest point (S) has a y value of b, and the lowest y value is 0. So the height of the triangle is $b - 0 = b$. Once the base ($c - 1$) and height (b) have been calculated, the area of the triangle can be determined.

Area $= \dfrac{b(c - 1)}{2}$ area of a triangle = $\dfrac{(\text{base})(\text{height})}{2}$

The correct answer is B.

86. Which of the following equations has a root in common with $x^2 - 6x + 5 = 0$?

    (A) $x^2 + 1 = 0$
    (B) $x^2 - x - 2 = 0$
    (C) $x^2 - 10x - 5 = 0$
    (D) $2x^2 - 2 = 0$
    (E) $x^2 - 2x - 3 = 0$

    Algebra Second-degree equations

    The first step is to find the roots of $x^2 - 6x + 5 = 0$:

    $x^2 - 6x + 5 = 0$

    $(x - 5)(x - 1) = 0$ factor the quadratic

    $x - 5 = 0, x - 1 = 0$ set each factor equal to zero

    $x = 5, x = 1$ solve for x to determine the roots

    Then, substitute these x values into the five answer choices to determine where the value might satisfy the equation. In answer choice D, the value of $x = 1$ satisfies the equation: $2(1)^2 - 2 = 0$.

    The correct answer is D.

87. One inlet pipe fills an empty tank in 5 hours. A second inlet pipe fills the same tank in 3 hours. If both pipes are used together, how long will it take to fill $\frac{2}{3}$ of the tank?

    (A) $\frac{8}{15}$ hr
    (B) $\frac{3}{4}$ hr
    (C) $\frac{5}{4}$ hr
    (D) $\frac{15}{8}$ hr
    (E) $\frac{8}{3}$ hr

    Algebra Applied problems

    Begin by determining each pipe's individual hourly rate and calculating their rate together. The first pipe fills $\frac{1}{5}$ of the tank in one hour, and the second pipe fills $\frac{1}{3}$ of the tank in one hour. Together, the two pipes fill $\frac{1}{5} + \frac{1}{3} = \frac{8}{15}$ of the tank in one hour.

    Next, let t = the number of hours needed to fill the tank to a certain level. Set up an equation multiplying the combined hourly fill rate by the needed number of hours to determine how many hours it will take to fill $\frac{2}{3}$ of the tank, and then solve for t.

    $\frac{8}{15}t = \frac{2}{3}$ solve for t

    $t = \frac{2}{3}\left(\frac{15}{8}\right)$

    $t = \frac{5}{4}$

    The correct answer is C.

88. $\left(\frac{1}{5}\right)^2 - \left(\frac{1}{5}\right)\left(\frac{1}{4}\right) =$

    (A) $-\frac{1}{20}$
    (B) $-\frac{1}{100}$
    (C) $\frac{1}{100}$
    (D) $\frac{1}{20}$
    (E) $\frac{1}{5}$

Arithmetic Operations on rational numbers

Simplify the expression.

$$\left(\frac{1}{5}\right)^2 - \left(\frac{1}{5}\right)\left(\frac{1}{4}\right)$$

$\dfrac{1}{25} - \dfrac{1}{20}$ simplify terms

$\dfrac{4}{100} - \dfrac{5}{100}$ convert to common denominator

$-\dfrac{1}{100}$ combine fractions

The correct answer is B.

89. If the length and width of a rectangular garden plot were each increased by 20 percent, what would be the percent increase in the area of the plot?

    (A)   20%
    (B)   24%
    (C)   36%
    (D)   40%
    (E)   44%

Geometry Area

Let L = original length and W = original width. Multiply each dimension by (1 + the percent as decimal) to reflect the 20% increase.

Original Area = LW area = (length)(width)

Increased Area = $(1.2L)(1.2W)$ multiply each by 1.2

Increased Area = $1.44LW$

The increased area would thus be 144% of the original area, or an increase of 44%.

The correct answer is E.

90. The population of a bacteria culture doubles every 2 minutes. Approximately how many minutes will it take for the population to grow from 1,000 to 500,000 bacteria?

    (A)   10
    (B)   12
    (C)   14
    (D)   16
    (E)   18

Arithmetic Estimation

Set up a table of values to see how the culture grows.

Number of Minutes	Bacteria Population
0	1,000
2	2,000
4	4,000
6	8,000
8	16,000
10	32,000
12	64,000
14	128,000
16	256,000
18	512,000

At 18 minutes, the population of bacteria is just over 500,000.

The correct answer is E.

91. For a light that has an intensity of 60 candles at its source, the intensity in candles, S, of the light at a point d feet from the source is given by the formula $S = \dfrac{60k}{d^2}$, where k is a constant. If the intensity of the light is 30 candles at a distance of 2 feet from the source, what is the intensity of the light at a distance of 20 feet from the source?

    (A) $\dfrac{3}{10}$ candle

    (B) $\dfrac{1}{2}$ candle

    (C)   1 candle
    (D)   2 candles
    (E)   3 candles

Algebra Applied problems

First, solve the equation for the constant k using the values where both the intensity (S) and distance (d) are known.

$$S = \frac{60k}{d^2}$$

$$30 = \frac{60k}{2^2}$$ substitute S = 30 candles and d = 2 feet

$120 = 60k$ solve for k

$2 = k$

Then, with this known value of k, solve the equation for S where only the distance (d) is known.

$$S = \frac{60k}{d^2}$$

$$S = \frac{60(2)}{20^2}$$ substitute k = 2 and d = 20 feet

$$S = \frac{120}{400} = \frac{3}{10}$$

The correct answer is A.

92. If $b < 2$ and $2x - 3b = 0$, which of the following must be true?

(A) $x > -3$
(B) $x < 2$
(C) $x = 3$
(D) $x < 3$
(E) $x > 3$

Algebra Inequalities

First, solve the equation for b.

$2x - 3b = 0$ solve for b

$2x = 3b$

$\frac{2}{3}x = b$

Then, substitute the value $\frac{2}{3}x$ for b in the inequality $b < 2$ to see the relationship for x.

$\frac{2}{3}x < 2$ solve for x

$x < 3$

The correct answer is D.

93. $\dfrac{(-1.5)(1.2) - (4.5)(0.4)}{30} =$

(A) -1.2
(B) -0.12
(C) 0
(D) 0.12
(E) 1.2

Arithmetic Operations on rational numbers

Simplify the expression.

$$\frac{(-1.5)(1.2) - (4.5)(0.4)}{30} =$$

$$\frac{-1.80 - 1.80}{30} = \frac{-3.60}{30} = -0.12$$

The correct answer is B.

94. René earns \$8.50 per hour on days other than Sundays and twice that rate on Sundays. Last week she worked a total of 40 hours, including 8 hours on Sunday. What were her earnings for the week?

(A) \$272
(B) \$340
(C) \$398
(D) \$408
(E) \$476

Arithmetic Operations on rational numbers

René worked a total of $40 - 8 = 32$ hours at a rate of \$8.50 per hour during the week. On Sunday she worked 8 hours at a rate of \$8.50(2) = \$17.00 per hour. Her total earnings for the week were thus 32(\$8.50) + 8(\$17) = \$408.

The correct answer is D.

95. In a shipment of 120 machine parts, 5 percent were defective. In a shipment of 80 machine parts, 10 percent were defective. For the two shipments combined, what percent of the machine parts were defective?

(A) 6.5%
(B) 7.0%
(C) 7.5%
(D) 8.0%
(E) 8.5%

Arithmetic Percents

The number of defective parts in the first shipment was $120(0.05) = 6$. The number of defective parts in the second shipment was $80(0.10) = 8$. The percent of machine parts that were defective in the two shipments combined was therefore $\dfrac{6+8}{120+80} = \dfrac{14}{200} = \dfrac{7}{100} = 7\%$.

The correct answer is B.

96. If $8^{2x+3} = 2^{3x+6}$, then $x =$

   (A) -3
   (B) -1
   (C) 0
   (D) 1
   (E) 3

Algebra First-degree equations

To work the problem, create a common base so that the exponents can be set equal to each other.

$8^{2x+3} = 2^{3x+6}$

$(2^3)^{2x+3} = 2^{3x+6}$ since $8 = 2 \times 2 \times 2$, can be expressed as 2^3

$2^{6x+9} = 2^{3x+6}$ multiply exponents

$6x + 9 = 3x + 6$ set exponents equal since they are on a common base (2)

$3x = -3$ solve for x

$x = -1$

The correct answer is B.

97. Of the following, the closest approximation to $\sqrt{\dfrac{5.98(601.5)}{15.79}}$ is

   (A) 5
   (B) 15
   (C) 20
   (D) 25
   (E) 225

Arithmetic Estimation

$$\sqrt{\dfrac{5.98(601.5)}{15.79}} \approx \sqrt{\dfrac{6(600)}{16}} = \sqrt{\dfrac{3600}{16}} = \sqrt{225} = 15$$

The correct answer is B.

98. Which of the following CANNOT be the greatest common divisor of two positive integers x and y?

   (A) 1
   (B) x
   (C) y
   (D) $x - y$
   (E) $x + y$

Arithmetic Properties of numbers

When deciding if something must be true, test the case with values known to be true. It takes only one counterexample to prove it false. Using the abbreviation "gcd" below to stand for the greatest common divisor:

A   If $x = 3$ and $y = 2$, gcd $= 1$ CAN be gcd

B   If $x = 2$ and $y = 4$, gcd $= 2 = x$ CAN be gcd

C   If $x = 4$ and $y = 2$, gcd $= 2 = y$ CAN be gcd

D   If $x = 3$ and $y = 2$, gcd $= 1 = x - y$ CAN be gcd

E   The gcd of 2 integers cannot be greater than either integer.   CANNOT be gcd

The correct answer is E.

99. If a, b, and c are nonzero numbers and $a + b = c$, which of the following is equal to 1?

   (A) $\dfrac{a-b}{c}$

   (B) $\dfrac{a-c}{b}$

   (C) $\dfrac{b-c}{a}$

   (D) $\dfrac{b-a}{c}$

   (E) $\dfrac{c-b}{a}$

Arithmetic Operations on rational numbers

Since $a + b = c$, substitute $a + b$ for c in each fraction, and work the problem to see if the fraction reduces to 1.

A $\dfrac{a-b}{c} = \dfrac{a-b}{a+b}$ cannot reduce further

B $\dfrac{a-c}{b} = \dfrac{a-(a+b)}{b} = \dfrac{a-a-b}{b} = \dfrac{-b}{b} = -1$

C $\dfrac{b-c}{a} = \dfrac{b-(a+b)}{a} = \dfrac{b-a-b}{a} = \dfrac{-a}{a} = -1$

D $\dfrac{b-a}{c} = \dfrac{b-a}{a+b} = \dfrac{-(a-b)}{a+b}$ cannot reduce further

E $\dfrac{c-b}{a} = \dfrac{(a+b)-b}{a} = \dfrac{a}{a} = 1$

The correct answer is E.

100. Last year Carlos saved 10 percent of his annual earnings. This year he earned 5 percent more than last year and he saved 12 percent of his annual earnings. The amount saved this year was what percent of the amount saved last year?

(A) 122%
(B) 124%
(C) 126%
(D) 128%
(E) 130%

Arithmetic Percent

Let x represent the amount of Carlos' annual earnings last year.

Carlos' savings last year = $0.1x$

Carlos' earning this year = $1.05x$

Carlos' savings this year = $(1.05x)(0.12) = 0.126x$

The amount saved this year as a percent of the amount saved last year is $\dfrac{0.126x}{0.1x} = 1.26 = 126\%$.

The correct answer is C.

101. A corporation that had $115.19 billion in profits for the year paid out $230.10 million in employee benefits. Approximately what percent of the profits were the employee benefits? (1 billion = 10^9)

(A) 50%
(B) 20%
(C) 5%
(D) 2%
(E) 0.2%

Arithmetic Percent + Estimation

The employee benefits as a fraction of profits can be expressed as $\dfrac{230.10 \times 10^6}{115.19 \times 10^9}$, which is

approximately $\dfrac{230}{115 \times 10^3} = \dfrac{230}{115,000} = \dfrac{23}{11,500} =$

$0.002 = 0.2\%$

The correct answer is E.

Questions 102–103 refer to the following definition.

For any positive integer n, $n > 1$, the "length" of n is the number of positive primes (not necessarily distinct) whose product is n. For example, the length of 50 is 3 since 50 = (2)(5)(5).

102. Which of the following integers has length 3?

(A) 3
(B) 15
(C) 60
(D) 64
(E) 105

Arithmetic Properties of numbers

Each number needs to be factored into primes to determine its "length."

A $3 = 3$ a prime number: therefore the "length" = 1

B $15 = (3)(5)$ "length" = 2

C $60 = (5)(3)(2)(2)$ "length" = 4

D $64 = (2)(2)(2)(2)(2)(2)$ "length" = 6

E $105 = (5)(3)(7)$ "length" = 3

The correct answer is E.

103. What is the greatest possible length of a positive integer less than 1,000?

   (A) 10
   (B) 9
   (C) 8
   (D) 7
   (E) 6

Arithmetic Properties of numbers

The greatest possible "length" comes from the number with the greatest number of prime factors. The greatest number of factors is created using the smallest prime number, 2, as a factor as many times as possible. Since $2^9 = 512$ and $2^{10} = 1,024$, the greatest possible "length" of a positive integer less than 1,000 is 9.

The correct answer is B.

104. If $x + y = 8z$, then which of the following represents the average (arithmetic mean) of x, y, and z, in terms of z?

   (A) $2z + 1$
   (B) $3z$
   (C) $5z$
   (D) $\dfrac{z}{3}$
   (E) $\dfrac{3z}{2}$

Arithmetic + Algebra Statistics + Simplifying algebraic expressions

Since the average (or the arithmetic mean) of three numbers is equal to $\dfrac{\text{sum of the numbers}}{3}$, the average of x, y, and z can be expressed as $\dfrac{x + y + z}{3}$.

Then, by substituting the given value for $x + y$ in this equation, and by simplifying the equation:

$$\frac{8z + z}{3} = \frac{9z}{3} = 3z.$$

The correct answer is B.

105. On the number line, if $r < s$, if p is halfway between r and s, and if t is halfway between p and r, then $\dfrac{s - t}{t - r} =$

   (A) $\dfrac{1}{4}$
   (B) $\dfrac{1}{3}$
   (C) $\dfrac{4}{3}$
   (D) 3
   (E) 4

Algebra Factoring + Simplifying algebraic expressions

Using a number line makes it possible to see these relationships more readily:

The given relative distances between r, s, t, and p are shown in the number line above. The distance between s and t can be expressed as $s - t$, or as $x + 2x$. The distance between t and r can be expressed as $t - r$, or as x. Thus, by substitution into the given equation:

$$\frac{s - t}{t - r} = \frac{x + 2x}{x} = \frac{3x}{x} 3.$$

The correct answer is D.

106. If x and y are different integers and $x^2 = xy$, which of the following must be true?

   I. $x = 0$
   II. $y = 0$
   III. $x = -y$

   (A) I only
   (B) II only
   (C) III only
   (D) I and III only
   (E) I, II, and III

Arithmetic + Algebra Operations on rational numbers + Second-degree equations

If $x \neq 0$, then both sides of the equation $x^2 = xy$ can be divided by x, resulting in $x = y$. This cannot be true because it is given that x and y are different integers; therefore, $x = 0$, and Statement I must be TRUE. Testing the case with the values $x = 0$ and $y = 3$ yields $x^2 = 0$ and $xy = 0$, which clearly satisfies $x^2 = xy$.

When deciding if something must be true, test the case with values known to be true. It takes only one counterexample to prove it false.

II   If $x = 3$ and $y = 0$, $x^2 = 9$ and $xy = 0$
      NEED NOT BE TRUE that $y = 0$

III   If $x = -3$ and $y = 3$, $x^2 = 9$ and $xy = -9$
      NEED NOT BE TRUE that $x = -y$

The correct answer is A.

107. If $\dfrac{3}{x} = 2$ and $\dfrac{y}{4} = 3$, then $\dfrac{3+y}{x+4} =$

(A) $\dfrac{10}{9}$

(B) $\dfrac{3}{2}$

(C) $\dfrac{20}{11}$

(D) $\dfrac{30}{11}$

(E) 5

Algebra First-degree equations + Simplifying algebraic expressions

Solving $\dfrac{3}{x} = 2$ and $\dfrac{y}{4} = 3$ for x and y respectively gives $x = \dfrac{3}{2}$ and $y = 12$. Then substituting these into the given expression gives

$$\frac{3+y}{x+4} = \frac{3+12}{\frac{3}{2}+4} = \frac{3+12}{\frac{3}{2}+\frac{8}{2}} = \frac{15}{\frac{11}{2}} = \frac{15 \times 2}{11} = \frac{30}{11}.$$

The correct answer is D.

108. Which of the following fractions has the greatest value?

(A) $\dfrac{6}{(2^2)(5^2)}$

(B) $\dfrac{1}{(2^3)(5^2)}$

(C) $\dfrac{28}{(2^2)(5^3)}$

(D) $\dfrac{62}{(2^3)(5^3)}$

(E) $\dfrac{122}{(2^4)(5^3)}$

Arithmetic Operations on rational expressions

Notice that $(2^2)(5^2)$ is a factor of the denominator of each of the answer choices. Factoring this out to identify the value by which $\dfrac{1}{(2^2)(5^2)}$ is multiplied in each fraction will make comparing the values of the fractions less complicated.

A $\dfrac{6}{(2^2)(5^2)} = 6 \times \dfrac{1}{(2^2)(5^2)}$

B $\dfrac{1}{(2^3)(5^2)} = \dfrac{1}{2} \times \dfrac{1}{(2^2)(5^2)}$

C $\dfrac{28}{(2^2)(5^3)} = \dfrac{28}{5} \times \dfrac{1}{(2^2)(5^2)}$

D $\dfrac{62}{(2^3)(5^3)} = \dfrac{62}{(2)(5)} \times \dfrac{1}{(2^2)(5^2)} =$

$\dfrac{62}{10} \times \dfrac{1}{(2^2)(5^2)} = \dfrac{31}{5} \times \dfrac{1}{(2^2)(5^2)}$

E $\dfrac{122}{(2^4)(5^3)} = \dfrac{122}{(2^2)(5)} \times \dfrac{1}{(2^2)(5^2)} =$

$\dfrac{61}{10} \times \dfrac{1}{(2^2)(5^2)}$

Of these fractions,

$\dfrac{31}{5} \times \dfrac{1}{(2^2)(5^2)}$ has the greatest value.

The correct answer is D.

109. Which of the following CANNOT yield an integer when divided by 10?

   (A)   The sum of two odd integers
   (B)   An integer less than 10
   (C)   The product of two primes
   (D)   The sum of three consecutive integers
   (E)   An odd integer

Arithmetic Operations on rational numbers

Test each answer choice with values that satisfy the condition in order to determine which one does NOT yield an integer when divided by 10.

A   3 and 7 are both odd integers, and
$\frac{3+7}{10} = 1$ IS an integer

B   −10 is an integer that is less than 10,
and $\frac{-10}{10} = 1$ IS an integer

C   2 and 5 are primes, and $\frac{(5)(2)}{10} = 1$
                 IS an integer

D   9, 10, and 11 are three consecutive integers,
and $\frac{9+10+11}{10} = 3$ IS an integer

E   All multiples of 10 are even integers; therefore, an odd integer divided by 10 CANNOT yield an integer.

The correct answer is E.

110. A certain clock marks every hour by striking a number of times equal to the hour, and the time required for a stroke is exactly equal to the time interval between strokes. At 6:00 the time lapse between the beginning of the first stroke and the end of the last stroke is 22 seconds. At 12:00, how many seconds elapse between the beginning of the first stroke and the end of the last stroke?

   (A)   72
   (B)   50
   (C)   48
   (D)   46
   (E)   44

Arithmetic Operations on rational numbers

At 6:00 there are 6 strokes and 5 intervals between strokes. Thus, there are 11 equal time intervals in the 22 seconds between the beginning of the first stroke and the end of the last stroke. Therefore, each time interval is $\frac{22}{11} = 2$ seconds long. At 12:00 there are 12 strokes and 11 intervals between strokes. Thus, there are 23 equal 2-second time intervals, or $23 \times 2 = 46$ seconds, between the beginning of the first stroke and the end of the last stroke.

The correct answer is D.

111. If $k \neq 0$ and $k - \frac{3-2k^2}{k} = \frac{x}{k}$, then $x =$

   (A) $-3 - k^2$
   (B) $k^2 - 3$
   (C) $3k^2 - 3$
   (D) $k - 3 - 2k^2$
   (E) $k - 3 + 2k^2$

Algebra Second-degree equations

Solve the equation for x.

$k - \frac{3-2k^2}{k} = \frac{x}{k}$

$k^2 - (3-2k^2) = x$ multiply through by k

$k^2 - 3 + 2k^2 = x$ simplify

$3k^2 - 3 = x$

The correct answer is C.

112. $\frac{\frac{1}{2}+\frac{1}{3}}{\frac{1}{4}} =$

   (A) $\frac{1}{12}$
   (B) $\frac{5}{24}$
   (C) $\frac{2}{3}$
   (D) $\frac{9}{4}$
   (E) $\frac{10}{3}$

Arithmetic Operations on rational numbers

This complex fraction can be simplified by multiplying both the numerator and the denominator by the lowest common denominator of 2, 3, and 4, which is 12.

$$\frac{12}{12}\left(\frac{\frac{1}{2}+\frac{1}{3}}{\frac{1}{4}}\right)=\frac{\left(\frac{12}{2}+\frac{12}{3}\right)}{\frac{12}{4}} \quad \text{multiply}$$

$$\frac{6+4}{3} \quad \text{simplify}$$

$$\frac{10}{3} \quad \text{simplify completely}$$

The correct answer is E.

113. For all numbers s and t, the operation $*$ is defined by $s * t = (s - 1)(t + 1)$. If $(-2) * x = -12$, then $x =$

(A) 2
(B) 3
(C) 5
(D) 6
(E) 11

Algebra Second-degree equations

The equivalent values established for this problem are $s = -2$ and $t = x$. So, substitute -2 for s and x for t in the given equation:

$$s * t = (s - 1)(t + 1)$$

$(-2) * x = ((-2) - 1)(x + 1)$ substitute -2 for s and x for t

$(-2) * x = (-3)(x + 1)$ simplify

Then, because

$(-2) * x = -12$

$-12 = (-3)(x + 1)$ substitute -12

$-12 = -3x - 3$

$-9 = -3x$ solve for x

$3 = x$

The correct answer is B.

114. Salesperson A's compensation for any week is $360 plus 6 percent of the portion of A's total sales above $1,000 for that week. Salesperson B's compensation for any week is 8 percent of B's total sales for that week. For what amount of total weekly sales would both salespeople earn the same compensation?

(A) $21,000
(B) $18,000
(C) $15,000
(D) $ 4,500
(E) $ 4,000

Algebra Applied problems + Simultaneous equations

Let x represent the total weekly sales amount at which both salespersons earn the same compensation. Then, the given information regarding when Salesperson A's weekly pay equals Salesperson B's weekly pay can be expressed as:

$360 + 0.06(x - 1,000) = 0.08x$

$360 + 0.06x - 60 = 0.08x$ solve for x

$300 = 0.02x$

$15,000 = x$

The correct answer is C.

115. The sum of the ages of Doris and Fred is y years. If Doris is 12 years older than Fred, how many years old will Fred be y years from now, in terms of y?

(A) $y - 6$
(B) $2y - 6$
(C) $\dfrac{y}{2} - 6$
(D) $\dfrac{3y}{2} - 6$
(E) $\dfrac{5y}{2} - 6$

Algebra Applied problems + Simultaneous equations

Letting d represent the current age of Doris and f represent the current age of Fred, the given information can be expressed as follows:

$d + f = y$ Doris's age + Fred's age = y

$d = f + 12$ Doris's age = Fred's age + 12

To find Fred's current age, substitute the value of d and solve for f:

$(f + 12) + f = y$

$2f + 12 = y$ combine like terms

$2f = y - 12$ subtract 12 from both sides

$f = \dfrac{y - 12}{2}$ divide both sides by 2

$f = \dfrac{y}{2} - 6$ simplify

Fred's age after y years can be expressed as $f + y$. First, substitute the value of $f = \dfrac{y}{2} - 6$ and then simplify. Thus, Fred's age y years from now will be:

$\dfrac{y}{2} - 6 + y$

$\dfrac{3y}{2} - 6$

The correct answer is D.

116. If a basketball team scores an average (arithmetic mean) of x points per game for n games and then scores y points in its next game, what is the team's average score for the n + 1 games?

(A) $\dfrac{nx + y}{n + 1}$

(B) $x + \dfrac{y}{n + 1}$

(C) $x + \dfrac{y}{n}$

(D) $\dfrac{n(x + y)}{n + 1}$

(E) $\dfrac{x + ny}{n + 1}$

Arithmetic Statistics

Using the formula average $= \dfrac{\text{total points}}{\text{number of games}}$, the average number of points per game for the first n games can be expressed as $x = \dfrac{\text{total points for } n \text{ games}}{n}$. Solving this equation shows that the total points for n games $= nx$. Then, the total points for $n + 1$ games can be expressed as $nx + y$, and the average number of points for $n + 1$ games $= \dfrac{nx + y}{n + 1}$.

The correct answer is A.

117. Of the following numbers, which one is third greatest?

(A) $2\sqrt{2} - 1$
(B) $\sqrt{2} + 1$
(C) $1 - \sqrt{2}$
(D) $\sqrt{2} - 1$
(E) $\sqrt{2}$

Arithmetic Operations on radical expressions

Since $\sqrt{2} \approx 1.41$, each option can be readily approximated.

A $2\sqrt{2} - 1 = 2(1.41) - 1 = 2.82 - 1 = 1.82$

B $\sqrt{2} + 1 = 1.41 + 1 = 2.41$

C $1 - \sqrt{2} = 1 - 1.41 = -0.41$

D $\sqrt{2} - 1 = 1.41 - 1 = 0.41$

E $\sqrt{2} = 1.41$

The order of the answer choices from least to greatest is C < D < E < A < B.

The correct answer is B.

118. At a certain pizzeria, $\dfrac{1}{8}$ of the pizzas sold in one week were mushroom and $\dfrac{1}{3}$ of the remaining pizzas sold were pepperoni. If n of the pizzas sold were pepperoni, how many were mushroom?

(A) $\dfrac{3}{8}n$

(B) $\dfrac{3}{7}n$

(C) $\dfrac{7}{16}n$

(D) $\dfrac{7}{8}n$

(E) $3n$

Algebra Simplifying algebraic expressions

Let t be the total number of pizzas sold.

Then $\dfrac{1}{8}t$ of the pizzas sold were mushroom,

and $\dfrac{1}{3}\left(\dfrac{7}{8}t\right) = \dfrac{7t}{24}$ of the pizzas sold were

pepperoni. Use these values and the given information to set up a proportion comparing the mushroom pizzas to the pepperoni pizzas.

$\dfrac{\frac{1}{8}t}{\frac{7}{24}t} = \dfrac{\text{mushroom}}{n}$ Simplify the fraction and solve for mushroom:

$\dfrac{3}{7} = \dfrac{\text{mushroom}}{n}$ $\quad$ (Note that $\dfrac{\frac{1}{8}t}{\frac{7}{24}t} = \dfrac{\frac{1}{8}}{\frac{7}{24}} = \dfrac{24}{56} = \dfrac{3}{7}$.)

$\dfrac{3}{7}n = \text{mushroom}$

The correct answer is B.

119. Two trains, X and Y, started simultaneously from opposite ends of a 100-mile route and traveled toward each other on parallel tracks. Train X, traveling at a constant rate, completed the 100-mile trip in 5 hours; train Y, traveling at a constant rate, completed the 100-mile trip in 3 hours. How many miles had train X traveled when it met train Y?

(A) 37.5
(B) 40.0
(C) 60.0
(D) 62.5
(E) 77.5

Algebra Applied problems

From the given information, it is known that train X was traveling at the rate of $\dfrac{100}{5} = 20$ miles per hour, and train Y was traveling at the rate of $\dfrac{100}{3} = 33\dfrac{1}{3}$ miles per hour. Use the formula distance = (rate)(time), and let t equal the number of hours the trains take to meet. Thus, when the trains meet, train X will have traveled a distance of $20t$ miles and train Y will have traveled a distance of $33\dfrac{1}{3}t$ miles.

Since between them the two trains will have traveled the entire route when they meet, the sum of the distances when they meet is 100 miles. Therefore, the information can be expressed in the following equation, which can be solved for t in hours:

$20t + 33\dfrac{1}{3}t = 100$ $\quad$ sum of distances traveled = 100 miles

$53\dfrac{1}{3}t = 100$

$t = 1.875$

Then, since train X had traveled $20t$ miles, substitute this value of t in train X's distance formula to determine its distance in miles:

$d = 20(1.875)$

$d = 37.5$

The correct answer is A.

120. One week a certain truck rental lot had a total of 20 trucks, all of which were on the lot Monday morning. If 50 percent of the trucks that were rented out during the week were returned to the lot on or before Saturday morning of that week, and if there were at least 12 trucks on the lot that Saturday morning, what is the greatest number of different trucks that could have been rented out during the week?

(A) 18
(B) 16
(C) 12
(D) 8
(E) 4

Arithmetic + Algebra Percents + Applied problems

The difference between the number of trucks on the lot on Monday (20) and the minimum number of trucks on the lot on Saturday (12) is $20 - 12 = 8$ trucks. So, 8 trucks is the maximum number of trucks not on the lot on that Saturday morning. If 50 percent of the trucks that were rented out were returned, then 50 percent were also not returned. Therefore, if the 8 trucks (at most) not on the lot on that Saturday morning represent 50 percent of the trucks rented out during the week, the maximum number of trucks rented out is $8(2) = 16$ trucks.

The correct answer is B.

121. What is the value of $2x^2 - 2.4x - 1.7$ for $x = 0.7$?

   (A) -0.72
   (B) -1.42
   (C) -1.98
   (D) -2.40
   (E) -2.89

Algebra Simplifying algebraic expressions

Work the problem by substituting $x = 0.7$.

$2x^2 - 2.4x - 1.7$

$2(0.7)^2 - 2.4(0.7) - 1.7$

$2(0.49) - 1.68 - 1.7$

$0.98 - 1.68 - 1.7$

-2.40

The correct answer is D.

122. If s, u, and v are positive integers and $2s = 2u + 2v$, which of the following must be true?

   I. $s = u$
   II. $u \neq v$
   III. $s > v$

   (A)   None
   (B)   I only
   (C)   II only
   (D)   III only
   (E)   II and III

Arithmetic Operations on rational numbers

Test each value in the equation to determine which statement[s] must be true.

I.   If $s = u$, then $2s = 2s + 2v$, or $v = 0$ which is not a positive integer. It is NOT true that $s = v$.

II. If, by counterexample, $u = v = 2$, then $2s = 2(2) + 2(2)$, or $2s = 8$ and $s = 4$, which is a positive integer. Thus, u can equal v, and it need NOT be true that $u \neq v$.

III. Since s, u, and v must all be positive integers, both $2u$ and $2v$ must be positive integers. If $2s = 2u + 2v$, then $2s$ must be greater than $2v$. Thus, it MUST be true that s is greater than v.

The correct answer is D.

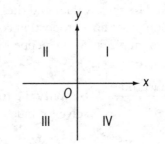

123. In the rectangular coordinate system shown above, which quadrant, if any, contains no point (x, y) that satisfies the inequality $2x - 3y \leq -6$?

   (A)   None
   (B)   I
   (C)   II
   (D)   III
   (E)   IV

Geometry Simple coordinate geometry

Work the given inequality to isolate the value of y to be able to graph the inequality.

$2x - 3y \leq -6$

$-3y \leq -2x - 6$

$y \geq \dfrac{2}{3}x + 2$ an inequality reverses when divided by a negative

Substitute values of x into this inequality to determine coordinates for plotting the line. For instance, when $x = -3$, $y = 0$, and when $x = 0$, $y = 2$. This is shown below:

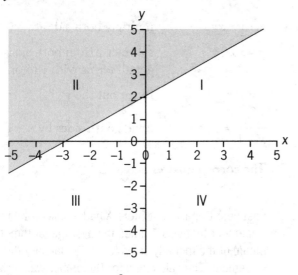

The inequality $y \geq \frac{2}{3}x + 2$ thus consists of a line that goes through every quadrant but quadrant IV and all values above the line into quadrants I, II, and III.

The correct answer is E.

124. The cost to rent a small bus for a trip is x dollars, which is to be shared equally among the people taking the trip. If 10 people take the trip rather than 16, how many more dollars, in terms of x, will it cost per person?

(A) $\dfrac{x}{6}$

(B) $\dfrac{x}{10}$

(C) $\dfrac{x}{16}$

(D) $\dfrac{3x}{40}$

(E) $\dfrac{3x}{80}$

Algebra Applied problems

If 16 take the trip, the cost per person would be $\dfrac{x}{16}$ dollars. If 10 take the trip, the cost per person would be $\dfrac{x}{10}$ dollars. (Note that the lowest common multiple of 10 and 16 is 80.)

Thus, if 10 take the trip, the increase in dollars per person would be $\dfrac{x}{10} - \dfrac{x}{16} = \dfrac{8x}{80} - \dfrac{5x}{80} = \dfrac{3x}{80}$.

The correct answer is E.

125. If x is an integer and $y = 3x + 2$, which of the following CANNOT be a divisor of y?

(A) 4

(B) 5

(C) 6

(D) 7

(E) 8

Arithmetic Properties of numbers

Although $3x$ is always divisible by 3, $3x + 2$ cannot be divisible by 3 since 2 is not divisible by 3. Thus, $3x + 2$ cannot be divisible by any multiple of 3, including 6.

The correct answer is C.

126. A certain electronic component is sold in boxes of 54 for $16.20 and in boxes of 27 for $13.20. A customer who needed only 54 components for a project had to buy 2 boxes of 27 because boxes of 54 were unavailable. Approximately how much more did the customer pay for each component due to the unavailability of the larger boxes?

(A) $0.33

(B) $0.19

(C) $0.11

(D) $0.06

(E) $0.03

Arithmetic Operations of rational numbers

The customer paid 2($13.20) = $26.40 for the 2 boxes of 27 components. This is $26.40 − $16.20 = $10.20 more than the cost of a single box of 54 components. So, the extra cost per component is $\frac{\$10.20}{54} = \$0.19$.

The correct answer is B.

127. As a salesperson, Phyllis can choose one of two methods of annual payment: either an annual salary of $35,000 with no commission or an annual salary of $10,000 plus a 20 percent commission on her total annual sales. What must her total annual sales be to give her the same annual pay with either method?

(A) $100,000
(B) $120,000
(C) $125,000
(D) $130,000
(E) $132,000

Algebra Applied problems

Letting s be Phyllis's total annual sales needed to generate the same annual pay with either method, the given information can be expressed as $35,000 = $10,000 + 0.2s$. Solve this equation for s.

$35,000 = $10,000 + 0.2s$

$25,000 = 0.2s$

$125,000 = s$

The correct answer is C.

128. If $\frac{x+y}{xy} = 1$, then $y =$

(A) $\frac{x}{x-1}$

(B) $\frac{x}{x+1}$

(C) $\frac{x-1}{x}$

(D) $\frac{x+1}{x}$

(E) x

Algebra First-degree equations

Solve the given equation for y.

$\frac{x+y}{xy} = 1$

$x + y = xy$	multiply both sides by xy
$x = xy - y$	subtract y from both sides to get all terms with y to one side
$x = y(x - 1)$	factor out the y
$\frac{x}{x-1} = y$	divide both sides by $x - 1$

The correct answer is A.

129. Last year Department Store X had a sales total for December that was 4 times the average (arithmetic mean) of the monthly sales totals for January through November. The sales total for December was what fraction of the sales total for the year?

(A) $\frac{1}{4}$

(B) $\frac{4}{15}$

(C) $\frac{1}{3}$

(D) $\frac{4}{11}$

(E) $\frac{4}{5}$

Algebra + Arithmetic Applied problems + Statistics

Let A equal the average sales per month for the first 11 months. The given information about the total sales for the year can then be expressed as $11A + 4A = 15A$. Thus, the ratio of the sales total for December to the sales total for the year was $\frac{4A}{15A} = \frac{4}{15}$.

The correct answer is B.

130. Working alone, printers X, Y, and Z can do a certain printing job, consisting of a large number of pages, in 12, 15, and 18 hours, respectively. What is the ratio of

the time it takes printer X to do the job, working alone at its rate, to the time it takes printers Y and Z to do the job, working together at their individual rates?

(A) $\dfrac{4}{11}$

(B) $\dfrac{1}{2}$

(C) $\dfrac{15}{22}$

(D) $\dfrac{22}{15}$

(E) $\dfrac{11}{4}$

Arithmetic Operations on rational numbers

From the given information, it can be stated that printer Y can do $\dfrac{1}{15}$ of the job per hour, and printer Z can do $\dfrac{1}{18}$ of the job per hour. Together, printers Y and Z can do $\left(\dfrac{1}{15} + \dfrac{1}{18} \right) = \left(\dfrac{6}{90} + \dfrac{5}{90} \right) = \dfrac{11}{90}$ of the job per hour, which means in turn that it takes them $\dfrac{90}{11}$ hours to complete the job. It is given that printer X completes the job in 12 hours. Therefore, the ratio of the time required for X to do the job to the time required for Y and Z working together to do the job is $\dfrac{12}{\frac{90}{11}} = \dfrac{12(11)}{90} = \dfrac{2(11)}{15} = \dfrac{22}{15}$.

The correct answer is D.

131. A rabbit on a controlled diet is fed daily 300 grams of a mixture of two foods, food X and food Y. Food X contains 10 percent protein and food Y contains 15 percent protein. If the rabbit's diet provides exactly 38 grams of protein daily, how many grams of food X are in the mixture?

(A) 100
(B) 140
(C) 150
(D) 160
(E) 200

Algebra Applied problems

Let x be the number of grams of food X in the mixture. Then the number of grams of food Y in the mixture can be expressed as $300 - x$. Since the sum of protein from X and Y is 38 grams, the given information about protein content can be expressed in the following equation, which can then be solved for x.

$0.10x + 0.15(300 - x) = 38$

$0.10x + 45 - 0.15x = 38$

$-0.05x = -7$

$x = 140$

The correct answer is B.

132. A company that ships boxes to a total of 12 distribution centers uses color coding to identify each center. If either a single color or a pair of two different colors is chosen to represent each center and if each center is uniquely represented by that choice of one or two colors, what is the minimum number of colors needed for the coding? (Assume that the order of the colors in a pair does not matter.)

(A) 4
(B) 5
(C) 6
(D) 12
(E) 24

Arithmetic Elementary combinatorics

Since the problem asks for the minimum number of colors needed, start with the lowest answer choice available. Calculate each successive option until finding the minimum number of colors that can represent at least 12 distribution centers.

Note that $_nC_r = \dfrac{n!}{r!(n-r)!}$ for the combination of n things taken r at a time.

# of Colors	Number represented by one color	Number represented by two colors	Total represented
4	4	$_4C_2 = \dfrac{4!}{2!2!} = 6$	4 + 6 = 10
5	5	$_5C_2 = \dfrac{5!}{2!3!} = \dfrac{(5)(4)}{2} = 10$	5 + 10 = 15

The correct answer is B.

133. If $x \neq 2$, then $\dfrac{3x^2(x-2)-x+2}{x-2} =$

(A) $3x^2 - x + 2$
(B) $3x^2 + 1$
(C) $3x^2$
(D) $3x^2 - 1$
(E) $3x^2 - 2$

Algebra Simplifying algebraic expressions

To simplify this expression, it is important to note that terms that are added and subtracted cannot be cancelled in a fraction. Only factors that are multiplied by all other items in the numerator or denominator can be cancelled. The first step in simplifying here is thus to factor out the negative from the last two terms to create a common factor. This allows the expression to be simplified as follows:

$\dfrac{3x^2(x-2)-x+2}{x-2}$

$\dfrac{3x^2(x-2)-(x-2)}{x-2}$

$\dfrac{3x^2(x-2)-1(x-2)}{x-2}$ — create the common factor of $(x-2)$

$\dfrac{(x-2)(3x^2-1)}{x-2}$ — factor $(x-2)$ to the front of the numerator

$3x^2-1$ — cancel the common factor of $(x-2)$

The correct answer is D.

134. If $d > 0$ and $0 < 1 - \dfrac{c}{d} < 1$, which of the following must be true?

I. $c > 0$

II. $\dfrac{c}{d} < 1$

III. $c^2 + d^2 > 1$

(A) I only
(B) II only
(C) I and II only
(D) II and III only
(E) I, II, and III

Algebra Inequalities

Consider each answer choice.

I.   Since $1 - \dfrac{c}{d} < 1$, it follows that $-\dfrac{c}{d} < 0$ or $\dfrac{c}{d} > 0$. Since it is given that $d > 0$, and since the quotient of $\dfrac{c}{d}$ is positive, then $c > 0$ must be TRUE.

II.   Since $0 < 1 - \dfrac{c}{d} < 1$, it follows that $-1 < -\dfrac{c}{d} < 0$, or $1 > \dfrac{c}{d} > 0$, which means $\dfrac{c}{d} < 1$ must be TRUE.

III. By counterexample, if $c = \dfrac{1}{4}$ and $d = \dfrac{1}{3}$,

then $0 < 1 - \dfrac{\frac{1}{4}}{\frac{1}{3}} < 1$ gives $0 < 1 - \dfrac{3}{4} < 1$,

which is true to the inequality. However,

$c^2 + d^2 = \left(\dfrac{1}{4}\right)^2 + \left(\dfrac{1}{3}\right)^2 = \dfrac{1}{16} + \dfrac{1}{9}$, which is

less than 1, and thus $c^2 + d^2 > 1$ NEED NOT BE TRUE.

The correct answer is C.

135. $\dfrac{\frac{1}{2}}{\frac{1}{4} + \frac{1}{6}} =$

(A) $\dfrac{6}{5}$

(B) $\dfrac{5}{6}$

(C) $\dfrac{5}{24}$

(D) $\dfrac{1}{5}$

(E) $\dfrac{1}{12}$

Arithmetic Operations on rational numbers

Simplify the expression using the least common denominator for the fractions in its denominator, and work the problem.

$$\dfrac{\frac{1}{2}}{\frac{1}{4} + \frac{1}{6}} = \dfrac{\frac{1}{2}}{\frac{3}{12} + \frac{2}{12}} = \dfrac{\frac{1}{2}}{\frac{5}{12}} = \dfrac{1}{2} \times \dfrac{12}{5} = \dfrac{12}{10} = \dfrac{6}{5}$$

The correct answer is A.

136. A train travels from New York City to Chicago, a distance of approximately 840 miles, at an average rate of 60 miles per hour and arrives in Chicago at 6:00 in the evening, Chicago time. At what hour in the morning, New York City time, did the train depart for Chicago? (Note: Chicago time is one hour earlier than New York City time.)

(A) 4:00
(B) 5:00
(C) 6:00
(D) 7:00
(E) 8:00

Arithmetic Operations on rational numbers

Using the formula $\dfrac{\text{distance}}{\text{rate}} = \text{time}$,

it can be calculated that it took the train

$\dfrac{840 \text{ miles}}{60 \text{ miles per hour}} = 14$ hours to travel from

New York City to Chicago. The train arrived in Chicago at 6:00 in the evening. Since it had departed 14 hours before that, it had therefore departed at 4:00 a.m. Chicago time. Then, since it is given that Chicago time is one hour earlier than New York City time, it had departed at 5:00 a.m. New York City time.

The correct answer is B.

137. Last year Manfred received 26 paychecks. Each of his first 6 paychecks was $750; each of his remaining paychecks was $30 more than each of his first 6 paychecks. To the nearest dollar, what was the average (arithmetic mean) amount of his paychecks for the year?

(A) $752
(B) $755
(C) $765
(D) $773
(E) $775

Arithmetic Statistics

In addition to the first 6 paychecks for $750 each, Manfred received $26 - 6 = 20$ paychecks for $750 + $30 or $780 each. Applying the formula

$\dfrac{\text{sum of values}}{\text{number of values}} = \text{average}$, this information

can be expressed in the following equation:

$$\dfrac{6(750) + 20(780)}{26} = \dfrac{20{,}100}{26} = 773.08.$$

The correct answer is D.

138. If 25 percent of p is equal to 10 percent of q, and pq ≠ 0, then p is what percent of q?

   (A)   2.5%
   (B)   15%
   (C)   20%
   (D)   35%
   (E)   40%

Arithmetic + Algebra Percent + Applied problems

The given information can be expressed as follows and solved for p.

$$0.25p = 0.10q$$

$$p = \frac{0.10}{0.25}q$$

$$p = 0.40q$$

The correct answer is E.

139. If the length of an edge of cube X is twice the length of an edge of cube Y, what is the ratio of the volume of cube Y to the volume of cube X?

   (A) $\dfrac{1}{2}$

   (B) $\dfrac{1}{4}$

   (C) $\dfrac{1}{6}$

   (D) $\dfrac{1}{8}$

   (E) $\dfrac{1}{27}$

Geometry Volume

When two similar three-dimensional objects are compared, the volume ratio will be the cube of the length ratio. Since it is given that the length of an edge of cube X is twice the length of an edge of cube Y, the length ratio for cube Y to cube X is $\dfrac{1}{2}$. This therefore makes the volume ratio $\left(\dfrac{1}{2}\right)^3 = \dfrac{1}{2} \times \dfrac{1}{2} \times \dfrac{1}{2} = \dfrac{1}{8}$.

The correct answer is D.

140. Machines A and B always operate independently and at their respective constant rates. When working alone, machine A can fill a production lot in 5 hours, and machine B can fill the same lot in x hours. When the two machines operate simultaneously to fill the production lot, it takes them 2 hours to complete the job. What is the value of x?

   (A) $3\dfrac{1}{3}$

   (B) 3

   (C) $2\dfrac{1}{2}$

   (D) $2\dfrac{1}{3}$

   (E) $1\dfrac{1}{2}$

Algebra Applied problems

From the given information, it can be stated that machine A can complete $\dfrac{1}{5}$ of the job in 1 hour, and machine B can complete $\dfrac{1}{x}$ of the job in 1 hour.

The two machines operating simultaneously can fill $\dfrac{1}{5} + \dfrac{1}{x}$ of the job in 1 hour. The fact that it takes them 2 hours to complete the job together can be expressed as $\dfrac{1}{5} + \dfrac{1}{x} = \dfrac{1}{2}$, which can be solved for x as follows:

$$\dfrac{1}{5} + \dfrac{1}{x} = \dfrac{1}{2}$$

$$\dfrac{x}{5x} + \dfrac{5}{5x} = \dfrac{1}{2} \qquad \text{create a common denominator on the left side}$$

$$\dfrac{x+5}{5x} = \dfrac{1}{2} \qquad \text{combine the fractions on the left side}$$

$$2x + 10 = 5x \qquad \text{multiply both sides by the common denominator } 10x$$

$$10 = 3x \qquad \text{solve for } x$$

$$3\dfrac{1}{3} = x$$

The correct answer is A.

141. An artist wishes to paint a circular region on a square poster that is 2 feet on a side. If the area of the circular region is to be $\frac{1}{2}$ the area of the poster, what must be the radius of the circular region in feet?

    (A) $\frac{1}{\pi}$

    (B) $\sqrt{\frac{2}{\pi}}$

    (C) 1

    (D) $\frac{2}{\sqrt{\pi}}$

    (E) $\frac{\pi}{1}$

Geometry Circles + Area

The area of the square poster is $2^2 = 4$ square feet. The area of a circle $= \pi r^2$, where r is the radius of the circle. The area of the circular region on the square poster can be expressed as $\pi r^2 = \frac{1}{2}(4)$, and this equation can be solved for r, the radius of the circular region:

$$\pi r^2 = 2$$
$$r^2 = \frac{2}{\pi}$$
$$r = \sqrt{\frac{2}{\pi}}$$

The correct answer is B.

142. If a is a positive integer, and if the units' digit of a^2 is 9 and the units' digit of $(a + 1)^2$ is 4, what is the units' digit of $(a + 2)^2$?

    (A) 1
    (B) 3
    (C) 5
    (D) 6
    (E) 14

Arithmetic Properties of numbers

Only numbers ending in 3 or 7 would yield a units' digit of 9 when squared. Thus, if 9 is the units' digit of a^2, then either 3 or 7 must be the units' digit of a.

If the units' digit is 3, then $a + 1 = 3 + 1 = 4$. This makes the units' digit of $(a + 1)^2$ the units' digit of 4^2, which is 6.

If, however, the units' digit is 7, then $a + 1 = 7 + 1 = 8$. This makes the units' digit of $(a + 1)^2$ the units' digit of 8^2, which is 4, as is needed in this problem. Therefore, the units' digit of a must be 7.

Thus, the units' digit of $a + 2$ is 9. This makes the units' digit of $(a + 2)^2$ the units' digit of 9^2, which is 1.

The correct answer is A.

143. A \$500 investment and a \$1,500 investment have a combined yearly return of 8.5 percent of the total of the two investments. If the \$500 investment has a yearly return of 7 percent, what percent yearly return does the \$1,500 investment have?

    (A) 9%
    (B) 10%
    (C) $10\frac{5}{8}$%
    (D) 11%
    (E) 12%

Algebra Percents

The total of the two investments is \$500 + \$1,500 = \$2,000, and the total yearly return for the two investments is thus $2,000(0.085) = \$170$. The return on the \$500 investment is $500(0.07) = \$35$, so the return on the \$1,500 investment is \$170 − \$35 = \$135. Then, $\frac{135}{1500} = 0.09 = 9\%$ is the percent return on the \$1,500 investment.

The correct answer is A.

144. For any integer n greater than 1, $\lfloor n$ denotes the product of all the integers from 1 to n, inclusive. How many prime numbers are there between $\lfloor 6 + 2$ and $\lfloor 6 + 6$, inclusive?

(A) None
(B) One
(C) Two
(D) Three
(E) Four

Arithmetic Properties of numbers

Calculate the product of all the integers, determine the problem's range of numbers, and consider whether each number in the range is a prime number.

$\lfloor 6 = (6)(5)(4)(3)(2)(1) = 720$

$\lfloor 6 + 2 = 720 + 2 = 722$

$\lfloor 6 + 6 = 720 + 6 = 726$

The range is thus 722 to 726, inclusive. The numbers 722, 724, and 726 are divisible by 2, and 725 is divisible by 5. The only remaining number is 723, which is divisible by 3.

The correct answer is A.

145. If $\left(7^{\frac{3}{4}}\right)^{n} = 7$, what is the value of n?

(A) $\dfrac{1}{3}$

(B) $\dfrac{2}{3}$

(C) $\dfrac{4}{3}$

(D) $\dfrac{5}{3}$

(E) s

Algebra First-degree equations

The common base means the exponents can be set equal to each other, and then the equation can be solved for n.

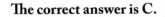

$\left(7^{\frac{3}{4}}\right)^{n} = 7$

$7^{\frac{3}{4}n} = 7^{1}$ set exponents equal to each other

$\dfrac{3}{4}n = 1$ solve for n

$n = \dfrac{4}{3}$

The correct answer is C.

146. Which of the following is equal to the average (arithmetic mean) of $(x + 2)^2$ and $(x - 2)^2$?

(A) x^2
(B) $x^2 + 2$
(C) $x^2 + 4$
(D) $x^2 + 2x$
(E) $x^2 + 4x$

Arithmetic + Algebra Statistics + Simplifying algebraic expressions

Since average $= \dfrac{\text{sum of values}}{\text{number of values}}$, the information in the problem can be expressed as shown.

$$\dfrac{(x + 2)^2 + (x - 2)^2}{2}$$

Simplify the expression as follows:

$$\dfrac{(x^2 + 4x + 4) + (x^2 - 4x + 4)}{2}$$

$$\dfrac{2x^2 + 8}{2}$$

$$x^2 + 4$$

The correct answer is C.

147. If $x^4 + y^4 = 100$ then the greatest possible value of x is between

(A) 0 and 3
(B) 3 and 6
(C) 6 and 9
(D) 9 and 12
(E) 12 and 15

Arithmetic Operations on rational numbers

The value of x is greatest when $y = 0$, that is, when $x^4 = 100$. Since $3^4 = 81$ and $4^4 = 256$, it follows that the greatest possible value of x is between 3 and 4.

The correct answer is B.

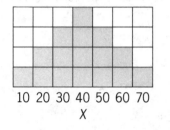

X

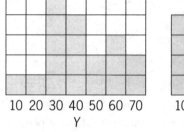

Y

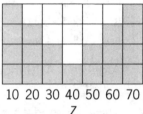

Z

148. If the variables, X, Y, and Z take on only the values 10, 20, 30, 40, 50, 60, or 70 with frequencies indicated by the shaded regions above, for which of the frequency distributions is the mean equal to the median?

    (A) X only
    (B) Y only
    (C) Z only
    (D) X and Y
    (E) X and Z

Arithmetic Statistics

The frequency distributions for both X and Z are symmetric about 40, and thus both X and Z have mean = median = 40. Since both X and Z satisfy the condition in the problem, and since there is no option of "X, Y, and Z" among the answer choices above, there is no need to calculate Y.

The correct answer is E.

149. For how many integers n is $2^n = n^2$?

    (A) None
    (B) One
    (C) Two
    (D) Three
    (E) More than three

Arithmetic Properties of numbers

For all negative values of n, 2^n would be less than 1, and n^2 would be 1 or more, so the statement $2^n = n^2$ would be false.

For $n \geq 0$, the table shown below applies; once $n \geq 5$, then $2^n > n^2$.

n	2^n	n^2
0	1	0
1	2	1
2	4	4
3	8	9
4	16	16
5	32	25
6	64	36

Therefore, $2^n = n^2$ for only two values of n, namely, 2 and 4.

The correct answer is C.

150. If r and s are integers and $rs + r$ is odd, which of the following must be even?

    (A) r
    (B) s
    (C) $r + s$
    (D) $rs - r$
    (E) $r^2 + s$

Arithmetic Properties of numbers

Since $rs + r$ is given as odd, then $rs + r = r(s + 1)$ is also odd. Only the product of two odd numbers equals an odd number, so both r and $s + 1$ must be odd numbers. Therefore, since r is odd and $s + 1$ is odd, s must be even. Since s is an answer choice, no further work is required to answer the problem.

The correct answer is B.

151. A box contains 100 balls, numbered from 1 to 100. If three balls are selected at random and with replacement from the box, what is the probability that the sum of the three numbers on the balls selected from the box will be odd?

    (A) $\dfrac{1}{4}$

    (B) $\dfrac{3}{8}$

    (C) $\dfrac{1}{2}$

    (D) $\dfrac{5}{8}$

    (E) $\dfrac{3}{4}$

Arithmetic Probability

Since there are 50 odd and 50 even balls in the box, the probability of selecting an odd ball at random is $\dfrac{50}{100} = \dfrac{1}{2}$; the probability of selecting an even ball is the same.

For the sum of the three numbers on the selected balls to be odd, either 1) the numbers must all be odd, or 2) exactly one of the numbers must be odd and the other two numbers must be even, which can occur in one of the three ways listed below.

1) Probability of selecting odd, odd, odd =
$$\left(\frac{1}{2}\right)\left(\frac{1}{2}\right)\left(\frac{1}{2}\right) = \frac{1}{8}$$

2) Probability of selecting odd, even, even =
$$\left(\frac{1}{2}\right)\left(\frac{1}{2}\right)\left(\frac{1}{2}\right) = \frac{1}{8}$$

Probability of selecting even, odd, even =
$$\left(\frac{1}{2}\right)\left(\frac{1}{2}\right)\left(\frac{1}{2}\right) = \frac{1}{8}$$

Probability of selecting even, even, odd =
$$\left(\frac{1}{2}\right)\left(\frac{1}{2}\right)\left(\frac{1}{2}\right) = \frac{1}{8}$$

Adding all four probabilities gives $4\left(\dfrac{1}{8}\right) = \dfrac{1}{2}$ as the probability that the sum of the three numbers will be odd.

The correct answer is C.

152. If $0 < x < 1$, which of the following inequalities must be true?

    I. $x^5 < x^3$
    II. $x^4 + x^5 < x^3 + x^2$
    III. $x^4 - x^5 < x^2 - x^3$

    (A) None
    (B) I only
    (C) II only
    (D) I and II only
    (E) I, II, and III

Algebra + Arithmetic Inequalities + Properties of numbers

The expression $0 < x < 1$ means that x is a positive fraction less than 1. The higher the exponent on a positive fraction less than 1, the lower the value of the number. Thus, Statements I and II must both be true.

From Statement III, $x^4 - x^5 < x^2 - x^3$, and thus $x^4(1 - x) < x^2(1 - x)$. Since $x^4 < x^2$ and since $1 - x$ is positive, then $x^4(1 - x) < x^2(1 - x)$ must also be true.

The correct answer is E.

153. If $(2^x)(2^y) = 8$ and $(9^x)(3^y) = 81$, then $(x, y) =$

    (A) (1, 2)
    (B) (2, 1)
    (C) (1, 1)
    (D) (2, 2)
    (E) (1, 3)

Algebra **Simultaneous equations**

Simplify both equations, and solve for x and y as shown.

$(2^x)(2^y) = 8$

$2^{x+y} = 2^3$ get both sides to a single term with the same base

$x + y = 3$ since the bases are now the same, set exponents equal

$y = 3 - x$ solve for y

$(9^x)(3^y) = 81$

$(3^{2x})(3^y) = 81$ get both sides to a single term with the same base

$(3^{2x})(3^y) = 3^4$

$3^{2x+y} = 3^4$ since the bases are now the same, set exponents equal

$2x + y = 4$

$2x + 3 - x = 4$ substitute $3 - x$ for y in this equation, and solve for x

$x + 3 = 4$

$x = 1$

$y = 3 - 1$ substitute 1 for x in the first equation, and solve for y

$y = 2$

The correct answer is A.

154. If $a = 1$ and $\dfrac{a - b}{c} = 1$, which of the following is NOT a possible value of b?

(A)   −2
(B)   −1
(C)   0
(D)   1
(E)   2

Arithmetic **Properties of numbers**

From $\dfrac{a - b}{c} = 1$, it follows that $a \neq b$ because that would cause $\dfrac{a - b}{c}$ to equal 0, which is not true. Since $a \neq b$ and since it is given that $a = 1$, then b CANNOT be equal to 1.

The correct answer is D.

155. If $\dfrac{x}{y} = \dfrac{2}{3}$, then $\dfrac{x - y}{x} =$

(A) $-\dfrac{1}{2}$

(B) $-\dfrac{1}{3}$

(C) $\dfrac{1}{3}$

(D) $\dfrac{1}{2}$

(E) $\dfrac{5}{2}$

Algebra **Simplifying algebraic expressions**

Simplifying the expression $\dfrac{x - y}{x}$ gives

$\dfrac{x - y}{x} = \dfrac{x}{x} - \dfrac{y}{x} = 1 - \dfrac{y}{x}$. If $\dfrac{x}{y} = \dfrac{2}{3}$, then $\dfrac{y}{x} = \dfrac{3}{2}$.

Thus, $\dfrac{x - y}{x} = 1 - \dfrac{3}{2} = -\dfrac{1}{2}$.

The correct answer is A.

156. The contents of a certain box consist of 14 apples and 23 oranges. How many oranges must be removed from the box so that 70 percent of the pieces of fruit in the box will be apples?

(A)   3
(B)   6
(C)   14
(D)   17
(E)   20

Arithmetic Percents

From the given information, it can be determined that 14 + 23 = 37 pieces of fruit are in the box to begin with. The information that, after the adjustment, apples will account for 70% of the fruit in the box can be expressed as $\frac{\text{apples}}{\text{new total}}$ = 70%. Letting x represent the number of oranges to be removed from the box, the problem can be expressed in the following equation, which can be solved for x.

$$\frac{14}{37 - x} = 0.70$$

$$14 = 25.9 - 0.70x$$

$$-11.9 = -0.70x \qquad \text{solve for } x$$

$$17 = x$$

The correct answer is D.

157. Last year, a certain public transportation system sold an average (arithmetic mean) of 41,000 tickets per day on weekdays (Monday through Friday) and an average of 18,000 tickets per day on Saturday and Sunday. Which of the following is closest to the total number of tickets sold last year?

   (A)   1 million
   (B)   1.25 million
   (C)   10 million
   (D)   12.5 million
   (E)   125 million

Arithmetic Statistics

Each week the number of tickets sold was 5(41,000) + 2(18,000) = 241,000. Since each year has approximately 52 weeks, the total number sold for the year was about (52)(241,000) = 12,532,000, which is approximately 12.5 million

The correct answer is D.

District	Number of Votes	Percent of Votes for Candidate P	Percent of Votes for Candidate Q
1	800	60	40
2	1,000	50	50
3	1,500	50	50
4	1,800	40	60
5	1,200	30	70

158. The table above shows the results of a recent school board election in which the candidate with the higher total number of votes from the five districts was declared the winner. Which district had the greatest number of votes for the winner?

   (A)   1
   (B)   2
   (C)   3
   (D)   4
   (E)   5

Arithmetic Interpretation of tables

A careful analysis of the table shows candidates P and Q were tied in districts 2 and 3 and had reverse percentages in districts 1 and 4. Since candidate Q won district 4, which is much larger than district 1, and also clearly won district 5, candidate Q won the election. Thus, it is not necessary to calculate the exact vote counts to determine the winner.

Calculate the number of votes each district cast for candidate Q based on the voting data in the table, and compare the districts' votes to find out which cast the most.

District 1 votes for Q = 800(0.40) = 320

District 2 votes for Q = 1,000(0.50) = 500

District 3 votes for Q = 1,500(0.50) = 750

District 4 votes for Q = 1,800(0.60) = 1,080

District 5 votes for Q = 1,200(0.70) = 840

The correct answer is D.

159. A group of store managers must assemble 280 displays for an upcoming sale. If they assemble 25 percent of the displays during the first hour and 40 percent of the remaining displays during the second hour, how many of the displays will not have been assembled by the end of the second hour?

   (A)   70
   (B)   98
   (C)   126
   (D)   168
   (E)   182

Arithmetic Percents

It follows from the given information that during the first hour, when 25% of the total displays were assembled, $280(0.25) = 70$ displays were assembled. It also follows that during the second hour, when 40% of the remaining displays were done, $(280 - 70)(0.40) = 84$ displays were assembled.

Let x be the number of displays that have NOT been assembled by the end of the second hour of assembly. The total number of displays minus the number of displays assembled in the first two hours is equal to the number still waiting to be assembled. This can be expressed as the following equation and solved for x.

$280 - (70 + 84) = x$ total – (first hour's assembly + second hour's assembly) = x

$280 - 154 = x$

$126 = x$

The correct answer is C.

1	2	3	4	5	6	7
–2	–4	–6	–8	–10	–12	–14
3	6	9	12	15	18	21
–4	–8	–12	–16	–20	–24	–28
5	10	15	20	25	30	35
–6	–12	–18	–24	–30	–36	–42
7	14	21	28	35	42	49

160. What is the sum of the integers in the table above?

   (A)   28
   (B)   112
   (C)   336
   (D)   448
   (E)   784

Arithmetic Operations on rational numbers

The sum of the numbers is the first row is $1 + 2 + 3 + 4 + 5 + 6 + 7 = 28$. Notice that in each of the remaining rows, the values are all integer multiples n of this first row. For the 7 rows, the values of n are 1, –2, 3, –4, 5, –6, and 7.

So, the total sum of all rows is the sum of the 7 values of n multiplied by 28, that is:

$(1 - 2 + 3 - 4 + 5 - 6 + 7)(28) = 4(28) = 112$

or

$(1)(28) + (-2)(28) + 3(28) + (-4)(28) + (5)(28) + (-6)(28) + (7)(28) = 4(28) = 112$

The correct answer is B.

$$3, k, 2, 8, m, 3$$

161. The arithmetic mean of the list of numbers above is 4. If k and m are integers and $k \neq m$, what is the median of the list?

   (A)   2
   (B)   2.5
   (C)   3
   (D)   3.5
   (E)   4

Arithmetic Statistics

Since the mean $= \dfrac{\text{sum of values}}{\text{number of values}}$, it follows from the given information that:

$$\frac{3+k+2+8+m+3}{6}=4$$

$$\frac{16+k+m}{6}=4$$

$$16+k+m=24$$

$$k+m=8$$

Since k and m are integers such that $k \neq m$, and since $k + m = 8$, one value must be less than 4 and the other must be greater than 4. The list's known values in ascending order are: 2, 3, 3, 8. One of the unknowns will be 3 or less, and the other 5 or greater; the ascending order will thus be 2, ?, 3, 3, ?, 8.

Since there is an even number of numbers, the median is the average of the middle two numbers. No matter which alternative is true of the unknowns, the value of the median will be $\dfrac{3+3}{2}=\dfrac{6}{2}=3$.

The correct answer is C.

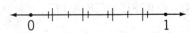

162. On the number line above, the segment from 0 to 1 has been divided into fifths, as indicated by the large tick marks, and also into sevenths, as indicated by the small tick marks. What is the least possible distance between any two of the tick marks?

(A) $\dfrac{1}{70}$

(B) $\dfrac{1}{35}$

(C) $\dfrac{2}{35}$

(D) $\dfrac{1}{12}$

(E) $\dfrac{1}{7}$

Arithmetic Operations on rational numbers

The small tick marks are placed at $\dfrac{1}{7}$, $\dfrac{2}{7}$, $\dfrac{3}{7}$, $\dfrac{4}{7}$, $\dfrac{5}{7}$, and $\dfrac{6}{7}$, and the large tick marks are at $\dfrac{1}{5}$, $\dfrac{2}{5}$, $\dfrac{3}{5}$, and $\dfrac{4}{5}$. The least common demominator is 35, so the tick marks in ascending order are placed at

$$\frac{5}{35},\ \frac{7}{35},\ \frac{10}{35},\ \frac{14}{35},\ \frac{15}{35},\ \frac{20}{35},\ \frac{21}{35},\ \frac{25}{35},\ \frac{28}{35},\ \frac{30}{35}.$$

The least distance between tick marks on this number line is $\dfrac{1}{35}$.

The correct answer is B.

163. $\dfrac{(8^2)(3^3)(2^4)}{96^2} =$

(A) 3
(B) 6
(C) 2
(D) 12
(E) 18

Arithmetic Operations on rational numbers

Simplify the expression.

$$\frac{(8^2)(3^3)(2^4)}{96^2}=\frac{(8^2)(3^3)(2^4)}{(8^2)(3^2)(2^4)}=3$$

The correct answer is A.

164. When 10 is divided by the positive integer n, the remainder is $n - 4$. Which of the following could be the value of n?

(A) 3
(B) 4
(C) 7
(D) 8
(E) 12

Algebra Applied problems

To have a remainder when dividing by a positive integer n, there must be an integer quotient, q, that has a fractional portion of n remaining.

$\dfrac{10}{n} = q + \dfrac{n-4}{n}$ quotient of $10/n$ = integer portion of quotient + remainder/divisor

$10 = qn + n - 4$ multiply through by n

$14 = n(q + 1)$ simplify by adding 4 to both sides and factoring out n

Since n and q are both integers, n is a factor of 14. The only factor of 14 among the answer choices is 7.

The correct answer is C.

165. If $\dfrac{1}{2}$ of the money in a certain trust fund was invested in stocks, $\dfrac{1}{4}$ in bonds, $\dfrac{1}{5}$ in a mutual fund, and the remaining $10,000 in a government certificate, what was the total amount of the trust fund?

(A) $ 100,000
(B) $ 150,000
(C) $ 200,000
(D) $ 500,000
(E) $2,000,000

Arithmetic Operations on rational numbers

First calculate what fraction of the fund is in stocks, bonds, and mutual funds by adding the fractions.

$\dfrac{1}{2} + \dfrac{1}{4} + \dfrac{1}{5} = \dfrac{19}{20}$

The remainder of the fund is in the government certificate, and the fraction of the fund in that government certificate is thus known.

$1 - \dfrac{19}{20} = \dfrac{1}{20}$

The total amount of the trust fund (F) can then be found using the following equation.

$\dfrac{1}{20} F = \$10,000$ solve for F

$F = \$200,000$

The correct answer is C.

166. If m is an integer such that $(-2)^{2m} = 2^{9-m}$, then $m =$

(A)   1
(B)   2
(C)   3
(D)   4
(E)   6

Algebra First-degree equations

To set exponents equal in an exponential equation, the bases must be the same

$(-2)^{2m} = ((-2)^2)^m = 4^m = 2^{2m}$.

Therefore, from the given equation,

$(-2)^{2m} = 2^{9-m}$.

$2^{2m} = 2^{9-m}$ substitute 2^{2m} for -2^{2m}

$2m = 9 - m$ set exponents of common bases equal to each other

$3m = 9$ solve for m

$m = 3$

The correct answer is C.

167. In a mayoral election, Candidate X received $\dfrac{1}{3}$ more votes than Candidate Y, and Candidate Y received $\dfrac{1}{4}$ fewer votes than Candidate Z. If Candidate Z received 24,000 votes, how many votes did Candidate X receive?

(A)   18,000
(B)   22,000
(C)   24,000
(D)   26,000
(E)   32,000

Algebra Applied problems

Let x, y, and z be the number of votes received by Candidates X, Y, and Z, respectively.

Build equations to express the relative votes each received:

$x = \dfrac{4}{3} y$ $y = \dfrac{3}{4} z$ $z = 24,000$

Substitute and solve for x:

$$x = \frac{4}{3}\left(\frac{3}{4}z\right) \qquad \text{substitute } \frac{3}{4}z \text{ for } y$$

$$x = z \qquad \text{simplify}$$

$$x = 24{,}000$$

The correct answer is C.

168. An airline passenger is planning a trip that involves three connecting flights that leave from Airports A, B, and C, respectively. The first flight leaves Airport A every hour, beginning at 8:00 a.m., and arrives at Airport B $2\frac{1}{2}$ hours later. The second flight leaves Airport B every 20 minutes, beginning at 8:00 a.m., and arrives at Airport C $1\frac{1}{6}$ hours later. The third flight leaves Airport C every hour, beginning at 8:45 a.m. What is the <u>least</u> total amount of time the passenger must spend between flights if all flights keep to their schedules?

(A) 25 min
(B) 1 hr 5 min
(C) 1 hr 15 min
(D) 2 hr 20 min
(E) 3 hr 40 min

Arithmetic Operations on rational numbers

Since the first flight always leaves Airport A on the hour, it will always arrive at Airport B at half-past the hour $2\frac{1}{2}$ hours later. The second flight leaves Airport B on the hour or at 20 or 40 minutes past the hour, so taking the flight leaving at 40 minutes past the hour would therefore result in a passenger's 10-minute wait between flights while at Airport B.

The flight from Airport B to Airport C takes $1\frac{1}{6}$ hours, or 1 hour 10 minutes. A flight taken at 40 minutes past the hour would arrive at Airport C at 50 minutes past the hour, causing the passenger to have missed the flight from Airport C by 5 minutes. The passenger therefore has a 55-minute wait at Airport C.

Thus, the least total amount of time the passenger must spend waiting between flights is 10 + 55 = 65 minutes, or 1 hour 5 minutes.

The correct answer is B.

169. If n is a positive integer and n^2 is divisible by 72, then the largest positive integer that must divide n is

(A) 6
(B) 12
(C) 24
(D) 36
(E) 48

Arithmetic Properties of numbers

It is given that n^2 is divisible by 72, so $n^2 = 72k$ for some positive integer k. Finding the largest positive integer that must divide n thus means finding the smallest value of k such that $n^2 = 72k$. Also, since it is given that n is a positive integer, n^2 must be a perfect square, that is, a positive integer that has an integer as its square root. The first positive integer for k that makes n^2 a perfect square is $k = 2$ because $72 \times 2 = 144$, which is a perfect square. Since $n^2 = 144$, then $n = 12$, so no integer greater than 12 will necessarily divide all n such that n^2 is divisible by 72.

Another approach to solving this problem is to recognize that finding the largest positive integer that must divide n also means finding the smallest multiple of 72 that is a perfect square. The first multiple of 72 that is a perfect square is $n^2 = 72(2) = 144$, so $n = 12$ is the largest integer that will necessarily divide all n such that n^2 is divisible by 72.

The correct answer is B.

170. If n is a positive integer and $k + 2 = 3^n$, which of the following could NOT be a value of k?

(A) 1
(B) 4
(C) 7
(D) 25
(E) 79

Arithmetic Operations on rational numbers

For a number to equal 3^n, the number must be a power of 3. Substitute the answer choices for k in the equation given, and determine which one does not yield a power of 3.

A $1 + 2 = 3$ power of 3 (3^1)

B $4 + 2 = 6$ multiple of 3, but NOT a power of 3

C $7 + 2 = 9$ power of 3 (3^2)

D $25 + 2 = 27$ power of 3 (3^3)

E $79 + 2 = 81$ power of 3 (3^4)

The correct answer is B.

171. A certain grocery purchased x pounds of produce for p dollars per pound. If y pounds of the produce had to be discarded due to spoilage and the grocery sold the rest for s dollars per pound, which of the following represents the gross profit on the sale of the produce?

(A) $(x - y) s - xp$
(B) $(x - y) p - ys$
(C) $(s - p) y - xp$
(D) $xp - ys$
(E) $(x - y) (s - p)$

Algebra Simplifying algebraic expressions + Applied problems

Set out the various unknowns for the produce as given in the problem:

x = pounds purchased

p = cost per pound

y = pounds discarded

s = selling price per pound

xp (pounds purchased)(cost per pound) = total cost of produce

$x - y$ (pounds purchased) less (pounds discarded) = pounds of produce sold

$(x - y)s$ (pounds sold)(selling price per pound) = income from produce sold

$(x - y)s - xp$ income − cost = gross profit

The correct answer is A.

172. If x, y, and z are positive integers such that x is a factor of y, and x is a multiple of z, which of the following is NOT necessarily an integer?

(A) $\dfrac{x + z}{z}$

(B) $\dfrac{y + z}{x}$

(C) $\dfrac{x + y}{z}$

(D) $\dfrac{xy}{z}$

(E) $\dfrac{yz}{x}$

Arithmetic Properties of numbers

Let c and k represent positive integers. Since it is given that the positive integer x is a factor of y, then the positive integer y can be set equal to kx. Since it is further given that x is a multiple of the positive integer z, then additionally $x = cz$.

Letting $y = kx$ and $x = cz$, make substitutions into each answer choice to find the one expression that is NOT an integer.

A $\dfrac{x + z}{z} = \dfrac{cz + z}{z} = \dfrac{(c + 1)z}{z} = (c + 1)$

   MUST be an integer

B $\dfrac{y + z}{x} = \dfrac{y}{x} + \dfrac{z}{x} = \dfrac{kx}{x} + \dfrac{z}{cz} = k + \dfrac{1}{c}$

   NEED NOT be an integer

C $\dfrac{x + y}{z} = \dfrac{cz + kx}{z} = \dfrac{cz}{z} + \dfrac{kx}{z} = c + \dfrac{k(cz)}{z} = c + kc$

   MUST be an integer

D $\dfrac{xy}{z} = \dfrac{(cz)y}{z} = cy$

   MUST be an integer

E $\dfrac{yz}{x} = \dfrac{(kx)z}{x} = kz$

   MUST be an integer

The correct answer is B.

173. If $\dfrac{a}{b} = \dfrac{2}{3}$, which of the following is NOT true?

(A) $\dfrac{a+b}{b} = \dfrac{5}{3}$

(B) $\dfrac{b}{b-a} = 3$

(C) $\dfrac{a-b}{b} = \dfrac{1}{3}$

(D) $\dfrac{2a}{3b} = \dfrac{4}{9}$

(E) $\dfrac{a+3b}{a} = \dfrac{11}{2}$

Algebra First-degree equations

Since it is a given that $\dfrac{a}{b} = \dfrac{2}{3}$, it is possible to substitute $\dfrac{2}{3}$ for $\dfrac{a}{b}$ and $\dfrac{3}{2}$ for $\dfrac{b}{a}$ when they appear in the algebraic expressions in each answer choice for this problem. By simplifying and substituting, it can be determined whether each expression is true or NOT true.

A $\dfrac{a+b}{b} = \dfrac{5}{3}$

$\dfrac{a}{b} + \dfrac{b}{b} = \dfrac{5}{3}$

$\dfrac{2}{3} + 1 = \dfrac{5}{3}$

$\dfrac{5}{3} = \dfrac{5}{3}$

True

B $\dfrac{b}{b-a} = 3$

$\dfrac{b-a}{b} = \dfrac{1}{3}$

$\dfrac{b}{b} - \dfrac{a}{b} = \dfrac{1}{3}$

$1 - \dfrac{2}{3} = \dfrac{1}{3}$

$\dfrac{1}{3} = \dfrac{1}{3}$

True

C $\dfrac{a-b}{b} = \dfrac{1}{3}$

$\dfrac{a}{b} - \dfrac{b}{b} = \dfrac{1}{3}$

$\dfrac{2}{3} - 1 = -\dfrac{1}{3}$

$-\dfrac{1}{3} \neq \dfrac{1}{3}$

NOT true

D $\dfrac{2a}{3b} = \dfrac{4}{9}$

$\dfrac{2(2)}{3(3)} = \dfrac{4}{9}$

$\dfrac{4}{9} = \dfrac{4}{9}$

True

E $\dfrac{a+3b}{a} = \dfrac{11}{2}$

$\dfrac{a}{a} + \dfrac{3b}{a} = \dfrac{11}{2}$

$1 + \dfrac{3(3)}{2} = \dfrac{11}{2}$

$\dfrac{2}{2} + \dfrac{9}{2} = \dfrac{11}{2}$

$\dfrac{11}{2} = \dfrac{11}{2}$

True

The correct answer is C.

$$\begin{array}{r} \square\,\triangle \\ \times\ \triangle\,\square \\ \hline \end{array}$$

174. The product of the two-digit numbers above is the three-digit number $\square\lozenge\square$, where $\square$, $\triangle$, and $\lozenge$, are three different nonzero digits. If $\square \times \triangle < 10$, what is the two-digit number $\square\triangle$?

(A) 11
(B) 12
(C) 13
(D) 21
(E) 31

Arithmetic Operations on rational numbers

According to the given information, the solution looks like this:

$$\begin{array}{r} \square\,\triangle \\ \times\ \triangle\,\square \\ \hline \square\,\lozenge\,\square \end{array}$$

Since it is given that $\square \times \triangle$ is less than 10, there is no carrying over from the first column being multiplied in the long multiplication. Thus $\square \times \triangle = \square$. Since the product of $(x)(1)$ is always x, this means $\triangle = 1$, and so $\square \neq 1$ because it is also given that all the values are different nonzero digits. Writing out the long multiplication gives:

Then notice that the hundreds digit in the solution is the same as the digit above (circled in the figure) so there is no carrying over from the tens column. This means $\square^2 + 1 < 10$ or $\square^2 < 9$, and thus $\square < 3$. Since $\triangle = 1$, it follows that $\square = 2$. The value of $\square\,\triangle$ is thus 21.

The correct answer is D.

175. A square countertop has a square tile inlay in the center, leaving an untiled strip of uniform width around the tile. If the ratio of the tiled area to the untiled area is 25 to 39, which of the following could be the width, in inches, of the strip?

    I.   1
    II.   3
    III. 4

    (A) I only
    (B) II only
    (C) I and II only
    (D) I and III only
    (E) I, II, and III

Geometry Area

Since the ratio of the tiled area to the untiled area is 25 to 39, the ratio of the tiled area to the total area of the countertop is $\dfrac{25}{39+25} = \dfrac{25}{64}$. Therefore, the ratio of the length of a side of the square tiled area to the length of a side of the square countertop is $\sqrt{\dfrac{25}{64}} = \dfrac{5}{8}$. Let x be the length of a side of the countertop; let y be the length of a side of the tiled area; and let w be the width of the untiled strip, as shown below.

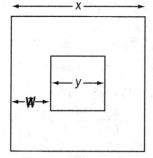

Not drawn to scale

Set up two equations to express the information that the length of the center tiled area is $\dfrac{5}{8}$ the length of the countertop and that the width of the untiled strip is half the difference between x and y:

$$y = \frac{5}{8}x$$

$$w = \frac{x-y}{2}$$

Substitute $\dfrac{5}{8}x$ for the value of y in the second equation, and solve for w:

$$w = \frac{x - \left(\frac{5}{8}x\right)}{2}$$

$$w = \frac{\frac{3}{8}x}{2} = \frac{3}{16}x$$

This means that, for ANY positive value of w, there exists a countertop width that can be found using $w = \dfrac{3}{16}x$. Therefore, all the answer choices are possible.

The correct answer is E.

176. $\dfrac{2\dfrac{3}{5} - 1\dfrac{2}{3}}{\dfrac{2}{3} - \dfrac{3}{5}}$

    (A)   16

    (B)   14

    (C)   3

    (D)   1

    (E)   −1

Arithmetic Operations on rational numbers

Work the problem:

$$\dfrac{2\dfrac{3}{5} - 1\dfrac{2}{3}}{\dfrac{2}{3} - \dfrac{3}{5}} =$$

$$\dfrac{\dfrac{13}{5} - \dfrac{5}{3}}{\dfrac{2}{3} - \dfrac{3}{5}} = \dfrac{\dfrac{39 - 25}{15}}{\dfrac{10 - 9}{15}} = \dfrac{\dfrac{14}{15}}{\dfrac{1}{15}} = \dfrac{14}{15} \times \dfrac{15}{1} = 14$$

The correct answer is B.

5.0 Data Sufficiency

5.0 Data Sufficiency

Data sufficiency questions appear in the Quantitative section of the GMAT® exam. Multiple-choice data sufficiency questions are intermingled with problem solving questions throughout the section. You will have 75 minutes to complete the Quantitative section of the GMAT® exam, or about 2 minutes to answer each question. These questions require knowledge of the following topics:

- Arithmetic
- Elementary algebra
- Commonly known concepts of geometry

Data sufficiency questions are designed to measure your ability to analyze a quantitative problem, recognize which given information is relevant, and determine at what point there is sufficient information to solve a problem. In these questions, you are to classify each problem according to the five fixed answer choices, rather than find a solution to the problem.

Each data sufficiency question consists of a question, often accompanied by some initial information, and two statements, labeled (1) and (2), which contain additional information. You must decide whether the information in each statement is sufficient to answer the question or—if neither statement provides enough information—whether the information in the two statements together is sufficient. It is also possible that the statements in combination do not give enough information to answer the question.

Begin by reading the initial information and the question carefully. Next, consider the first statement. Does the information provided by the first statement enable you to answer the question? Go on to the second statement. Try to ignore the information given in the first statement when you consider whether the second statement provides information that, by itself, allows you to answer the question. Now you should be able to say, for each statement, whether it is sufficient to determine the answer.

Next, consider the two statements in tandem. Do they, together, enable you to answer the question?

Look again at your answer choices. Select the one that most accurately reflects whether the statements provide the information required to answer the question.

5.1 Test-Taking Strategies for Data Sufficiency Questions

1. **Do not waste valuable time solving a problem.**
   You only need to determine whether sufficient information is given to solve it.

2. **Consider each statement separately first.**
   Then you can decide whether each alone gives sufficient information to solve the problem. Be sure to disregard the information given in statement (1) when you evaluate the information given in statement (2). If either, or both, of the statements give(s) sufficient information to solve the problem, select the answer corresponding to the description of which statement(s) give(s) sufficient information to solve the problem.

3. **Judge the statements in tandem if neither statement is sufficient by itself.**
   It is possible that the two statements together do not provide sufficient information. Once you decide, select the answer corresponding to the description of whether the statements together give sufficient information to solve the problem.

4. **Answer the question asked.**
   For example, if the question asks, "What is the value of y?" for an answer statement to be sufficient, you must be able to find one and only one value for y. Being able to determine minimum or maximum values for an answer (e.g., $y = x + 2$) is not sufficient, because such answers constitute a range of values rather than the specific value of y.

5. **Be very careful not to make unwarranted assumptions based on the images represented.**
   Figures are not necessarily drawn to scale; they are generalized figures showing little more than intersecting line segments and the relationships of points, angles, and regions. So, for example, if a figure described as a rectangle looks like a square, do not conclude that it is, in fact, a square just by looking at the figure.

If statement 1 is sufficient, then the answer must be **A or D**.

If statement 2 is not sufficient, then the answer must be **A**.

If statement 2 is sufficient, then the answer must be **D**.

If statement 1 is not sufficient, then the answer must be **B, C, or E**.

If statement 2 is sufficient, then the answer must be **B**.

If statement 2 is not sufficient, then the answer must be **C or E**.

If both statements together are sufficient, then the answer must be **C**.

If both statements together are still not sufficient, then the answer must be **E**.

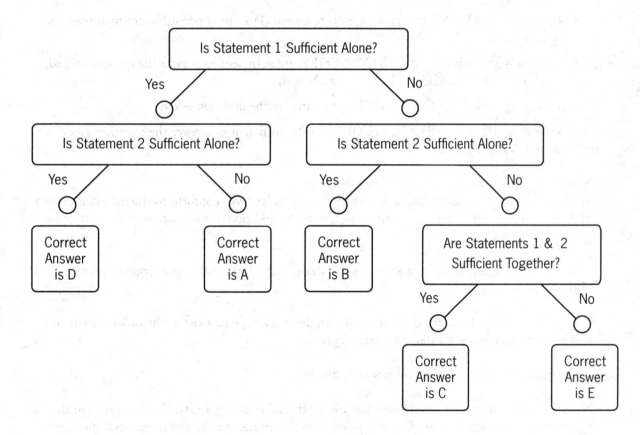

5.2 The Directions

These directions are very similar to those you will see for data sufficiency questions when you take the GMAT® test. If you read the directions carefully and understand them clearly before going to sit for the exam, you will not need to spend too much time reviewing them when you take the GMAT® exam.

This data sufficiency problem consists of a question and two statements, labeled (1) and (2), that give data. You have to decide whether the data given in the statements are sufficient for answering the question. Using the data given in the statements plus your knowledge of mathematics and everyday facts (such as the number of days in July or the meaning of counterclockwise), you must indicate whether the data given in the statements are sufficient for answering the questions and then indicate one of the following answer choices—

- statement (1) ALONE is sufficient, but statement (2) alone is not sufficient to answer the question asked;

- statement (2) ALONE is sufficient, but statement (1) alone is not sufficient to answer the question asked;

- BOTH statements (1) and (2) TOGETHER are sufficient to answer the question asked, but NEITHER statement ALONE is sufficient;

- EACH statement ALONE is sufficient to answer the question asked;

- statements (1) and (2) TOGETHER are NOT sufficient to answer the question asked, and additional data are needed.

Numbers: All numbers used are real numbers.
Figures: A figure accompanying a data sufficiency problem will conform to the information given in the question but will not necessarily conform to the additional information given in statements (1) and (2).

Lines shown as straight can be assumed to be straight and lines that appear jagged can also be assumed to be straight.

You may assume that the positions of points, angles, regions, etc., exist in the order shown and that angle measures are greater than zero degrees.

All figures lie in a plane unless otherwise indicated.

NOTE: In data sufficiency problems that ask for the value of a quantity, the data given in the statements are sufficient only when it is possible to determine exactly one numerical value for the quantity.

5.3 Data Sufficiency Sample Questions

A   Statement (1) ALONE is sufficient, but statement (2) alone is not sufficient.
B   Statement (2) ALONE is sufficient, but statement (1) alone is not sufficient.
C   BOTH statements TOGETHER are sufficient, but NEITHER statement ALONE is sufficient.
D   EACH statement ALONE is sufficient.
E   Statements (1) and (2) TOGETHER are NOT sufficient.

1.   John and David each received a salary increase. Which one received the greater dollar increase?

  (1)   John's salary increased 8 percent.
  (2)   David's salary increased 5 percent.

2.   What is the value of $\dfrac{r}{2} + \dfrac{s}{2}$?

  (1) $\dfrac{r+s}{2} = 5$
  (2) $r + s = 10$

3.   If n is an integer, then n is divisible by how many positive integers?

  (1) n is the product of two different prime numbers.
  (2) n and 2^3 are each divisible by the same number of positive integers.

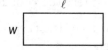

4.   If ℓ and w represent the length and width, respectively, of the rectangle above, what is the perimeter?

  (1) $2\ell + w = 40$
  (2) $\ell + w = 25$

5.   A retailer purchased a television set for x percent less than its list price, and then sold it for y percent less than its list price. What was the list price of the television set?

  (1) $x = 15$
  (2) $x - y = 5$

6.   If x and y are positive, what is the value of x?

  (1) $x = 3.927\,y$
  (2) $y = 2.279$

7.   If n is a member of the set {33, 36, 38, 39, 41, 42}, what is the value of n?

  (1) n is even.
  (2) n is a multiple of 3.

8.   Committee member W wants to schedule a one-hour meeting on Thursday for himself and three other committee members, X, Y, and Z. Is there a one-hour period on Thursday that is open for all four members?

  (1)   On Thursday W and X have an open period from 9:00 a.m. to 12:00 noon.
  (2)   On Thursday Y has an open period from 10:00 a.m. to 1:00 p.m. and Z has an open period from 8:00 a.m. to 11:00 a.m.

9.   If $x + 2y + 1 = y - x$, what is the value of x?

  (1) $y^2 = 9$
  (2) $y = 3$

10.   Of the 230 single-family homes built in City X last year, how many were occupied at the end of the year?

  (1)   Of all single-family homes in City X, 90 percent were occupied at the end of last year.
  (2)   A total of 7,200 single-family homes in City X were occupied at the end of last year.

11.   What is the ratio of x to y?

  (1) x is 4 more than twice y.
  (2)   The ratio of $0.5x$ to $2y$ is 3 to 5.

12. What were the gross revenues from ticket sales for a certain film during the second week in which it was shown?

(1) Gross revenues during the second week were $1.5 million less than during the first week.
(2) Gross revenues during the third week were $2.0 million less than during the first week.

13. If r and s are positive integers, is $r + s$ divisible by 3?

(1) s is divisible by 3.
(2) r is divisible by 3.

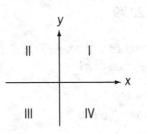

14. Point (x, y) lies in which quadrant of the rectangular coordinate system shown above?

(1) $x + y < 0$
(2) $x = 4$ and $y = -7$.

15. What is the value of x?

(1) $x + 1 = 2 - 3x$
(2) $\dfrac{1}{2x} = 2$

16. Is the prime number p equal to 37?

(1) $p = n^2 + 1$, where n is an integer.
(2) p^2 is greater than 200.

17. What was the amount of money donated to a certain charity?

(1) Of the amount donated, 40 percent came from corporate donations.
(2) Of the amount donated, $1.5 million came from noncorporate donations.

18. What is the value of the positive integer n?

(1) $n^4 < 25$
(2) $n \neq n^2$

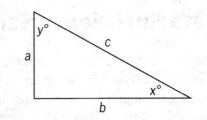

19. In the triangle above, does $a^2 + b^2 = c^2$?

(1) $x + y = 90$
(2) $x = y$

20. If x, y, and z are three integers, are they consecutive integers?

(1) $z - x = 2$
(2) $x < y < z$

21. The symbol ∇ represents one of the following operations: addition, subtraction, multiplication, or division. What is the value of $3 \nabla 2$?

(1) $0 \nabla 1 = 1$
(2) $1 \nabla 0 = 1$

22. A sum of $200,000 from a certain estate was divided among a spouse and three children. How much of the estate did the youngest child receive?

(1) The spouse received $\dfrac{1}{2}$ of the sum from the estate, and the oldest child received $\dfrac{1}{4}$ of the remainder.
(2) Each of the two younger children received $12,500 more than the oldest child and $62,500 less than the spouse.

23. What is the value of x?

(1) $-(x + y) = x - y$
(2) $x + y = 2$

24. A certain 4-liter solution of vinegar and water consists of x liters of vinegar and y liters of water. How many liters of vinegar does the solution contain?

(1) $\dfrac{x}{4} = \dfrac{3}{8}$
(2) $\dfrac{y}{4} = \dfrac{5}{8}$

25. If x and y are integers, what is the value of y?

    (1) $xy = 27$
    (2) $x = y^2$

26. How many newspapers were sold at a certain newsstand today?

    (1) A total of 100 newspapers were sold at the newsstand yesterday, 10 fewer than twice the number sold today.
    (2) The number of newspapers sold at the newsstand yesterday was 45 more than the number sold today.

27. What is Ricky's age now?

    (1) Ricky is now twice as old as he was exactly 8 years ago.
    (2) Ricky's sister Teresa is now 3 times as old as Ricky was exactly 8 years ago.

28. If both x and y are nonzero numbers, what is the value of $\frac{y}{x}$?

    (1) $x = 6$
    (2) $y^2 = x^2$

29. John took a test that had 60 questions numbered from 1 to 60. How many of the questions did he answer correctly?

    (1) The number of questions he answered correctly in the first half of the test was 7 more than the number he answered correctly in the second half of the test.
    (2) He answered $\frac{5}{6}$ of the odd-numbered questions correctly and $\frac{4}{5}$ of the even numbered questions correctly.

30. If $x = 0.rstu$, where r, s, t, and u each represent a nonzero digit of x, what is the value of x?

    (1) $r = 3s = 2t = 6u$
    (2) The product of r and u is equal to the product of s and t.

31. An empty rectangular swimming pool has uniform depth. How long will it take to fill the pool with water?

    (1) Water will be pumped in at the rate of 240 gallons per hour (1 cubic foot = 7.5 gallons).
    (2) The pool is 60 feet long and 25 feet wide.

32. Is the value of n closer to 50 than to 75?

    (1) $75 - n > n - 50$
    (2) $n > 60$

33. If n is an integer, is $\frac{100 - n}{n}$ an integer?

    (1) $n > 4$
    (2) $n^2 = 25$

34. If p, q, x, y, and z are different positive integers, which of the five integers is the median?

    (1) $p + x < q$
    (2) $y < z$

35. If $w + z = 28$, what is the value of wz?

    (1) w and z are positive integers.
    (2) w and z are consecutive odd integers.

36. Elena receives a salary plus a commission that is equal to a fixed percentage of her sales revenue. What was the total of Elena's salary and commission last month?

    (1) Elena's monthly salary is $1,000.
    (2) Elena's commission is 5 percent of her sales revenue.

37. What is the value of $a - b$?

    (1) $a = b + 4$
    (2) $(a - b)^2 = 16$

38. Machine X runs at a constant rate and produces a lot consisting of 100 cans in 2 hours. How much less time would it take to produce the lot of cans if both machines X and Y were run simultaneously?

    (1) Both machines X and Y produce the same number of cans per hour.
    (2) It takes machine X twice as long to produce the lot of cans as it takes machines X and Y running simultaneously to produce the lot.

39. Can the positive integer p be expressed as the product of two integers, each of which is greater than 1?

    (1) $31 < p < 37$
    (2) p is odd.

40. Is $x < y$?

    (1) $z < y$
    (2) $z < x$

41. If S is a set of four numbers w, x, y, and z, is the range of the numbers in S greater than 2?

    (1) $w - z > 2$
    (2) z is the least number in S.

42. If y is greater than 110 percent of x, is y greater than 75?

    (1) $x > 75$
    (2) $y - x = 10$

43. Is $x < 0$?

    (1) $-2x > 0$
    (2) $x^3 < 0$

44. If Q is an integer between 10 and 100, what is the value of Q?

    (1) One of Q's digits is 3 more than the other, and the sum of its digits is 9.
    (2) $Q < 50$

45. If p and q are positive integers and $pq = 24$, what is the value of p?

    (1) $\dfrac{q}{6}$ is an integer.
    (2) $\dfrac{p}{2}$ is an integer.

46. What is the value of $x^2 - y^2$?

    (1) $x - y = y + 2$
    (2) $x - y = \dfrac{1}{x + y}$

47. Hoses X and Y simultaneously fill an empty swimming pool that has a capacity of 50,000 liters. If the flow in each hose is independent of the flow in the other hose, how many hours will it take to fill the pool?

    (1) Hose X alone would take 28 hours to fill the pool.
    (2) Hose Y alone would take 36 hours to fill the pool.

48. How many integers n are there such that $r < n < s$?

    (1) $s - r = 5$
    (2) r and s are not integers.

49. If the total price of n equally priced shares of a certain stock was $12,000, what was the price per share of the stock?

    (1) If the price per share of the stock had been $1 more, the total price of the n shares would have been $300 more.
    (2) If the price per share of the stock had been $2 less, the total price of the n shares would have been 5 percent less.

50. What is the ratio of $x : y : z$?

    (1) $z = 1$ and $xy = 32$.
    (2) $\dfrac{x}{y} = 2$ and $\dfrac{z}{y} = \dfrac{1}{4}$.

51. Is $xy > 5$?

    (1) $1 \le x \le 3$ and $2 \le y \le 4$.
    (2) $x + y = 5$

52. In year X, 8.7 percent of the men in the labor force were unemployed in June compared with 8.4 percent in May. If the number of men in the labor force was the same for both months, how many men were unemployed in June of that year?

    (1) In May of year X, the number of unemployed men in the labor force was 3.36 million.
    (2) In year X, 120,000 more men in the labor force were unemployed in June than in May.

53. If $x \neq 0$, what is the value of $\left(\dfrac{x^p}{x^q}\right)^4$?

    (1) $p = q$
    (2) $x = 3$

54. On Monday morning a certain machine ran continuously at a uniform rate to fill a production order. At what time did it completely fill the order that morning?

    (1) The machine began filling the order at 9:30 a.m.
    (2) The machine had filled $\dfrac{1}{2}$ of the order by 10:30 a.m. and $\dfrac{5}{6}$ of the order by 11:10 a.m.

55. If $xy < 3$, is $x < 1$?

    (1) $y > 3$
    (2) $x < 3$

56. If $\dfrac{m}{n} = \dfrac{5}{3}$, what is the value of $m + n$?

    (1) $m > 0$
    (2) $2m + n = 26$

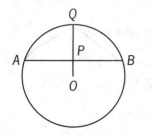

57. What is the radius of the circle above with center O?

    (1) The ratio of OP to PQ is 1 to 2.
    (2) P is the midpoint of chord AB.

58. What is the number of 360-degree rotations that a bicycle wheel made while rolling 100 meters in a straight line without slipping?

    (1) The diameter of the bicycle wheel, including the tire, was 0.5 meter.
    (2) The wheel made twenty 360-degree rotations per minute.

59. The perimeter of a rectangular garden is 360 feet. What is the length of the garden?

    (1) The length of the garden is twice the width.
    (2) The difference between the length and width of the garden is 60 feet.

60. If $2x(5n) = t$, what is the value of t?

    (1) $x = n + 3$
    (2) $2x = 32$

61. In the equation $x^2 + bx + 12 = 0$, x is a variable and b is a constant. What is the value of b?

    (1) $x - 3$ is a factor of $x^2 + bx + 12$.
    (2) 4 is a root of the equation $x^2 + bx + 12 = 0$.

62. A Town T has 20,000 residents, 60 percent of whom are female. What percent of the residents were born in Town T?

    (1) The number of female residents who were born in Town T is twice the number of male residents who were <u>not</u> born in Town T.
    (2) The number of female residents who were not born in Town T is twice the number of female residents who were born in Town T.

63. If y is an integer, is y^3 divisible by 9?

    (1) y is divisible by 4.
    (2) y is divisible by 6.

64. In $\triangle XYZ$, what is the length of YZ?

    (1) The length of XY is 3.
    (2) The length of XZ is 5.

65. What was the ratio of the number of cars to the number of trucks produced by Company X last year?

(1) Last year, if the number of cars produced by Company X had been 8 percent greater, the number of cars produced would have been 150 percent of the number of trucks produced by Company X.

(2) Last year Company X produced 565,000 cars and 406,800 trucks.

66. Is $xy < 6$?

(1) $x < 3$ and $y < 2$.

(2) $\frac{1}{2} < x < \frac{2}{3}$ and $y^2 < 64$.

67. If x, y, and z are positive numbers, is $x > y > z$?

(1) $xz > yz$

(2) $yx > yz$

68. An infinite sequence of positive integers is called an "alpha sequence" if the number of even integers in the sequence is finite. If S is an infinite sequence of positive integers, is S an alpha sequence?

(1) The first ten integers in S are even.

(2) An infinite number of integers in S are odd.

69. How long did it take Betty to drive nonstop on a trip from her home to Denver, Colorado?

(1) If Betty's average speed for the trip had been $1\frac{1}{2}$ times as fast, the trip would have taken 2 hours.

(2) Betty's average speed for the trip was 50 miles per hour.

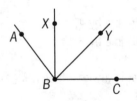

70. In the figure above, what is the measure of $\angle ABC$?

(1) BX bisects $\angle ABY$ and BY bisects $\angle XBC$.

(2) The measure of $\angle ABX$ is 40°.

71. If x, y, and z are numbers, is $z = 18$?

(1) The average (arithmetic mean) of x, y, and z is 6.

(2) $x = -y$

72. After winning 50 percent of the first 20 games it played, Team A won all of the remaining games it played. What was the total number of games that Team A won?

(1) Team A played 25 games altogether.

(2) Team A won 60 percent of all the games it played.

73. Is x between 0 and 1?

(1) x^2 is less than x.

(2) x^3 is positive.

74. A jar contains 30 marbles, of which 20 are red and 10 are blue. If 9 of the marbles are removed, how many of the marbles left in the jar are red?

(1) Of the marbles removed, the ratio of the number of red ones to the number of blue ones is 2:1.

(2) Of the first 6 marbles removed, 4 are red.

75. Is p^2 an odd integer?

(1) p is an odd integer.

(2) $\sqrt{p}$ is an odd integer.

76. If $-10 < k < 10$, is $k > 0$?

(1) $\frac{1}{k} > 0$

(2) $k^2 > 0$

77. What is the value of xy?

(1) $x + y = 10$

(2) $x - y = 6$

78. Is x^2 greater than x?

(1) x^2 is greater than 1.

(2) x is greater than −1.

79. Is $y = 6$?

    (1) $y^2 = 36$
    (2) $y^2 - 7y + 6 = 0$

80. If $xy > 0$, does $(x - 1)(y - 1) = 1$?

    (1) $x + y = xy$
    (2) $x = y$

81. The only contents of a parcel are 25 photographs and 30 negatives. What is the total weight, in ounces, of the parcel's contents?

    (1) The weight of each photograph is 3 times the weight of each negative.
    (2) The total weight of 1 of the photographs and 2 of the negatives is $\frac{1}{3}$ ounce.

82. If m and n are consecutive positive integers, is m greater than n?

    (1) $m - 1$ and $n + 1$ are consecutive positive integers.
    (2) m is an even integer.

83. If k and n are integers, is n divisible by 7?

    (1) $n - 3 = 2k$
    (2) $2k - 4$ is divisible by 7.

84. Is the perimeter of square S greater than the perimeter of equilateral triangle T?

    (1) The ratio of the length of a side of S to the length of a side of T is 4:5.
    (2) The sum of the lengths of a side of S and a side of T is 18.

85. If $x + y + z > 0$, is $z > 1$?

    (1) $z > x + y + 1$
    (2) $x + y + 1 < 0$

86. Can the positive integer n be written as the sum of two different positive prime numbers?

    (1) n is greater than 3.
    (2) n is odd.

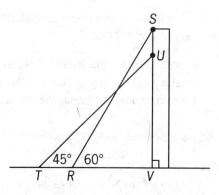

87. In the figure above, segments RS and TU represent two positions of the same ladder leaning against the side SV of a wall. The length of TV is how much greater than the length of RV?

    (1) The length of TU is 10 meters.
    (2) The length of RV is 5 meters.

88. Is the integer x divisible by 36?

    (1) x is divisible by 12.
    (2) x is divisible by 9.

Cancellation Fees	
Days Prior to Departure	Percent of Package Price
46 or more	10%
45–31	35%
30–16	50%
15–5	65%
4 or fewer	100%

89. The table above shows the cancellation fee schedule that a travel agency uses to determine the fee charged to a tourist who cancels a trip prior to departure. If a tourist canceled a trip with a package price of $1,700 and a departure date of September 4, on what day was the trip canceled?

    (1) The cancellation fee was $595.
    (2) If the trip had been canceled one day later, the cancellation fee would have been $255 more.

90. What is the value of $\frac{x}{yz}$?

    (1) $x = \frac{y}{2}$ and $z = \frac{2x}{5}$.
    (2) $\frac{x}{z} = \frac{5}{2}$ and $\frac{1}{y} = \frac{1}{10}$.

91. If P and Q are each circular regions, what is the radius of the larger of these regions?

    (1) The area of P plus the area of Q is equal to 90π.
    (2) The larger circular region has a radius that is 3 times the radius of the smaller circular region.

92. If x and y are positive, what is the value of x?

    (1) 200 percent of x equals 400 percent of y.
    (2) xy is the square of a positive integer.

93. If Aaron, Lee, and Tony have a total of $36, how much money does Tony have?

    (1) Tony has twice as much money as Lee and $\frac{1}{3}$ as much as Aaron.
    (2) The sum of the amounts of money that Tony and Lee have is half the amount that Aaron has.

94. Is z less than 0?

    (1) $xy > 0$ and $yz < 0$.
    (2) $x > 0$

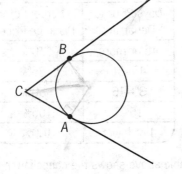

95. The circular base of an above-ground swimming pool lies in a level yard and just touches two straight sides of a fence at points A and B, as shown in the figure above. Point C is on the ground where the two sides of the fence meet. How far from the center of the pool's base is point A?

    (1) The base has area 250 square feet.
    (2) The center of the base is 20 feet from point C.

96. If $xy = -6$, what is the value of $xy(x + y)$?

    (1) $x - y = 5$
    (2) $xy^2 = 18$

97. If the average (arithmetic mean) of 4 numbers is 50, how many of the numbers are greater than 50?

    (1) None of the four numbers is equal to 50.
    (2) Two of the numbers are equal to 25.

98. Is the positive square root of x an integer?

    (1) $x = n^4$ and n is an integer.
    (2) $x = 16$

99. If x is a positive number less than 10, is z greater than the average (arithmetic mean) of x and 10?

    (1) On the number line, z is closer to 10 than it is to x.
    (2) $z = 5x$

100. If n is an integer, is n + 2 a prime number?

    (1) n is a prime number.
    (2) n + 1 is not a prime number.

101. If $t \neq 0$, is r greater than zero?

    (1) $rt = 12$
    (2) $r + t = 7$

102. Is $\frac{x}{m}(m^2 + n^2 + k^2) = xm + yn + zk$?

    (1) $\frac{z}{k} = \frac{x}{m}$
    (2) $\frac{x}{m} = \frac{y}{n}$

103. If $R = \frac{8x}{3y}$ and $y \neq 0$, what is the value of R?

    (1) $x = \frac{2}{3}$
    (2) $x = 2y$

104. A bookstore that sells used books sells each of its paperback books for a certain price and each of its hardcover books for a certain price. If Joe, Maria, and Paul bought books in this store, how much did Maria pay for 1 paperback book and 1 hardcover book?

    (1) Joe bought 2 paperback books and 3 hardcover books for $12.50.
    (2) Paul bought 4 paperback books and 6 hardcover books for $25.00.

105. If x, y, and z are positive, is $x = \dfrac{y}{z^2}$?

   (1) $z = \dfrac{y}{xz}$

   (2) $z = \sqrt{\dfrac{y}{x}}$

106. If n is an integer between 2 and 100 and if n is also the square of an integer, what is the value of n?

   (1) n is even.
   (2) The cube root of n is an integer.

107. For a certain set of n numbers, where $n > 1$, is the average (arithmetic mean) equal to the median?

   (1) If the n numbers in the set are listed in increasing order, then the difference between any pair of successive numbers in the set is 2.
   (2) The range of the n numbers in the set is $2(n - 1)$.

108. If d is a positive integer, is $\sqrt{d}$ an integer?

   (1) d is the square of an integer.
   (2) $\sqrt{d}$ is the square of an integer.

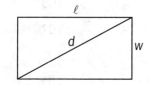

109. What is the area of the rectangular region above?

   (1) $\ell + w = 6$
   (2) $d^2 = 20$

110. Is the positive integer n a multiple of 24?

   (1) n is a multiple of 4.
   (2) n is a multiple of 6.

111. If x is a positive integer and w is a negative integer, what is the value of xw?

   (1) $x^w = \dfrac{1}{2}$

   (2) $w = -1$

112. If x is an integer, is y an integer?

   (1) The average (arithmetic mean) of x, y, and $y - 2$ is x.
   (2) The average (arithmetic mean) of x and y is <u>not</u> an integer.

113. In the fraction $\dfrac{x}{y}$, where x and y are positive integers, what is the value of y?

   (1) The least common denominator of $\dfrac{x}{y}$ and $\dfrac{1}{3}$ is 6.
   (2) $x = 1$

114. Is $\dfrac{1}{a - b} < b - a$?

   (1) $a < b$
   (2) $1 < |a - b|$

115. If x and y are nonzero integers, is $x^y < y^x$?

   (1) $x = y^2$
   (2) $y > 2$

116. If x is a positive integer, is $\sqrt{x}$ an integer?

   (1) $\sqrt{4x}$ is an integer.
   (2) $\sqrt{3x}$ is not an integer.

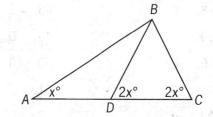

117. In triangle ABC above, what is the length of side BC?

   (1) Line segment AD has length 6.
   (2) $x = 36$

118. If $rs \neq 0$, is $\dfrac{1}{r} + \dfrac{1}{s} = 4$?

   (1) $r + s = 4rs$
   (2) $r = s$

5.4 Data Sufficiency Answer Key

1.	E	31.	E	61.	D	91.	C
2.	D	32.	A	62.	C	92.	E
3.	D	33.	B	63.	B	93.	A
4.	B	34.	E	64.	E	94.	C
5.	E	35.	B	65.	D	95.	A
6.	C	36.	E	66.	B	96.	B
7.	E	37.	A	67.	E	97.	E
8.	C	38.	D	68.	E	98.	D
9.	B	39.	A	69.	A	99.	A
10.	E	40.	E	70.	C	100.	E
11.	B	41.	A	71.	C	101.	C
12.	E	42.	A	72.	D	102.	C
13.	C	43.	D	73.	A	103.	B
14.	B	44.	C	74.	A	104.	E
15.	D	45.	E	75.	D	105.	D
16.	E	46.	B	76.	A	106.	B
17.	C	47.	C	77.	C	107.	A
18.	C	48.	C	78.	A	108.	D
19.	A	49.	D	79.	C	109.	C
20.	C	50.	B	80.	A	110.	E
21.	A	51.	E	81.	C	111.	A
22.	B	52.	D	82.	A	112.	A
23.	A	53.	A	83.	C	113.	E
24.	D	54.	B	84.	A	114.	A
25.	C	55.	A	85.	B	115.	C
26.	A	56.	B	86.	E	116.	A
27.	A	57.	E	87.	D	117.	A
28.	E	58.	A	88.	C	118.	A
29.	B	59.	D	89.	C		
30.	A	60.	C	90.	B		

5.5 Data Sufficiency Answer Explanations

The following discussion of data sufficiency is intended to familiarize you with the most efficient and effective approaches to the kinds of problems common to data sufficiency. The particular questions in this chapter are generally representative of the kinds of reading comprehension questions you will encounter on the GMAT®. Remember that it is the problem solving strategy that is important, not the specific details of a particular question.

1. John and David each received a salary increase. Which one received the greater dollar increase?

   (1) John's salary increased 8 percent.
   (2) David's salary increased 5 percent.

   Arithmetic Percent

   (1) There is no information about David's salary to compare with John's salary increase; NOT sufficient.

   (2) There is no information about John's salary to compare with David's salary increase; NOT sufficient.

   To calculate and compare the dollar amounts of the salary increases, it is necessary to know or have the means to know the original salary amounts. Since (1) and (2) together give only the percentage increases in salary, it cannot be determined which person received the greater dollar increase.

   The correct answer is E; both statements together are still not sufficient.

2. What is the value of $\frac{r}{2} + \frac{s}{2}$?

   (1) $\frac{r+s}{2} = 5$
   (2) $r + s = 10$

   Arithmetic Arithmetic operations with fractions

   The sum $\frac{r}{2} + \frac{s}{2} = \frac{r+s}{2}$.

   (1) Since $\frac{r+s}{2} = 5$, the value of $\frac{r}{2} + \frac{s}{2}$ also equals 5; SUFFICIENT.

   (2) If $r + s = 10$, then, when both sides are divided by 2, the resultant equation is $\frac{r+s}{2} = 5$.

   As proved in (1), this is also the value of $\frac{r}{2} + \frac{s}{2}$; SUFFICIENT.

   The correct answer is D; each statement alone is sufficient.

3. If n is an integer, then n is divisible by how many positive integers?

   (1) n is the product of two different prime numbers.
   (2) n and 2^3 are each divisible by the same number of positive integers.

   Arithmetic Properties of numbers

   (1) $n = pq$, where both p and q are prime numbers and $p \neq q$. Thus, n is divisible by the positive integers 1, p, q, pq, and no others; SUFFICIENT.

   (2) Given $2^3 = 8$, the number of positive divisors of 8 (and thus n) can be determined; SUFFICIENT.

   The correct answer is D; each statement alone is sufficient.

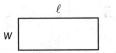

4. If ℓ and w represent the length and width, respectively, of the rectangle above, what is the perimeter?

(1) $2\ell + w = 40$
(2) $\ell + w = 25$

Geometry Perimeter

The formula for the perimeter of a rectangle is $P = 2\ell + 2w = 2(\ell + w)$, where ℓ and w represent the length and width, respectively.

(1) $2\ell + w = 40$ is equivalent to $w = 40 - 2\ell$. This cannot be solved without further information regarding either w or ℓ; NOT sufficient.

(2) Since $\ell + w = 25$, it can be substituted into the equation $P = 2(\ell + w)$ to find the perimeter, P; SUFFICIENT.

The correct answer is B; statement 2 alone is sufficient.

5. A retailer purchased a television set for x percent less than its list price, and then sold it for y percent less than its list price. What was the list price of the television set?

(1) $x = 15$
(2) $x - y = 5$

Arithmetic Percents

(1) This provides information only about the value of x. The list price cannot be determined using x because no dollar value for the purchase price is given; NOT sufficient.

(2) This provides information about the relationship between x and y but does not provide dollar values for either of these variables; NOT sufficient.

The list price cannot be determined without a dollar value for either the retailer's purchase price or the retailer's selling price. Even though the values for x or y are given or can be determined, taking (1) and (2) together provides no dollar values for either.

The correct answer is E; both statements together are still not sufficient.

6. If x and y are positive, what is the value of x?

(1) $x = 3.927y$
(2) $y = 2.279$

Algebra First- and second-degree equations

(1) While the value of x is 3.927 times the value of y, the value of y is not given; NOT sufficient.

(2) While the value of y is given, the relationship between x and y is not known; NOT sufficient.

When both the value of y and the relationship between x and y are known, the value of x can be determined by substitution: $x = (3.927)(2.279)$.

The correct answer is C; both statements together are sufficient.

7. If n is a member of the set {33, 36, 38, 39, 41, 42}, what is the value of n?

(1) n is even.
(2) n is a multiple of 3.

Arithmetic Sets

(1) This implies that n is 36, or 38, or 42. However, there is no further way to choose among these numbers as the single value of n; NOT sufficient.

(2) This implies that n could be 33, 36, 39, or 42. Again there is no further way to distinguish the value of n; NOT sufficient.

From (1) and (2) together, it can be determined that n could be either 36 or 42.

The correct answer is E; both statements together are still not sufficient.

8. Committee member *W* wants to schedule a one-hour meeting on Thursday for himself and three other committee members, *X*, *Y*, and *Z*. Is there a one-hour period on Thursday that is open for all four members?

   (1) On Thursday *W* and *X* have an open period from 9:00 a.m. to 12:00 noon.
   (2) On Thursday *Y* has an open period from 10:00 a.m. to 1:00 p.m. and *Z* has an open period from 8:00 a.m. to 11:00 a.m.

   Arithmetic Sets

   (1) There is no information about *Y* and *Z*, only information about *W* and *X*; NOT sufficient.

   (2) Similarly, there is no information about *W* and *X*, only information about *Y* and *Z*; NOT sufficient.

   Together, (1) and (2) detail information about all four committee members, and it can be determined that on Thursday all four members have an open one-hour period from 10:00 a.m. to 11:00 a.m.

   The correct answer is C; both statements together are sufficient.

9. If $x + 2y + 1 = y - x$, what is the value of *x*?

   (1) $y^2 = 9$
   (2) $y = 3$

   Algebra First- and second-degree equations

   The equation $x + 2y + 1 = y - x$ is equivalent to $2x = -y - 1$, or $x = -\frac{1}{2}(y + 1)$. Thus, the value of *x* can be determined if and only if the value of *y* is known.

   (1) It follows that either $y = 3$ or $y = -3$ and thus, by substitutions into the equation $x = -\frac{1}{2}(3 + 1)$ and $x = -\frac{1}{2}(-3 + 1)$, that *x* has two possible values as well (either –2 or 1); NOT sufficient.

   (2) The value of *y* is given, and therefore, by the same substitution, the value of *x* can be determined; SUFFICIENT.

   The correct answer is B; statement 2 alone is sufficient.

10. Of the 230 single-family homes built in City *X* last year, how many were occupied at the end of the year?

    (1) Of all single-family homes in City *X*, 90 percent were occupied at the end of last year.
    (2) A total of 7,200 single-family homes in City *X* were occupied at the end of last year.

    Arithmetic Percent

    (1) The percentage of the occupied single-family homes that were built last year is not given, and so the number occupied cannot be found; NOT sufficient.

    (2) Again, there is no information about the occupancy of the single-family homes that were built last year; NOT sufficient.

    Together (1) and (2) only yield the total number of the single-family homes that were occupied. Neither statement offers the needed information as to how many of the single-family homes built last year were indeed occupied at the end of last year.

    The correct answer is E; both statements together are still not sufficient.

11. What is the ratio of *x* to *y*?

    (1) *x* is 4 more than twice *y*.
    (2) The ratio of 0.5x to 2y is 3 to 5.

    Arithmetic Percents

    (1) This can be expressed as $x = 2y + 4$. Therefore, $\frac{x}{y} = 2 + \frac{4}{y}$, which cannot be solved without further information regarding either *x* or *y*; NOT sufficient.

    (2) This can be expressed as $\frac{0.5x}{2y} = \frac{3}{5}$ or $\frac{x}{y} = \frac{3}{5} \div \frac{0.5}{2}$; SUFFICIENT.

    The correct answer is B; statement 2 alone is sufficient.

12. What were the gross revenues from ticket sales for a certain film during the second week in which it was shown?

    (1) Gross revenues during the second week were $1.5 million less than during the first week.
    (2) Gross revenues during the third week were $2.0 million less than during the first week.

    Arithmetic Arithmetic operations

    (1) Since the amount of gross revenues during the first week is not given, the gross revenues during the second week cannot be determined; NOT sufficient.

    (2) No information is provided, directly or indirectly, about gross revenues during the second week; NOT sufficient.

    With (1) and (2) taken together, additional information, such as the amount of gross revenues during either the first or the third week, is still needed.

    The correct answer is E; both statements together are still not sufficient.

13. If r and s are positive integers, is $r + s$ divisible by 3?

    (1) s is divisible by 3.
    (2) r is divisible by 3.

    Arithmetic Properties of numbers

    In general terms, $r + s$ is divisible by 3 if both r and s are divisible by 3. If either r or s is not divisible by 3, then $r + s$ may or may not be divisible by 3.

    (1) Only gives information about s; NOT sufficient.

    (2) Only gives information about r; NOT sufficient.

    Taken together, (1) and (2) state that both r and s are divisible by 3, and thus $r + s$ is known to be divisible by 3.

    The correct answer is C; both statements together are sufficient.

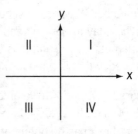

14. Point (x, y) lies in which quadrant of the rectangular coordinate system shown above?

    (1) $x + y < 0$
    (2) $x = 4$ and $y = -7$.

    Geometry Coordinate geometry

    (1) It is not possible to determine whether x, or y, or both x and y are negative. The only quadrant that can be ruled out is quadrant I, where any point in that quadrant has positive values for both x and y values; NOT sufficient.

    (2) It can be determined that the point $(4, -7)$ lies in quadrant IV because x has a positive value and y has a negative value; SUFFICIENT.

    The correct answer is B; statement 2 alone is sufficient.

15. What is the value of x?

    (1) $x + 1 = 2 - 3x$
    (2) $\dfrac{1}{2x} = 2$

    Algebra First- and second-degree equations

    (1) The equation can be reduced to $4x = 1$ and thus successfully solved for a single value of x; SUFFICIENT.

    (2) The equation can be reduced to $1 = 4x$ and thus successfully solved for a single value of x; SUFFICIENT.

    The correct answer is D; each statement alone is sufficient.

16. Is the prime number p equal to 37?

    (1) $p = n^2 + 1$, where n is an integer.
    (2) p^2 is greater than 200.

Arithmetic Properties of numbers

(1) Depending on the value of n, $n^2 + 1$ can represent a prime number that is less than, equal to, or greater than 37 (that is, if $n = 4$, $4^2 + 1 = 17$; if $n = 6$, $6^2 + 1 = 37$; and if $n = 10$, $10^2 + 1 = 101$); NOT sufficient.

(2) Since $14^2 = 196$ and $15^2 = 225$, it follows that $p > 14$, but p may or may not equal 37; NOT sufficient.

Taken together, (1) and (2) do not specify whether the value of p equals 17 or 37; thus, it cannot be determined if $p = 37$.

The correct answer is E; both statements together are still not sufficient.

17. What was the amount of money donated to a certain charity?

(1) Of the amount donated, 40 percent came from corporate donations.

(2) Of the amount donated, $1.5 million came from noncorporate donations.

Arithmetic Percents

The amount of money donated was the total of the corporate and the noncorporate portions of the donations.

(1) From this, only the portion that represented corporate donations is known, with no means of determining the amount donated; NOT sufficient.

(2) From this, only the dollar amount that represented noncorporate donations is known, with no means of determining the portion of the donations that it represents; NOT sufficient.

Letting x represent the total dollar amount donated, the amount known to be donated from corporate sources (1) can be represented as $0.40x$. Combining the information from (1) and (2) yields the equation $0.40x + \$1,500,000 = x$ or, by subtracting $0.40x$ from both sides, $\$1,500,000 = 0.60x$, which can be solved successfully for x.

The correct answer is C; both statements together are sufficient.

18. What is the value of the positive integer n?

(1) $n^4 < 25$
(2) $n \neq n^2$

Arithmetic Arithmetic operations

(1) If n is a positive integer and $n^4 < 25$, then n must equal either 1 or 2, since $1^4 = 1 \times 1 \times 1 \times 1 = 1$ and $2^4 = 2 \times 2 \times 2 \times 2 = 16$. If $n \geq 3$, then $n^4 \geq 3 \times 3 \times 3 \times 3 \geq 81$. However, there is no way to determine which value, 1 or 2, is equal to n; NOT sufficient.

(2) If the positive integer n does not equal n^2 or $n \times n$, it implies only that n is not equal to 1; NOT sufficient.

Using (1) and (2) together, it is possible to determine that either $n = 1$ or $n = 2$ and then to eliminate the value $n = 1$, thus establishing that $n = 2$.

The correct answer is C; both statements together are sufficient.

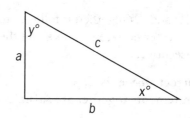

19. In the triangle above, does $a^2 + b^2 = c^2$?

(1) $x + y = 90$
(2) $x = y$

Geometry Triangles

The Pythagorean theorem states that $a^2 + b^2 = c^2$ for any right triangle with legs of lengths a and b and hypotenuse of length c. A right triangle is a triangle whose largest angle measures 90°.

(1) The sum of the three angles in a triangle equals 180°. Since $180° - (x + y)°$ is equivalent to $180° - 90°$ or 90°, the largest angle of the triangle measures 90°. This triangle is thus a right triangle, and the Pythagorean theorem thus holds true; SUFFICIENT.

(2) Knowing that $x = y$ provides many combinations of measurements for the three angles, but not enough information is provided to determine that the largest angle measures 90 degrees; NOT sufficient.

The correct answer is A; statement 1 alone is sufficient.

20. If x, y, and z are three integers, are they consecutive integers?

 (1) $z - x = 2$
 (2) $x < y < z$

Arithmetic Properties of numbers

 (1) From this information it follows that there is one integer between x and z, but there is no information about y; NOT sufficient.

 (2) There could be other integers between x and z besides y because there is no information as to how many integers are between x and z; NOT sufficient.

Using (1) and (2) together, it follows that y is the unique integer between x and z and the integers are consecutive.

The correct answer is C; both statements together are sufficient.

21. The symbol ∇ represents one of the following operations: addition, subtraction, multiplication, or division. What is the value of 3 ∇ 2?

 (1) $0 \nabla 1 = 1$
 (2) $1 \nabla 0 = 1$

Arithmetic Properties of numbers

 (1) $0 + 1 = 1; 0 - 1 = -1; 0 \times 1 = 0;$ and $0 \div 1 = 0.$ Therefore, the symbol shown can only represent addition, and the value of 3∇2 can be determined; SUFFICIENT.

 (2) $1 + 0 = 1; 1 - 0 = 1; 1 \times 0 = 0;$ and $1 \div 0$ is undefined. Therefore, the symbol shown could represent either addition or subtraction, and the value of 3∇2 cannot be determined; NOT sufficient.

The correct answer is A; statement 1 alone is sufficient.

22. A sum of $200,000 from a certain estate was divided among a spouse and three children. How much of the estate did the youngest child receive?

 (1) The spouse received $\frac{1}{2}$ of the sum from the estate, and the oldest child received $\frac{1}{4}$ of the remainder.
 (2) Each of the two younger children received $12,500 more than the oldest child and $62,500 less than the spouse.

Algebra First- and second-degree equations

 (1) The combined amount that the two youngest children together received can be determined, but not the specific amount that either one of them received; NOT sufficient.

 (2) An equation can be set up expressing the relationships given in terms of x, with x being the amount that each of the two younger children received: $200,000 = x + x + (x - 12,500) + (x + 62,500)$. The amount that the youngest child received (x) can thus be determined; SUFFICIENT.

The correct answer is B; statement 2 alone is sufficient.

23. What is the value of x?

 (1) $-(x + y) = x - y$
 (2) $x + y = 2$

Algebra First- and second-degree equations

 (1) This equation can be reduced to $2x = 0$, or $x = 0$; SUFFICIENT.

 (2) This equation cannot be solved without further information regarding either x or y; NOT sufficient.

The correct answer is A; statement 1 alone is sufficient.

24. A certain 4-liter solution of vinegar and water consists of x liters of vinegar and y liters of water. How many liters of vinegar does the solution contain?

 (1) $\dfrac{x}{4} = \dfrac{3}{8}$
 (2) $\dfrac{y}{4} = \dfrac{5}{8}$

Arithmetic Percent

(1) This proportion can be solved for x to determine the liters of vinegar in the solution; SUFFICIENT.

(2) This proportion can be solved for y to determine the liters of water in the solution. Then, substituting this value of y in the equation $x + y = 4$, which can be formulated from the given information, will give the value of x; SUFFICIENT.

The correct answer is D; each statement alone is sufficient.

25. If x and y are integers, what is the value of y?

(1) $xy = 27$
(2) $x = y^2$

Arithmetic Arithmetic operations

(1) Many different pairs of integers could have the product 27, for example, $(-3)(-9)$ or $(1)(27)$. There is no way of knowing which pair of integers is represented here, and there is also no way of knowing which member of a pair is x and which member of a pair is y; NOT sufficient.

(2) The given $x = y^2$ does not determine the value of y, since x could have many different values; NOT sufficient.

Using both (1) and (2), it is possible to substitute y^2, from (2), for the value of x in (1). The result, $y^3 = 27$, establishes that $y = 3$.

The correct answer is C; both statements together are sufficient.

26. How many newspapers were sold at a certain newsstand today?

(1) A total of 100 newspapers were sold at the newsstand yesterday, 10 fewer than twice the number sold today.

(2) The number of newspapers sold at the newsstand yesterday was 45 more than the number sold today.

Algebra First- and second-degree equations

Let t be the number of newspapers sold today.

(1) This can be expressed as $100 = 2t - 10$ and successfully solved for t; SUFFICIENT.

(2) It can only be determined that the number of newspapers sold yesterday was 45 more than the number of newspapers sold today. Since the number sold yesterday is unknown, t cannot be determined; NOT sufficient.

The correct answer is A; statement 1 alone is sufficient.

27. What is Ricky's age now?

(1) Ricky is now twice as old as he was exactly 8 years ago.

(2) Ricky's sister Teresa is now 3 times as old as Ricky was exactly 8 years ago.

Algebra Translation into equations

Let r represent Ricky's age now, and let t represent Teresa's age now.

(1) This can be represented as $r = 2(r - 8)$, which can be solved for r, where $r = 16$; SUFFICIENT.

(2) This can be represented as $t = 3(r - 8)$, which cannot be solved for Ricky's age now, since there are two unknowns; NOT sufficient.

The correct answer is A; statement 1 alone is sufficient.

28. If both x and y are nonzero numbers, what is the value of $\frac{y}{x}$?

(1) $x = 6$
(2) $y^2 = x^2$

Arithmetic Powers of numbers

(1) This states only the value of x, with the value of y not determined and no means for it to be determined; NOT sufficient.

(2) Although the squares of x and y are equal, their square roots are not necessarily equal. For example, y could be a negative number and x could be a positive number, and when squared, their squares would still be equal. Therefore, the value of $\frac{y}{x}$ could be either -1 or 1; NOT sufficient.

The two statements together are not sufficient since y could be either 6 or -6, which implies that $\frac{y}{x}$ could be either 1 or -1.

**The correct answer is E;
both statements together are still not sufficient.**

29. John took a test that had 60 questions numbered from 1 to 60. How many of the questions did he answer correctly?

 (1) The number of questions he answered correctly in the first half of the test was 7 more than the number he answered correctly in the second half of the test.
 (2) He answered $\frac{5}{6}$ of the odd-numbered questions correctly and $\frac{4}{5}$ of the even-numbered questions correctly.

Arithmetic Fractions

(1) Letting f represent the number of questions answered correctly in the first half of the test and s represent the number answered correctly in the second half, this can be expressed in the equation $f = 7 + s$. Because there are two unknowns, this equation cannot be solved for either f or s, and therefore $f + s$, the total number of questions answered correctly, cannot be found; NOT sufficient.

(2) Since there are 30 odd-numbered questions and 30 even-numbered questions in a 60-question test, it can be determined that the number of questions answered correctly was equal to $\frac{5}{6}(30) + \frac{4}{5}(30)$; SUFFICIENT.

**The correct answer is B;
statement 2 alone is sufficient.**

30. If $x = 0.rstu$, where r, s, t, and u each represent a nonzero digit of x, what is the value of x?

 (1) $r = 3s = 2t = 6u$
 (2) The product of r and u is equal to the product of s and t.

Arithmetic Decimals + Properties of numbers

If the values of r, s, t, and u were known, the value of x could be found.

(1) Since $r = 6u$ and r and u must be nonzero digits, it must be that $u = 1$ and $r = 6$. If u were any larger than 1, r could not be a single digit (i.e., 0, 1, 2, 3, 4, 5, 6, 7, 8, or 9) because $2 \times 6 = 12$, a two-digit number. Since $u = 1$ and $2t = 6u$, $2t = 6$ and $t = 3$. Since $3s = 6u$, $3s = 6$ and $s = 2$. With the values established for r, s, t, and u, $x = 0.6231$; SUFFICIENT.

(2) Any digits where $r = s$ and $u = t$ (such as 3366, 2299, or 1188) would satisfy this statement, and there is no way to determine which digits define the value of x; NOT sufficient.

**The correct answer is A;
statement 1 alone is sufficient.**

31. An empty rectangular swimming pool has uniform depth. How long will it take to fill the pool with water?

 (1) Water will be pumped in at the rate of 240 gallons per hour (1 cubic foot = 7.5 gallons).
 (2) The pool is 60 feet long and 25 feet wide.

Geometry Volume

To determine how long it will take to fill the pool, it is necessary to know both the capacity of the pool and the filling rate, that is, the rate at which water will be pumped into the pool.

(1) The filling rate is given, but there is no information about the capacity of the pool; NOT sufficient.

(2) While this gives the length and width of the pool, the pool's depth is also needed to make a determination of the pool's capacity; additionally, no information is given about the filling rate; NOT sufficient.

Statements (1) and (2) together are still not sufficient, since the capacity of the pool cannot be determined.

**The correct answer is E;
both statements together are still not sufficient.**

32. Is the value of n closer to 50 than to 75?

    (1) $75 - n > n - 50$
    (2) $n > 60$

Algebra Inequalities

Begin by considering the value of n when it is at the exact same distance from both 50 and 75. The value of n is equidistant between 50 and 75 when n is the midpoint between 75 and 50, that is, when $n = \dfrac{50 + 75}{2} = 62.5$. Alternatively stated, n is equidistant between 50 and 75 when the distance that n is below 75 is equal to the distance that n is above 50, i.e., when $75 - n = n - 50$, as indicated on the number line below.

(1) Since here $75 - n > n - 50$, it follows that the value of n is closer to 50 than to 75; SUFFICIENT.

(2) Although n is greater than 60, for all values of n between 60 and 62.5, n is closer to 50, and for all values of n greater than 62.5, n is closer to 75. Without further information, the value of n relative to 50 and 75 cannot be determined; NOT sufficient.

**The correct answer is A;
statement 1 alone is sufficient.**

33. If n is an integer, is $\dfrac{100 - n}{n}$ an integer?

    (1) $n > 4$
    (2) $n^2 = 25$

Arithmetic Properties of numbers

(1) This information states that $n > 4$, which means that n could be 5 or 6 (among many other possibilities). If $n = 5$, $\dfrac{100 - n}{n} = \dfrac{100 - 5}{5} = 19$, which is an integer. If $n = 6$, $\dfrac{100 - n}{n} = \dfrac{100 - 6}{6} = 15.7$, which is not an integer. From this wide generalization of n, some values yield integers and others do not; NOT sufficient.

(2) If $n^2 = 25$, then $n = 5$ or -5. If $n = 5$, $\dfrac{100 - n}{n}$ is an integer as shown above. If $n = -5$, $\dfrac{100 - n}{n} = \dfrac{100 - (-5)}{n} = \dfrac{105}{-5} = -21$, which is an integer. For either possible value of n, the given expression is an integer; SUFFICIENT.

**The correct answer is B;
statement 2 alone is sufficient.**

34. If p, q, x, y, and z are different positive integers, which of the five integers is the median?

    (1) $p + x < q$
    (2) $y < z$

Arithmetic Statistics

Since there are five different integers, there are two integers greater and two integers less than the median, which is the middle number.

(1) No information is given about the order of y and z with respect to the other three numbers; NOT sufficient.

(2) This statement does not relate y and z to the other three integers; NOT sufficient.

Because (1) and (2) taken together do not relate p, x, and q to y and z, it is impossible to tell which is the median.

**The correct answer is E;
both statements together are still not sufficient.**

35. If $w + z = 28$, what is the value of wz?

    (1) w and z are positive integers.
    (2) w and z are consecutive odd integers.

Arithmetic Arithmetic operations

(1) The fact that w and z are both positive does not help to specify the values of w and z because, for example, if $w = 20$ and $z = 8$, then $wz = 160$, and if $w = 10$ and $z = 18$, then $wz = 180$; NOT sufficient.

(2) Since w and z are consecutive odd integers, consider some consecutive odd integers that are less than 28, e.g., 11, 13, 15, 17, 19, 21, 23, and note that the only two consecutive odd integers that add to 28 are 13 and 15. From this it is possible to determine that the value of wz must be $(13)(15)$, or 195.

To look at this problem more formally, let the consecutive odd integers w and z be represented by $2n + 1$ and $2n + 3$, where n is any integer. The equation in the problem can thus be expressed as $w + z = (2n + 1) + (2n + 3)$ and solved for n as follows:

$w + z = (2n + 1) + (2n + 3)$

$28 = 4n + 4$ simplify

$24 = 4n$ subtract 4 from both sides

$6 = n$ divide both sides by 4

Thus, $w = 2(6) + 1 = 13$, and $z = 2(6) + 3 = 15$; SUFFICIENT.

The correct answer is B; statement 2 alone is sufficient.

36. Elena receives a salary plus a commission that is equal to a fixed percentage of her sales revenue. What was the total of Elena's salary and commission last month?

    (1) Elena's monthly salary is $1,000.
    (2) Elena's commission is 5 percent of her sales revenue.

Arithmetic Percents

In order to find the total of Elena's salary and commission last month, it is necessary to have the following information: her monthly salary, her sales revenue last month, and the percent of her sales revenue that is her commission.

(1) Elena's monthly salary is given, but there is no information about the other factors that made up her salary last month; NOT sufficient.

(2) The percent of Elena's sales revenue that is her commission is given, but there is no information about her sales revenue for the month or her monthly salary; NOT sufficient.

Using both (1) and (2) still yields no information about Elena's sales revenue from last month, and thus the total of her salary and commission last month cannot be determined.

The correct answer is E; both statements together are still not sufficient.

37. What is the value of $a - b$?

    (1) $a = b + 4$
    (2) $(a - b)^2 = 16$

Algebra First- and second-degree equations

(1) If $a = b + 4$ then, when b is subtracted from both sides, the resultant equation is $a - b = 4$; SUFFICIENT.

(2) Since $(a - b)^2 = 16$, either $a - b = 4$ or $a - b = -4$. There is no further information available to determine a single numerical value of $a - b$; NOT sufficient.

The correct answer is A; statement 1 alone is sufficient.

38. Machine X runs at a constant rate and produces a lot consisting of 100 cans in 2 hours. How much less time would it take to produce the lot of cans if both machines X and Y were run simultaneously?

(1) Both machines *X* and *Y* produce the same number of cans per hour.

(2) It takes machine *X* twice as long to produce the lot of cans as it takes machines *X* and *Y* running simultaneously to produce the lot.

Arithmetic Rate problem

The problem states that the job is to produce 100 cans and that machine *X* can do it in 2 hours. Thus, the only information needed to answer this question about the decreased time necessary for both of them to produce that number of cans is either the rate for machine *Y* or the time that machines *X* and *Y* together take to get the job done.

(1) This states that the rate for *Y* is the same as that for *X*, which is given; SUFFICIENT.

(2) Since the rate for *X* is twice that for *X* and *Y* running simultaneously, it can be determined that *X* and *Y* together would take one-half the time, or 1 hour, to produce the lot; SUFFICIENT.

**The correct answer is D;
each statement alone is sufficient.**

39. Can the positive integer *p* be expressed as the product of two integers, each of which is greater than 1?

(1) $31 < p < 37$
(2) *p* is odd.

Arithmetic Properties of numbers

(1) This statement implies that *p* can be any of the integers 32, 33, 34, 35, or 36. Because each of these integers can be expressed as the product of two integers, each of which is greater than 1, the question can be answered even though the specific value of *p* is not known; SUFFICIENT.

(2) Some odd numbers are prime and so cannot be expressed as a product of two integers, each of which is greater than 1; other odd numbers are composite and so can be expressed as a product of two integers, each of which is greater than 1; NOT sufficient.

**The correct answer is A;
statement 1 alone is sufficient.**

40. Is $x < y$?

(1) $z < y$
(2) $z < x$

Algebra Inequalities

(1) This gives no information about *x* and its relationship to *y*; NOT sufficient.

(2) This gives no information about *y* and its relationship to *x*; NOT sufficient.

From (1) and (2) together, it can only be determined that *z* is less than either *x* or *y*. It is still not possible to determine the relationship of *x* and *y*, and *x* might be greater than, equal to, or less than *y*.

**The correct answer is E;
both statements together are still not sufficient.**

41. If *S* is a set of four numbers *w*, *x*, *y*, and *z*, is the range of the numbers in *S* greater than 2?

(1) $w - z > 2$
(2) *z* is the least number in *S*.

Arithmetic Statistics

The range of the numbers *w*, *x*, *y*, and *z* is equal to the greatest of those numbers minus the least of those numbers.

(1) This reveals that the difference between two of the numbers in the set is greater than 2, which means that the range of the four numbers must also be greater than 2; SUFFICIENT.

(2) The information that *z* is the least number gives no information regarding the other numbers or their range; NOT sufficient.

**The correct answer is A;
statement 1 alone is sufficient.**

42. If *y* is greater than 110 percent of *x*, is *y* greater than 75?

(1) $x > 75$
(2) $y - x = 10$

Arithmetic + Algebra Percents + Inequalities

(1) It is known that $x > 75$. Since it is given that $y > 110$ percent of x, and since 110 percent of $75 > 75$, then $y > 75$; SUFFICIENT.

(2) Although the relationship between x and y is known to be $y - x = 10$, more information about the value of x is needed to determine the value of y. For example, using examples where $y > 110$ percent of x, if $x = 20$, then $y = 30$, which is less than 75. If, however, $x = 80$, then $y = 90$, which is greater than 75; NOT sufficient.

The correct answer is A; statement 1 alone is sufficient.

43. Is $x < 0$?

   (1) $-2x > 0$
   (2) $x^3 < 0$

Algebra Inequalities

(1) A negative number times a positive number is negative, whereas a negative number times a negative number is positive. Thus, since -2 times x is positive, x must be a negative number; SUFFICIENT.

(2) The cube of a positive number is positive, and the cube of a negative number is negative; SUFFICIENT.

The correct answer is D; each statement alone is sufficient.

44. If Q is an integer between 10 and 100, what is the value of Q?

   (1) One of Q's digits is 3 more than the other, and the sum of its digits is 9.
   (2) $Q < 50$

Algebra Properties of numbers

(1) While it is quite possible to guess that the two integers that satisfy these stipulations are 36 and 63, this can also be determined algebraically. Letting x and y be the digits of Q, this can be expressed as $x = y + 3$ and $x + y = 9$. These equations can be solved simultaneously to identify the digits of 3

and 6, with the resultant integers of 36 and 63. However, it is unknown which of these integers is Q; NOT sufficient.

(2) There is a range of integers between 10 and 49; NOT sufficient.

When the information from (1) and (2) is integrated, the value of Q can be determined to be 36.

The correct answer is C; both statements together are sufficient.

45. If p and q are positive integers and $pq = 24$, what is the value of p?

   (1) $\dfrac{q}{6}$ is an integer.
   (2) $\dfrac{p}{2}$ is an integer.

Arithmetic Arithmetic operations

There are four pairs of positive integers whose product is 24: 1 and 24, 2 and 12, 3 and 8, and 4 and 6.

(1) The possible values of q are therefore 6, 12, and 24, and for each of these there is a different value of p (4, 2, and 1); NOT sufficient.

(2) The possible values of p are therefore 2, 4, 6, 8, 12, and 24; NOT sufficient.

From (1) and (2) together, the possible values of q can only be narrowed down to 6 or 12, with corresponding values of p being either 4 or 2.

The correct answer is E; both statements together are still not sufficient.

46. What is the value of $x^2 - y^2$?

   (1) $x - y = y + 2$
   (2) $x - y = \dfrac{1}{x + y}$

Algebra First- and second-degree equations

(1) If $x - y = y + 2$, then $x = 2y + 2$. When $2y + 2$ is substituted for x in the expression $x^2 - y^2$, the resultant expression is $(2y + 2)^2 - y^2$. The value of the expression cannot be determined any further since the value of y is unknown; NOT sufficient.

(2) Since $x - y = \dfrac{1}{x + y}$, $(x - y)(x + y) = 1$, or $x^2 - y^2 = 1$. Thus, the value can be determined for $-y^2$; SUFFICIENT.

The correct answer is B; statement 2 alone is sufficient.

47. Hoses X and Y simultaneously fill an empty swimming pool that has a capacity of 50,000 liters. If the flow in each hose is independent of the flow in the other hose, how many hours will it take to fill the pool?

(1) Hose X alone would take 28 hours to fill the pool.
(2) Hose Y alone would take 36 hours to fill the pool.

Arithmetic Arithmetic operations

In order to answer this problem about *two* hoses being used *simultaneously* to fill a pool, information about the filling rate for *both* hoses is needed.

(1) Only the filling rate for hose X is given; NOT sufficient.
(2) Only the filling rate for hose Y is given; NOT sufficient.

Using both (1) and (2) the filling rates for both hoses are known, and thus the time needed to fill the pool can be determined. Since hose X fills the pool in 28 hours, hose X fills $\dfrac{1}{28}$ of the pool in 1 hour. Since hose Y fills the pool in 36 hours, hose Y fills $\dfrac{1}{36}$ of the pool in 1 hour. Therefore, together they fill $\dfrac{1}{28} + \dfrac{1}{36} = \dfrac{9}{252} + \dfrac{7}{252} = \dfrac{16}{252} = \dfrac{4}{63}$ in 1 hour. The time (t) that it will take them to fill the pool together can be found by solving for t in $\dfrac{4}{63}(t) = 1$. Remember in answering that it is enough to establish the sufficiency of the data; it is not actually necessary to do the computations.

The correct answer is C; both statements together are sufficient.

48. How many integers n are there such that $r < n < s$?

(1) $s - r = 5$
(2) r and s are not integers.

Arithmetic Properties of numbers

(1) The difference between s and r is 5. If r and s are integers (e.g., 7 and 12), the number of integers, n, between them (i.e., 8, 9, 10, and 11) is 4. If r and s are not integers (e.g., 6.5 and 11.5), then the number of integers between them (i.e., 7, 8, 9, 10, and 11) is 5. No information is given that allows a determination of whether s and r are integers or not; NOT sufficient.

(2) No information is given about the difference between r and s. They could be two unit fractions with no integer between them, or they could be two decimals with a difference of 100 and 99 integers between them; NOT sufficient.

Using the information from both (1) and (2), it can be determined that, because r and s are not integers, there are 5 integers between them.

The correct answer is C; both statements together are sufficient.

49. If the total price of n equally priced shares of a certain stock was $12,000, what was the price per share of the stock?

(1) If the price per share of the stock had been $1 more, the total price of the n shares would have been $300 more.
(2) If the price per share of the stock had been $2 less, the total price of the n shares would have been 5 percent less.

Arithmetic Arithmetic operations + Percent

Since the price per share of the stock can be expressed as $\dfrac{\$12{,}000}{n}$, determining the value of n is sufficient to answer this question.

(1) A per-share increase of $1 and a total increase of $300 for n shares of stock mean together that $n(\$1) = \$300$. It follows that $n = 300$; SUFFICIENT.

(2) If the price of each of the n shares had been reduced by \$2, the total reduction in price would have been 5 percent less or 0.05(\$12,000). The equation $2n = 0.05(\$12,000)$ expresses this relationship. The value of n can be determined to be 300 from this equation; SUFFICIENT.

**The correct answer is D;
each statement alone is sufficient.**

50. What is the ratio of $x : y : z$?

(1) $z = 1$ and $xy = 32$.

(2) $\dfrac{x}{y} = 2$ and $\dfrac{z}{y} = \dfrac{1}{4}$.

Arithmetic Ratio and proportion

(1) The knowledge that $xy = 32$ still yields several choices for the values of x and y, and inconsistent ratios can result. For example, if $x = 4$ and $y = 8$, the ratio among the three variables is $4 : 8 : 1$, but if $x = 16$ and $y = 2$, then the ratio among the variables is $16 : 2 : 1$; NOT sufficient.

(2) Multiplying each of these two equations by y yields $x = 2y$ and $z = \dfrac{1}{4}y$. Therefore, the ratio can be expressed entirely in terms of y, and thus $x : y : z$ can be rendered as $2y : y : \dfrac{1}{4}y$ or $2 : 1 : \dfrac{1}{4}$; SUFFICIENT.

**The correct answer is B;
statement 2 alone is sufficient.**

51. Is $xy > 5$?

(1) $1 \le x \le 3$ and $2 \le y \le 4$.

(2) $x + y = 5$

Algebra Inequalities

(1) While it is known that x is greater than or equal to 1 but less than or equal to 3 and that y is greater than or equal to 2 but less than 4, the product of xy could thus be as small as $(1)(2) = 2$ or as large as $(3)(4) = 12$. Nothing definitively shows that $xy > 5$; NOT sufficient.

(2) If x were 1, y would be 4 and $xy = 4$; if x were 2, y would be 3 and $xy = 6$. Again, there is nothing definite to say that $xy > 5$; NOT sufficient.

Both (1) and (2) together are not sufficient since the two examples $x = 1$, $y = 4$ and $x = 2$, $y = 3$ are consistent with the statements but yield one xy that is less than 5 and one xy that is greater than 5.

**The correct answer is E;
both statements together are still not sufficient.**

52. In year X, 8.7 percent of the men in the labor force were unemployed in June compared with 8.4 percent in May. If the number of men in the labor force was the same for both months, how many men were unemployed in June of that year?

(1) In May of year X, the number of unemployed men in the labor force was 3.36 million.

(2) In year X, 120,000 more men in the labor force were unemployed in June than in May.

Arithmetic Percents

Since 8.7 percent of the men in the labor force were unemployed in June, the number of unemployed men could be calculated if the total number of men in the labor force was known. Let t represent the total number of men in the labor force.

(1) This implies that for May $(8.4\%)t = 3,360,000$, from which the value of t can be determined; SUFFICIENT.

(2) This implies that $(8.7\% - 8.4\%)t = 120,000$ or $(0.3\%)t = 120,000$. This equation can be solved for t; SUFFICIENT.

**The correct answer is D;
each statement alone is sufficient.**

53. If $x \ne 0$, what is the value of $\left(\dfrac{x^p}{x^q}\right)^4$?

(1) $p = q$

(2) $x = 3$

Arithmetic + Algebra Arithmetic operations + Simplifying expressions

(1) Since $p = q$, it follows that
$$\left(\frac{x^p}{x^q}\right)^4 = \left(\frac{x^p}{x^p}\right)^4 = (1)^4; \text{ SUFFICIENT.}$$

(2) While the value of x is defined, there is no information about the values of p or q. Because these values are still unknown, the value of the expression $\left(\dfrac{x^p}{x^q}\right)^4$ cannot be determined; NOT sufficient.

The correct answer is A; statement 1 alone is sufficient.

54. On Monday morning a certain machine ran continuously at a uniform rate to fill a production order. At what time did it completely fill the order that morning?

   (1) The machine began filling the order at 9:30 a.m.

   (2) The machine had filled $\dfrac{1}{2}$ of the order by 10:30 a.m. and $\dfrac{5}{6}$ of the order by 11:10 a.m.

Arithmetic Arithmetic operations

(1) This merely states what time the machine began filling the order; NOT sufficient.

(2) In the 40 minutes between 10:30 a.m. and 11:10 a.m., $\dfrac{5}{6} - \dfrac{1}{2} = \dfrac{1}{3}$ of the order was filled. Therefore, the entire order was completely filled in $3 \times 40 = 120$ minutes, or 2 hours. Since half the order took 1 hour and was filled by 10:30 a.m., the second half of the order, and thus the entire order, was filled by 11:30 a.m.; SUFFICIENT.

The correct answer is B; statement 2 alone is sufficient.

55. If $xy < 3$, is $x < 1$?

   (1) $y > 3$
   (2) $x < 3$

Algebra Inequalities

(1) If $y > 3$ and ≥ 1, then $xy > 3$. Since this contradicts the given $xy < 3$, it can therefore be determined that $x < 1$; SUFFICIENT.

(2) The information that $x < 3$ is not enough to determine whether $x < 1$ since there are many possible values of x between the parameters of 1 and 3; NOT sufficient.

The correct answer is A; statement 1 alone is sufficient.

56. If $\dfrac{m}{n} = \dfrac{5}{3}$, what is the value of $m + n$?

   (1) $m > 0$
   (2) $2m + n = 26$

Algebra Simultaneous equations

(1) From this, m and n could be any positive numbers in the ratio $5 : 3$, e.g., 10 and 6, or 5 and 3; NOT sufficient.

(2) The given equation $\dfrac{m}{n} = \dfrac{5}{3}$ and the equation $2m + n = 26$ can be solved simultaneously for the two unknowns. From $2m + n = 26$, it can be determined that $n = 26 - 2m$. Substituting this value of n in the given equation produces $\dfrac{m}{26 - 2m} = \dfrac{5}{3}$, which by cross-multiplying yields $3m = 130 - 10m$, and thus $13m = 130$ or $m = 10$. The value of n can be determined by substituting 10 for m in either one of the equations, and therefore the sum of $m + n$ can also be determined; SUFFICIENT.

The correct answer is B; statement 2 alone is sufficient.

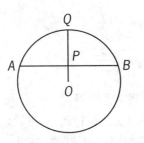

57. What is the radius of the circle above with center O?

(1) The ratio of OP to PQ is 1 to 2.
(2) P is the midpoint of chord AB.

Geometry Circles

(1) It can only be concluded that the radius is 3 times the length of OP, which is unknown; NOT sufficient.

(2) It can only be concluded that AP = PB, and the chord is irrelevant to the radius; NOT sufficient.

Together, (1) and (2) do not give the length of any line segment shown in the circle, so they are not sufficient to determine the radius.

The correct answer is E; both statements together are still not sufficient.

58. What is the number of 360-degree rotations that a bicycle wheel made while rolling 100 meters in a straight line without slipping?

(1) The diameter of the bicycle wheel, including the tire, was 0.5 meter.
(2) The wheel made twenty 360-degree rotations per minute.

Geometry Circles

For each 360-degree rotation, the wheel has traveled a distance equal to its circumference. Given either the circumference of the wheel or the means to calculate its circumference, it is thus possible to determine the number of times the circumference of the wheel was laid out along the straight-line path of 100 meters.

(1) The circumference of the bicycle wheel can be determined from the given diameter using the equation $C = 2\pi r$, where r = the radius, or one-half the diameter; SUFFICIENT.

(2) The speed of the rotations is irrelevant, and no dimensions of the wheel are given; NOT sufficient.

The correct answer is A; statement 1 alone is sufficient.

59. The perimeter of a rectangular garden is 360 feet. What is the length of the garden?

(1) The length of the garden is twice the width.
(2) The difference between the length and width of the garden is 60 feet.

Geometry + Algebra Perimeter + Simultaneous Equations

If ℓ and w denote the length and width of the garden, respectively, then it is given that the perimeter is $2(\ell + w) = 360$. When both sides of the equation are divided by 2, the result is $\ell + w = 180$.

(1) This can be represented as $\ell = 2w$, or $w = \dfrac{\ell}{2}$. By substituting $\dfrac{\ell}{2}$ for w in the equation $\ell + w = 180$, the resulting equation of $\ell + \dfrac{\ell}{2} = 180$ can be solved for ℓ; SUFFICIENT.

(2) This can be represented as $\ell - w = 60$. The length can then be determined by solving the two equations, $\ell - w = 60$ and $\ell + w = 180$, simultaneously. Adding the two equations yields $2\ell - w + w = 240$ or $\ell = 120$; SUFFICIENT.

The correct answer is D; each statement alone is sufficient.

60. If $2x(5n) = t$, what is the value of t?

(1) $x = n + 3$
(2) $2x = 32$

Algebra First- and second-degree equations

To determine the value of t, the values of x and n must both be known.

(1) This merely provides the relationship between x and n. If $n + 3$ were substituted for x, the given equation would be $2(n + 3)(5n) = t$, or when simplified, $10n^2 + 30n = t$. Because there are two variables, this equation cannot be solved for t as is; NOT sufficient.

(2) This provides only the value of x (that is, $x = 16$). This yields $32(5n) = t$ in the given equation, leaving no way to determine the value of n and thus the value of t; NOT sufficient.

The value of x determined from equation (2) can be substituted in equation (1) to determine the value of n, and thus $16 = n + 3$, which can readily be solved for n. So the value of t can be found when both statements are used together to determine the values of x and n.

The correct answer is C; both statements together are sufficient.

61. In the equation $x^2 + bx + 12 = 0$, x is a variable and b is a constant. What is the value of b?

(1) $x - 3$ is a factor of $x^2 + bx + 12$.
(2) 4 is a root of the equation $x^2 + bx + 12 = 0$.

Algebra First- and second-degree equations

(1) If $x - 3$ is a factor, then the root or value of x is 3, since $x - 3 = 0$ and thus $x = 3$. The other factor can then be found by dividing 12 by -3 from the first factor, or $\frac{12}{-3} = -4$. Therefore, the other factor of the equation is $x - 4$. Thus $(x - 3)(x - 4) = x^2 + bx + 12$ or, when the factors are multiplied, $x^2 - 7x + 12$. From this, it can be inferred that $b = -7$; SUFFICIENT.

(2) If 4 is a root of the equation, then $x = 4$, and 4 can be substituted for x in the equation $x^2 + bx + 12 = 0$, yielding $4^2 + 4b + 12 = 0$. From this, the value of b can again be determined; SUFFICIENT.

The correct answer is D; each statement alone is sufficient.

62. A Town T has 20,000 residents, 60 percent of whom are female. What percent of the residents were born in Town T?

(1) The number of female residents who were born in Town T is twice the number of male residents who were <u>not</u> born in Town T.
(2) The number of female residents who were not born in Town T is twice the number of female residents who were born in Town T.

Arithmetic Percents

It is given that 60% of the 20,000 residents of Town T are females, or thus that $(0.60)(20,000) = 12,000$ females are residents. Thus, the number of male residents is 20,000 total residents − 12,000 female residents = 8,000 male residents. To determine the percent of residents born in Town T, it is necessary to know or have the means to know the *number* of residents, both male and female, *who were born* in Town T so that:

$$\frac{\text{number of residents born in Town } T}{\text{total number of residents in Town } T} = \begin{array}{l}\text{percent of}\\ \text{residents born}\\ \text{in Town } T\end{array}$$

or thus:

$$\frac{\text{number of residents born in Town } T}{20,000} = \begin{array}{l}\text{percent of}\\ \text{residents born}\\ \text{in Town } T\end{array}$$

(1) The total number of male and female residents born in Town T is not given and cannot be determined from this information; NOT sufficient.

(2) Letting the number of females not born in Town T be represented by n and the number of females born in Town T be represented by b, this can be expressed as $n = 2b$. From the given statement, it is known that $n + b = 12,000$. By substitution, $2b + b = 12,000$.

Thus $\frac{1}{3}$, or 4,000, of the female residents of Town T were born there. However, no information is given about the male residents born in Town T; NOT sufficient.

From (1) and (2) together, the number of residents born in Town T can be determined. From (2) it is known that 4,000 of the female residents were born there. (1) states that the number of male residents who were not born in Town T is half the number of females who were born in Town T, or 2,000.

Thus, the number of males born in Town T is 8,000 male residents − 2,000 male residents not born there = 6,000 male residents who were born there. So, out of 20,000 residents, 4,000 females + 6,000 males = 10,000 residents were born in Town T. This number of residents born in Town T can now be substituted in the equation above to determine the percent of the residents who were born in Town T.

**The correct answer is C;
both statements together are sufficient.**

63. If y is an integer, is y^3 divisible by 9?

    (1) y is divisible by 4.
    (2) y is divisible by 6.

Arithmetic Properties of numbers

In order for y^3 to be divisible by 9, the integer y must also be divisible by 3.

    (1) Not all multiples of 4 are divisible by 3 (e.g., y = 12 is divisible by 3, but y = 16 is not divisible by 3); NOT sufficient.

    (2) Any number divisible by 6 is also divisible by 3; SUFFICIENT.

**The correct answer is B;
statement 2 alone is sufficient.**

64. In $\triangle XYZ$, what is the length of YZ?

    (1) The length of XY is 3.
    (2) The length of XZ is 5.

Geometry Triangles

Given the length of one side of a triangle, it is known that the sum of the lengths of the other two sides is greater than that given length. The length of either of the other two sides, however, can be any positive number.

    (1) Only the length of one side, XY, is given, and that is not enough to determine the length of YZ; NOT sufficient.

    (2) Again, only the length of one side, XZ, is given and that is not enough to determine the length of YZ; NOT sufficient.

Even by using the triangle inequality stated above, only a range of values for YZ can be determined from (1) and (2). If the length of side YZ is represented by k, then it is known both that $3 + 5 > k$ and that $3 + k > 5$, or $k > 2$. Combining these inequalities to determine the length of k yields only that $8 > k > 2$.

**The correct answer is E;
both statements together are still not sufficient.**

65. What was the ratio of the number of cars to the number of trucks produced by Company X last year?

    (1) Last year, if the number of cars produced by Company X had been 8 percent greater, the number of cars produced would have been 150 percent of the number of trucks produced by Company X.

    (2) Last year Company X produced 565,000 cars and 406,800 trucks.

Arithmetic Ratio + Percents

Let c equal the number of cars and t the number of trucks produced by Company X last year. The ratio of cars to trucks produced last year can be expressed as $\frac{c}{t}$.

    (1) An 8% increase in the number of cars produced can be expressed as 108% of c, or $1.08c$. Similarly, a 150% increase in the number of trucks produced can be expressed as $1.5t$. The relationship between the two can be expressed in the equation $1.08c = 1.5t$. From this:

    $$\frac{1.08c}{t} = 1.5 \qquad \text{divide both sides by } t$$

    $$\frac{c}{t} = \frac{1.5}{1.08} \qquad \text{divide both sides by } 1.08$$

    Thus the ratio of cars to trucks produced last year can be determined; SUFFICIENT.

    (2) The values of c and t are given; so the ratio $\frac{c}{t}$ can be determined; SUFFICIENT.

**The correct answer is D;
each statement alone is sufficient.**

66. Is $xy < 6$?

    (1) $x < 3$ and $y < 2$.
    (2) $\dfrac{1}{2} < x < \dfrac{2}{3}$ and $y^2 < 64$.

Algebra Inequalities

(1) For some values of $x < 3$ and $y < 2$, $xy < 6$, but for other values, $xy > 6$. If x and y were restricted to nonnegative values, then $xy < 6$. However, if x and y were both negative and sufficiently large, xy would not be less than 6. For example, if $x = y = -3$, then xy would be $(-3)^2$, or 9, which is clearly greater than 6; NOT sufficient.

(2) This restricts x to the interval $\dfrac{1}{3} < x < \dfrac{2}{3}$ and y to the interval $-8 < y < 8$. Thus, the largest value possible for xy is less than $\left(\dfrac{2}{3}\right)(8)$, or less than $5\dfrac{1}{3}$, which is clearly less than 6; SUFFICIENT.

**The correct answer is B;
statement 2 alone is sufficient.**

67. If x, y, and z are positive numbers, is $x > y > z$?

    (1) $xz > yz$
    (2) $yx > yz$

Algebra Inequalities

(1) Dividing both sides of the inequality by z yields $x > y$. However, there is no information relating z to either x or y; NOT sufficient.

(2) Dividing both sides of the inequality by y yields only that $x > z$, with no further information relating y to either x or z; NOT sufficient.

From (1) and (2) it can be determined that x is greater than both y and z. Since it still cannot be determined whether y or z is least, the correct ordering of the three numbers also cannot be determined.

**The correct answer is E;
both statements together are still not sufficient.**

68. An infinite sequence of positive integers is called an "alpha sequence" if the number of even integers in the sequence is finite. If S is an infinite sequence of positive integers, is S an alpha sequence?

    (1) The first ten integers in S are even.
    (2) An infinite number of integers in S are odd.

Arithmetic Properties of numbers

(1) This gives no information about the integers in the sequence S other than the first ten. In addition to the first ten integers in S, there could be any number of other even integers; NOT sufficient.

(2) This statement is irrelevant because, while it gives information about the number of odd integers in sequence S, it gives no information about the number of even integers in S. S could have an infinite number of even integers (as in the case of the set of all positive integers), or S could have a finite number of even integers; NOT sufficient.

Taken together, (1) and (2) do not give enough information about even integers to determine whether sequence S is an alpha sequence.

**The correct answer is E;
both statements together are still not sufficient.**

69. How long did it take Betty to drive nonstop on a trip from her home to Denver, Colorado?

    (1) If Betty's average speed for the trip had been $1\dfrac{1}{2}$ times as fast, the trip would have taken 2 hours.
    (2) Betty's average speed for the trip was 50 miles per hour.

Arithmetic Distance/rate problem

The formula for calculating distance is $rt = d$, where r is the rate in miles per hour, t is the time in hours, and d is the distance in miles.

(1) If Betty had driven $1\frac{1}{2}$ times as fast, then her driving rate could be expressed as $\frac{3}{2}r$. By definition, $\left(\frac{3}{2}r\right)\left(\frac{2}{3}t\right) = rt$; and thus, since Betty's rate was $\frac{3}{2}r$, her time to cover the distance was $\frac{2}{3}t$. Then, because Betty's trip time, $\frac{2}{3}t$, is given as equaling 2 hours, $\frac{2}{3}t = 2$, or $t = 3$; SUFFICIENT.

(2) The distance d that Betty drove is equal to her rate (or speed) multiplied by the time she drove, or rt. The fact that the rate was 50 miles per hour can be expressed as $50t = d$, or as $t = \frac{d}{50}t$, but the time t cannot be determined without knowing the distance; NOT sufficient.

**The correct answer is A;
statement 1 alone is sufficient.**

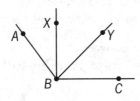

70. In the figure above, what is the measure of $\angle ABC$?

(1) BX bisects $\angle ABY$ and BY bisects $\angle XBC$.
(2) The measure of $\angle ABX$ is 40°.

Geometry Angles

(1) From this, it can be determined that $\angle ABX = \angle XBY$, and $\angle XBY = \angle YBC$ so that all three angles are equal in measure. The measure of $\angle ABC$ cannot be determined without information on the measure of any one of the three equal angles; NOT sufficient.

(2) Part of the measure of $\angle ABC$ is given, but there is no information about the measure of $\angle XBC$; NOT sufficient.

From (1) and (2) together, it can be determined that the measure of $\angle ABX$ = the measure of $\angle XBY$ = the measure of $\angle YBC$ = 40°, so $\angle ABC$ measures 3(40) = 120°.

The correct answer is C; both statements together are sufficient.

71. If x, y, and z are numbers, is $z = 18$?

(1) The average (arithmetic mean) of x, y, and z is 6.
(2) $x = -y$

Arithmetic Statistics

(1) From this, it is known that $\frac{x + y + z}{3} = 6$, or, when both sides are multiplied by 3, $x + y + z = 18$.

Since nothing is known about the value of $x + y$, no conclusion can be drawn about the value of z; NOT sufficient.

(2) This implies that $x + y = 0$ but gives no further information about the values of x, y, and z; NOT sufficient.

Taking (1) and (2) together is sufficient since 0 can be substituted for $x + y$ in the equation $x + y + z = 18$ to yield $z = 18$.

The correct answer is C; both statements together are sufficient.

72. After winning 50 percent of the first 20 games it played, Team A won all of the remaining games it played. What was the total number of games that Team A won?

(1) Team A played 25 games altogether.
(2) Team A won 60 percent of all the games it played.

Arithmetic Percents

Letting r equal the number of the remaining games that the team played, the total number of games that the team played can be expressed as $20 + r$. The fact that the team won 50 percent of its first 20 games can be expressed as .50(20), and it is given that the team won all its remaining games.

Therefore, the total number of games that the team won can be expressed as $.50(20) + r$ or thus as $10 + r$. To solve this problem, the value of r is needed.

(1) If 25 games were played altogether, then $20 + r = 25$, which can be solved for r; SUFFICIENT.

(2) From this, the total number of games won by the team can be expressed as $.60(20 + r)$. Since it is also known that the number of games won by the team is $10 + r$, then $.60(20 + r) = 10 + r$. This equation can be simplified to $12 + .6r = 10 + r$ or $2 = .4r$ and then solved for r; SUFFICIENT.

**The correct answer is D;
each statement alone is sufficient.**

73. Is x between 0 and 1?

(1) x^2 is less than x.
(2) x^3 is positive.

Arithmetic Arithmetic operations

(1) Since x^2 is always positive, it follows that here x must also be positive, that is, greater than 0. Furthermore, if x is greater than 1, then x^2 is also greater than 1. If $x = 0$ or 1, then $x^2 = x$. Therefore, x must be between 0 and 1; SUFFICIENT.

(2) If x^3 is positive, then x is positive, but x can be any positive number; NOT sufficient.

**The correct answer is A;
statement 1 alone is sufficient.**

74. A jar contains 30 marbles, of which 20 are red and 10 are blue. If 9 of the marbles are removed, how many of the marbles left in the jar are red?

(1) Of the marbles removed, the ratio of the number of red ones to the number of blue ones is 2:1.
(2) Of the first 6 marbles removed, 4 are red.

Arithmetic Discrete probability

(1) Of the 9 marbles removed, the ratio of red to blue was 2 to 1; thus 6 red and 3 blue marbles were removed. Since there were originally 20 red marbles in the jar, the number of red marbles remaining in the jar is $20 - 6 = 14$; SUFFICIENT.

(2) Knowing that 4 of the first 6 marbles removed were red does not tell how many of the other 3 marbles removed were red. It cannot be determined how many red marbles were left in the jar; NOT sufficient.

**The correct answer is A;
statement 1 alone is sufficient.**

75. Is p^2 an odd integer?

(1) p is an odd integer.
(2) $\sqrt{p}$ is an odd integer.

Arithmetic Properties of numbers

The product of two or more odd integers is always odd.

(1) Since p is an odd integer, $p \times p$, or p^2, will be an odd integer; SUFFICIENT.

(2) If $\sqrt{p}$ is an odd integer, then $\sqrt{p} \times \sqrt{p} = p$, also an odd number. Therefore, $p \times p$ or p^2 is also an odd integer; SUFFICIENT.

**The correct answer is D;
each statement alone is sufficient.**

76. If $-10 < k < 10$, is $k > 0$?

(1) $\dfrac{1}{k} > 0$
(2) $k^2 > 0$

Algebra Inequalities

(1) If the reciprocal of k, $\dfrac{1}{k}$, is positive, then k must also be positive; SUFFICIENT.

(2) This statement permits k to be positive or negative; NOT sufficient.

**The correct answer is A;
statement 1 alone is sufficient.**

77. What is the value of xy?

    (1) $x + y = 10$
    (2) $x - y = 6$

    Algebra First- and second-degree equations
    + Simultaneous equations

    (1) If $x + y = 10$, then subtracting y from both
         sides results in the equation $x = 10 - y$. Since
         there are two unknowns, there is no way to
         determine either their value or their product;
         NOT sufficient.

    (2) If $x - y = 6$, then adding y to both sides
         results in the equation $x = 6 + y$. Again,
         since there are two unknowns with no way
         to determine either value, their product
         cannot be determined; NOT sufficient.

    Using (1) and (2) together, the two equations can
    be solved simultaneously for x and y. Adding the
    two equations, $x + y = 10$ plus $x - y = 6$, yields
    $2x = 16$, or $x = 8$. Then, substituting for x in the
    first equation gives $(8) + y = 10$ and $y = 2$. Thus,
    xy can be determined to be 16.

    **The correct answer is C;
    both statements together are sufficient.**

78. Is x^2 greater than x?

    (1) x^2 is greater than 1.
    (2) x is greater than -1.

    Arithmetic + Algebra Exponents + Inequalities

    (1) From $x^2 > 1$, it follows that either $x > 1$ or
         $x < -1$. If $x > 1$, multiplying both sides of the
         inequality by x gives $x^2 > x$. Also, for all
         nonzero values of x, $x^2 > 0$. If $x^2 > 0$, then
         clearly $x^2 > -1$. It therefore follows that, if
         $x < -1$ and thus $-1 > x$, then $x^2 > -1 > x$, or
         $x^2 > x$; SUFFICIENT.

    (2) Using $x > -1$ in the given problem, possible
         values of x are:

         $x^2 = \dfrac{1}{4}$, $x = \dfrac{1}{2}$, where thus $x^2 < x$;

         $x^2 = 0$, $x = 0$, where thus $x^2 = x$; and

         $x^2 = 2$, $x = \sqrt{2}$, where thus $x^2 > x$;
         NOT sufficient.

    **The correct answer is A;
    statement 1 alone is sufficient.**

79. Is $y = 6$?

    (1) $y^2 = 36$
    (2) $y^2 - 7y + 6 = 0$

    Algebra First- and second-degree equations

    (1) From this, it cannot be determined
         whether $y = 6$ or $y = -6$; NOT sufficient.

    (2) Factoring this equation yields
         $(y - 6)(y - 1) = 0$, which implies that
         $y = 1$ or $y = 6$. Thus a single numerical
         value of y cannot be determined from this
         equation; NOT sufficient.

    Taking both (1) and (2) together, it can be
    determined that $y = 6$.

    **The correct answer is C;
    both statements together are sufficient.**

80. If $xy > 0$, does $(x - 1)(y - 1) = 1$?

    (1) $x + y = xy$
    (2) $x = y$

    Algebra First- and second-degree equations

    When multiplied, $(x - 1)(y - 1) = xy - y - x + 1$.

    (1) If $x + y = xy$, then $x + y$ can be substituted
         for xy in the equation $(x - 1)(y - 1) = xy - y -$
         $x + 1$, so that $(x - 1)(y - 1) = x + y - y - x + 1$,
         and thus $(x - 1)(y - 1) = 1$; SUFFICIENT.

    (2) Substituting y for x in $(x - 1)(y - 1) = 1$
         gives $(y - 1)(y - 1) = 1$ or thus only that
         $y^2 - 2y + 1 = 1$; this cannot be solved
         uniquely for y; NOT sufficient.

    **The correct answer is A;
    statement 1 alone is sufficient.**

81. The only contents of a parcel are 25 photographs and 30 negatives. What is the total weight, in ounces, of the parcel's contents?

    (1) The weight of each photograph is 3 times the weight of each negative.
    (2) The total weight of 1 of the photographs and 2 of the negatives is $\frac{1}{3}$ ounce.

Algebra Simultaneous equations

Let p and n denote the weight, in ounces, of a photograph and a negative, respectively, and let W denote the total weight of the parcel's contents in ounces. Then the total weight of the parcel's contents can be expressed as $W = 25p + 30n$.

(1) This information can be written as $p = 3n$. When $3n$ is substituted for p in the above equation, $W = 25(3n) + 30n$, the equation cannot be solved for W because there is no way to discover the value of n; NOT sufficient.

(2) This information can be written as $p + 2 = \frac{1}{3}$, or $p = \frac{1}{3} - 2n$. After substituting for p, the equation $W = 25(\frac{1}{3} - 2n) + 30n$ cannot be solved for W because again there is no way to discover the value of n. Similarly, the equation $p + 2n = \frac{1}{3}$ is also equivalent to $2n = \frac{1}{3} - p$, or $n = \frac{1}{6} - \frac{p}{2}$. After substituting for n, the equation

$$W = 25p + 30\left(\frac{1}{6} - \frac{p}{2}\right)$$ cannot be solved

for W because there is no way to discover the value of p; NOT sufficient.

The two linear equations from (1) and (2) can be solved simultaneously for p and n, since $p = 3n$ and $p + 2n = \frac{1}{3}$, where $3n$ can be substituted for p. Thus, by substitution $(3n) + 2n = \frac{1}{3}$, by simplification $5n = \frac{1}{3}$, and by division of both sides by 5 then $n = \frac{1}{15}$. This value of n, $\frac{1}{15}$, can in turn be substituted in $p = 3n$, and a value of $\frac{1}{5}$ can be determined for p. Using these values of n and p,

it is possible to solve the equation $W = 25p + 30n$ and answer the original question about the total weight of the package's contents.

The correct answer is C; both statements together are sufficient.

82. If m and n are consecutive positive integers, is m greater than n?

    (1) $m - 1$ and $n + 1$ are consecutive positive integers.
    (2) m is an even integer.

Arithmetic Properties of numbers

For two integers to be consecutive, the larger integer must be 1 more than the smaller integer. Here, since m and n are consecutive, by definition either $n = m + 1$ or instead $m = n + 1$.

(1) Working out which one of these two equations is true in this case:

    If $\quad n = m + 1$
    then $n + 1 = (m + 1) + 1$ (add 1 to both sides)
    and $\quad n + 1 = m + 2 \quad$ (simplify)

    There is a difference of 3 between $m - 1$ and $m + 2$ (which was shown to equal $n + 1$), and this result contradicts the information that $m - 1$ and $n + 1$ are consecutive integers. Thus, the equation $n = m + 1$ cannot be the one that is true in this case. Therefore, the equation $m = n + 1$ must be true instead, and it follows that $m > n$; SUFFICIENT.

    Alternatively, specific values for m and n can be used to confirm this determination. In the example of $m = 4$, the consecutive number n could be either 3 or 5. So here, $m - 1$ equals 3, and $n + 1$ can equal either 4 or 6. Since (1) states that $m - 1$ and $n + 1$ are consecutive, here n must have the value of 3 rather than 5. As $4 > 3$, the relationship $m > n$ can be shown; SUFFICIENT.

(2) The fact that m is even is irrelevant because it does not contribute to solving the relationship between m and n; NOT sufficient.

The correct answer is A; statement 1 alone is sufficient.

83. If k and n are integers, is n divisible by 7?

    (1) $n - 3 = 2k$
    (2) $2k - 4$ is divisible by 7.

Arithmetic Properties of numbers

(1)   This yields the equation $n = 2k + 3$. The quantity $2k$ will always produce an even number that, when added to 3, will always produce an odd number. However, since not all odd numbers are divisible by 7, the equation $n = 2k + 3$ can yield odd numbers that are or are not divisible by 7; NOT sufficient.

(2)   While $2k - 4$ is divisible by 7, there is no corresponding information about n or the relationship between k and n to determine if n is divisible by 7; NOT sufficient.

Applying both (1) and (2), it is possible to answer the question. Through addition and subtraction, the equation $n = 2k + 3$ from (1) can be expressed as $n = 2k - 4 + 7$. From (2) it is known that the term $(2k - 4)$ of this equation is divisible by 7. Also, 7 is by definition divisible by 7, and n is therefore composed of two terms, both of which are divisible by 7. Therefore, n is divisible by 7.

**The correct answer is C;
both statements together are sufficient.**

84. Is the perimeter of square S greater than the perimeter of equilateral triangle T?

    (1)   The ratio of the length of a side of S to the length of a side of T is 4:5.
    (2)   The sum of the lengths of a side of S and a side of T is 18.

Geometry Perimeter

(1)   Working with the given ratio of $4 : 5$, let $4x$ represent the length of a side of square S, and let $5x$ represent the length of a side of equilateral triangle T. Then, the perimeter of S is $4(4x)$ and the perimeter of T is $3(5x)$. It can therefore be determined that the perimeter of S is greater than the perimeter of T, no matter what the value of x is; SUFFICIENT.

(2)   Many possible pairs of numbers have the sum of 18. For some of these pairs (length of a side of $S = 2$ and length of a side of $T = 16$), the perimeter of S (or 4×2) is less than that of T (or 3×16). For others (length of a side of $S = 12$ and length of a side of $T = 6$), the perimeter of S (or 4×12) is greater than that of T (or 3×6); NOT sufficient.

**The correct answer is A;
statement 1 alone is sufficient.**

85. If $x + y + z > 0$, is $z > 1$?

    (1) $z > x + y + 1$
    (2) $x + y + 1 < 0$

Algebra Inequalities

(1)   First, if $x + y + z > 0$, then, by subtracting z from both sides, it can be determined that $x + y > -z$. To see if it is possible to solve for z, add 1 to both sides of the inequality $x + y > -z$ to get $x + y + 1 > -z + 1$. It is given here that $z > x + y + 1$, so it follows that $z > x + y + 1 > -z + 1$. From this, $z > -z + 1$. By adding z to both sides to get $2z > 1$, and then dividing both sides by 2, it can only be determined that $z > \dfrac{1}{2}$ or 0.5. There are many opportunities for z to be a value between 0.5 and 1, for example, if $z = 0.7$, then $z < 1$. So this information does not conclusively prove that $z > 1$; NOT sufficient.

(2)   The inequality $x + y + 1 < 0$ is equivalent to $x + y < -1$ by subtracting 1 from both sides. It was given in the question that $x + y + z > 0$, and since $x + y < -1$, the only way for $x + y + z > 0$ is for z to be at least greater than 1; SUFFICIENT.

**The correct answer is B;
statement 2 alone is sufficient.**

86. Can the positive integer n be written as the sum of two different positive prime numbers?

    (1) n is greater than 3.
    (2) n is odd.

Arithmetic Properties of numbers

The prime numbers are 2, 3, 5, 7, 11, 13, 17, 19, etc., that is, those integers $p > 1$ whose only positive factors are 1 and p.

(1) If $n = 5$, then n can be written as the sum of two different primes ($5 = 2 + 3$). If $n = 4$, however, then n cannot be written as the sum of two different primes. (Note that while $4 = 1 + 3 = 2 + 2$, neither of these sums satisfies both requirements of the question.) This value of n does not allow an answer to be determined; NOT sufficient.

(2) While some odd integers can be written as the sum of two different primes (e.g., $5 = 2 + 3$), others cannot (e.g., 11). This value of n does not allow an answer to be determined; NOT sufficient.

Since the sum of two odd integers is always even, for an odd integer greater than 3 to be the sum of two prime numbers, one of those prime numbers must be an even number. The only even prime number is 2. Thus, the only odd integers that can be expressed as the sum of two different prime numbers are those for which $n - 2$ is an odd prime number. Using the example of 11 (an odd integer greater than 3), $11 - 2 = 9$, which is not a prime number. Statements (1) and (2) together do not define n well enough to determine the answer.

**The correct answer is E;
both statements together are still not sufficient.**

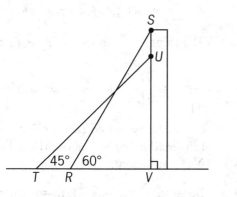

87. In the figure above, segments *RS* and *TU* represent two positions of the same ladder leaning against the side *SV* of a wall. The length of *TV* is how much greater than the length of *RV*?

(1) The length of *TU* is 10 meters.
(2) The length of *RV* is 5 meters.

Geometry Triangles

The Pythagorean Theorem ($a^2 + b^2 = c^2$) can be applied here. Since the triangle *TUV* is a 45°–45°–90° triangle, the lengths of the sides are in the ratio $1 : 1 : \sqrt{2}$; so the length of any one side determines the length of the other two sides. Similarly, the triangle *RSV* is a 30°–60°–90° triangle with the lengths of the sides in the ratio $1 : \sqrt{3} : 2$; so the length of any one side determines the length of the other two sides. Also, the length of the hypotenuse is the same in both triangles, because it is the length of the ladder. Hence, the length of any one side of either triangle determines the lengths of all sides of both triangles.

(1) Since the length of one side of *TUV* is given, the length of any side of either triangle can be found. Therefore, the difference between *TV* and *RV* can also be found; SUFFICIENT.

(2) Since the length of one side of *RSV* is given, the length of any side of either triangle can be found. Therefore, the difference between *TV* and *RV* can also be found; SUFFICIENT.

**The correct answer is D;
both statements alone are sufficient.**

88. Is the integer *x* divisible by 36?

(1) *x* is divisible by 12.
(2) *x* is divisible by 9.

Arithmetic Properties of numbers

When discussing divisibility, it is helpful to express a number as the product of prime factors. The integer 36 can be expressed as the product of prime numbers, i.e., $36 = 2 \times 2 \times 3 \times 3$. If *x* is divisible by 36, it would follow that when *x* is expressed as a product of prime numbers, this product would contain at least two 2's and two 3's (from the prime factorization of 36).

(1) The prime factorization of 12 is 12 = $2 \times 2 \times 3$, which implies that the prime factorization of x contains at least two 2's and at least one 3. This does not contain at least two 2's and two 3's, but does not exclude these factors, either; NOT sufficient.

(2) The prime factorization of 9 is 9 = 3×3, which implies that the prime factorization of x contains at least two 3's. Again, this does not contain at least two 2's and two 3's, but does not exclude these factors, either; NOT sufficient.

However, both (1) and (2) together imply that the prime factorization of x contains at least two 2's (1) and two 3's (2), so x must be divisible by 36.

**The correct answer is C;
both statements together are sufficient.**

Cancellation Fees	
Days Prior to Departure	Percent of Package Price
46 or more	10%
45–31	35%
30–16	50%
15–5	65%
4 or fewer	100%

89. The table above shows the cancellation fee schedule that a travel agency uses to determine the fee charged to a tourist who cancels a trip prior to departure. If a tourist canceled a trip with a package price of $1,700 and a departure date of September 4, on what day was the trip canceled?

(1) The cancellation fee was $595.
(2) If the trip had been canceled one day later, the cancellation fee would have been $255 more.

Arithmetic Percents

(1) The cancellation fee given is $\frac{\$595}{\$1,700} = 35\%$ of the package price, which is the percent charged for cancellation 45-31 days prior to the departure date of September 4. However, there is no further information to determine exactly when within this interval the trip was cancelled; NOT sufficient.

(2) This implies that the increase in the cancellation fee for canceling one day later would have been $\frac{\$595}{\$1,700} = 15\%$ of the package price. The $1,700 cancellation could thus have occurred either 31 days or 16 days prior to the departure date of September 4 because the cancellation fee would have increased by that percentage either 30 days before departure or 15 days before departure. However, there is no further information to establish whether the interval before departure was 31 days or 16 days; NOT sufficient.

Taking (1) and (2) together establishes that the trip was canceled 31 days prior to September 4.

**The correct answer is C;
both statements together are sufficient.**

90. What is the value of $\frac{x}{yz}$?

(1) $x = \frac{y}{2}$ and $z = \frac{2x}{5}$.

(2) $\frac{x}{z} = \frac{5}{2}$ and $\frac{1}{y} = \frac{1}{10}$.

Algebra Evaluating expressions

(1) From this, z can be expressed in terms of y by substituting $\frac{y}{2}$ for x in the equation $z = \frac{2x}{5}$, which gives $z = \frac{2\left(\frac{y}{2}\right)}{5} = \frac{y}{5}$. The value of $\frac{x}{yz}$ in terms of y is then $\frac{\frac{y}{2}}{y\left(\frac{y}{5}\right)} = \frac{y}{2}\left(\frac{5}{y^2}\right) = \frac{5}{2y}$. This expression cannot be evaluated further since no information is given about the value of y; NOT sufficient.

(2) Because $\frac{x}{yz} = \left(\frac{1}{y}\right)\left(\frac{x}{z}\right)$, by substitution the given information can be stated as $\left(\frac{1}{10}\right)\left(\frac{5}{2}\right)$, or $\frac{1}{4}$; SUFFICIENT.

**The correct answer is B;
statement 2 alone is sufficient.**

91. If *P* and *Q* are each circular regions, what is the radius of the larger of these regions?

    (1) The area of *P* plus the area of *Q* is equal to 90π.
    (2) The larger circular region has a radius that is 3 times the radius of the smaller circular region.

Geometry Circles

The area of a circle with a radius of *r* is equal to πr^2. For this problem, let *r* represent the radius of the smaller circular region, and let *R* represent the radius of the larger circular region.

(1) This can be expressed as $\pi r^2 + \pi R^2 = 90\pi$, which means that, when all terms are divided by π, $r^2 + R^2 = 90$, and this is not enough information to determine *R*; NOT sufficient.

(2) This can be expressed as $R = 3r$, which by itself is not enough to determine *R*; NOT sufficient.

Using (1) and (2), the value of *R*, or the radius of the larger circular region, can be determined. In (2), $R = 3r$, and thus $r = \frac{R}{3}$. Therefore, $\frac{R}{3}$ can be substituted for *r* in the equation $\pi r^2 + \pi R^2 = 90\pi$ from (1). The result is the following single equation in *R* that can be worked to determine *R*:

$\pi\left(\frac{R}{3}\right)^2 + \pi R^2 = 90\pi$. Remember that it is only necessary to establish the sufficiency of the data; there is no need to solve the problem.

The correct answer is C; both statements together are sufficient.

92. If *x* and *y* are positive, what is the value of *x*?

    (1) 200 percent of *x* equals 400 percent of *y*.
    (2) *xy* is the square of a positive integer.

Arithmetic Arithmetic operations + Percents

(1) From this, it can only be determined that $x = 2y$. This equation has an infinite number of solutions, so a single value of *x* cannot be determined; NOT sufficient.

(2) From this, it can only be determined that $xy = k^2$, where *k* is a positive integer. This equation also has an infinite number of solutions, so a single value of *x* cannot be determined; NOT sufficient.

If (1) and (2) are taken together, the two equations have three unknowns and cannot be solved for a unique value of *x*.

The correct answer is E; both statements together are still not sufficient.

93. If Aaron, Lee, and Tony have a total of $36, how much money does Tony have?

    (1) Tony has twice as much money as Lee and $\frac{1}{3}$ as much as Aaron.
    (2) The sum of the amounts of money that Tony and Lee have is half the amount that Aaron has.

Algebra Applied problem + Equations

(1) From this, it can be determined that Lee has *x* dollars, Tony has 2*x* dollars, Aaron has 6*x* dollars, and together they have $9x = 36$ dollars, or $x = 4$. Thus, the amount that Tony has can be determined $(2x = 8)$; SUFFICIENT.

(2) If the sum of the amounts that Tony and Lee have is *y* dollars, then Aaron has 2*y* dollars, and *y* can be determined $(3y = 36$, or $y = 12)$. However, the individual amounts for Tony and Lee cannot be determined; NOT sufficient.

The correct answer is A; statement 1 alone is sufficient.

94. Is *z* less than 0?

    (1) $xy > 0$ and $yz < 0$.
    (2) $x > 0$

Arithmetic Properties of numbers

When multiplying positive and negative numbers, that is, numbers greater than 0 and numbers less than 0, the products must always be (positive)(positive) = positive, (negative)(negative) = positive, and (negative)(positive) = negative.

(1) Many sets of values consistent with this statement can be found when using values of z that are greater than, less than, or equal to 1. For example, the set of values $x = 1$, $y = 1$, $z = -1$ and the set of values $x = -1$, $y = -1$, $z = 1$ both yield values of z that are less than or equal to 1; NOT sufficient.

(2) This gives no information about z or y, and the information about x is not useful in determining the positive or negative value of the other variables; NOT sufficient.

Taken together, since from (1) $xy > 0$, and from (2) $x > 0$, y must also be greater than 0, that is, positive. Then, since $y > 0$ and from (1) $yz < 0$, it can be concluded that z must be negative, or less than 0, since the product of yz is negative.

The correct answer is C;
both statements together are sufficient.

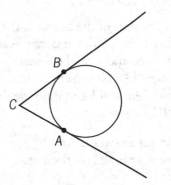

95. The circular base of an above-ground swimming pool lies in a level yard and just touches two straight sides of a fence at points A and B, as shown in the figure above. Point C is on the ground where the two sides of the fence meet. How far from the center of the pool's base is point A?

(1) The base has area 250 square feet.
(2) The center of the base is 20 feet from point C.

Geometry Circles

Let Q be the center of the pool's base and r be the distance from Q to A, as shown in the figure below.

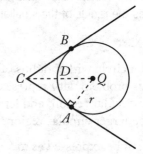

Since A is a point on the circular base, QA is a radius (r) of the base. The area of the circle = πr^2.

(1) Since the formula for the area of a circle is Area = πr^2, this information can stated as $250 = \pi r^2$ or $\dfrac{\sqrt{250}}{\sqrt{\pi}} = r$, which can be solved for r; SUFFICIENT.

(2) Since CA is tangent to the base, $\triangle QAC$ is a right triangle. It is given that $QC = 20$, but there is not enough information to use the Pythagorean theorem to determine the length of QA; NOT sufficient.

The correct answer is A;
statement 1 alone is sufficient.

96. If $xy = -6$, what is the value of $xy(x + y)$?

(1) $x - y = 5$
(2) $xy^2 = 18$

Algebra First- and second-degree equations

By substituting -6 as the value of xy, the question can be simplified to "What is the value of $-6(x + y)$?"

(1) If $x - y = 5$, then $x = y + 5$ when y is added to both sides. When $y + 5$ is substituted for x in the equation $xy = -6$, the equation yields $(y + 5)y = -6$, or $y^2 + 5y + 6 = 0$. Factoring this equation gives $(y + 2)(y + 3) = 0$. Thus y may have a value of -2 or -3. Since a single value of y is not known, neither the value of x nor the value of $x + y$ can be determined; NOT sufficient.

(2)   Since $xy^2 = (xy)y$, it follows that $xy^2 = (xy)y = 18$. When -6 is substituted for xy, this equation yields $-6y = 18$, thus $y = -3$. Since $y = -3$ and $xy = -6$, it follows that $x = 2$. Therefore, the value of $x + y$ and thus of $-6(x + y)$ can be determined; SUFFICIENT.

**The correct answer is B;
statement 2 alone is sufficient.**

97.   If the average (arithmetic mean) of 4 numbers is 50, how many of the numbers are greater than 50?

(1)   None of the four numbers is equal to 50.
(2)   Two of the numbers are equal to 25.

Arithmetic Statistics

The mean of 4 numbers, w, x, y, and $z = 50$ can be represented by the equation:

$$\frac{w + x + y + z}{4} = 50$$

(1)   The only information about the four numbers is that none is equal to 50. If the four numbers were 25, 25, 26, and 124, their average would be 50. If the four numbers were 25, 25, 75, and 75, their average would also be 50. Many sets of numbers would satisfy this statement; NOT sufficient.

(2)   In the previous example of 25, 25, 26, and 124, which also satisfies this statement, only one number is greater than 50. In the second example of 25, 25, 75, and 75, which again satisfies this statement, two of the numbers are greater than 50. Here as well, there is no way to determine the four numbers; NOT sufficient.

As shown in (2), it is possible to offer multiple examples that can satisfy the givens in both (1) and (2).

**The correct answer is E;
both statements together are still not sufficient.**

98.   Is the positive square root of x an integer?

(1) $x = n^4$ and n is an integer.
(2) $x = 16$

Arithmetic Arithmetic operations + Properties of numbers

(1)   If n is an integer, then n^2 is also an integer. Since the positive square root of x is here equal to n^2, the positive square root of x is also an integer; SUFFICIENT.

(2)   Since the positive square root of 16 is the integer 4, the positive square root of x is here an integer; SUFFICIENT.

**The correct answer is D;
each statement alone is sufficient.**

99.   If x is a positive number less than 10, is z greater than the average (arithmetic mean) of x and 10?

(1)   On the number line, z is closer to 10 than it is to x.
(2) $z = 5x$

Arithmetic + Algebra Statistics + Inequalities

(1)   The average of x and 10 is $\frac{x + 10}{2}$, which is necessarily the number (or point) half the distance between x and 10 on the number line. Here it is given that, on the number line, z is closer to 10 than it is to x. So, with the average of x and 10 being the number half way between x and 10, and with z being closer to 10 than it is to x, z must lie beyond the half-way point between x and 10 and must thus be greater than the average of x and 10; SUFFICIENT.

(2)   If, for example, $x = 1$, then $z = 5$. In this case, the average of x and 10 is $\frac{1 + 10}{2} = 5.5$, which is greater than z. If, however, $x = 1.6$, then $z = 8$, and the average of 1.6 and 10 is $\frac{1.6 + 10}{2} = 5.8$, which is less than z; NOT sufficient.

**The correct answer is A;
statement 1 alone is sufficient.**

100.   If n is an integer, is $n + 2$ a prime number?

(1) n is a prime number.
(2) $n + 1$ is <u>not</u> a prime number.

Arithmetic Properties of numbers

For problems such as this, testing the truth of two or three values of n can be helpful.

(1) Consider the prime numbers 2, 3, or 7, as examples. For these values, $n + 2 = 4$, 5, or 9, respectively, with 5 as the only prime number. Therefore $n + 2$ is not necessarily a prime number; NOT sufficient.

(2) If $n = 3$ or 7, then $n + 1 = 4$ or 8, which are not prime numbers. Additionally, $n + 2 = 5$ or 9. Again, $n + 2$ is not necessarily a prime number; NOT sufficient.

Neither (1) nor (2) gives any definitive information about $n + 2$, and taken together they are still not sufficient to determine whether $n + 2$ is a prime number.

**The correct answer is E;
both statements together are still not sufficient.**

101. If $t \neq 0$, is r greater than zero?

    (1) $rt = 12$
    (2) $r + t = 7$

Arithmetic + Algebra Arithmetic operations + Properties of numbers + Simultaneous equations

(1) Since the product of rt is positive, r and t can be either both positive or both negative; NOT sufficient.

(2) In this case, both r and t can be positive (e.g., $r = 3$ and $t = 4$) or r can be positive and t can be negative (e.g., $r = 10$ and $t = -4$) or t can be positive and r negative (e.g., $t = 10$ and $r = -3$); NOT sufficient.

If (1) and (2) are considered together, the system of equations can be solved to show that r must be positive. From (2), since $r + t = 7$, then $t = 7 - r$. Substituting this value for t in the equation of (1) and working through the problem by simplifying and factoring yields positive 3 or positive 4 for the value of r.

$$rt = 12$$
$r(7 - r) = 12$	substitution
$7r - r^2 = 12$	distribution property
$r^2 - 7r + 12 = 0$	bring all terms to one side
$(r - 4)(r - 3) = 0$	factor
$r = 3$ or $r = 4$	solve for r

**The correct answer is C;
both statements together are sufficient.**

102. Is $\dfrac{x}{m}(m^2 + n^2 + k^2) = xm + yn + zk$?

    (1) $\dfrac{z}{k} = \dfrac{x}{m}$

    (2) $\dfrac{x}{m} = \dfrac{y}{n}$

Algebra First- and second-degree equations

The equation $\dfrac{x}{m}(m^2 + n^2 + k^2) = xm + yn + zk$ becomes $x(m^2 + n^2 + k^2) = m(xm + yn + zk)$ when both sides of the equation are multiplied by m. When simplified, this is equivalent to $xm^2 + xn^2 + xk^2 = m^2x + myn + mzk$. This in turn is equivalent to $xn^2 + xk^2 = myn + mzk$ when xm^2 is subtracted from both sides of the equation.

(1) When cross-multiplied, $\dfrac{z}{k} = \dfrac{x}{m}$ becomes $xk = mz$. Looking above for any familiar terms, note that when both sides of the equation $xk = mz$ are multiplied by k, it yields $xk^2 = mzk$, 2 terms in the above equation. However, it cannot be determined whether $xn^2 + xk^2 = myn + mzk$, since it cannot be concluded that $xn^2 = myn$; NOT sufficient.

(2) When cross-multiplied, $\dfrac{x}{m} = \dfrac{y}{n}$ becomes $xn = my$. Again looking above, when both sides of this equation are multiplied by n, it yields $xn^2 = myn$. However, it cannot be concluded that $xn^2 + xk^2 = myn + mzk$ unless it is known that $xk^2 = mzk$; NOT sufficient.

Combining the information in both (1) and (2) gives $xn^2 + xk^2 = myn + mzk$.

**The correct answer is C;
both statements together are sufficient.**

103. If $R = \dfrac{8x}{3y}$ and $y \neq 0$, what is the value of R?

    (1) $x = \dfrac{2}{3}$

    (2) $x = 2y$

Algebra First- and second-degree equations

(1)   If $\dfrac{2}{3}$ is substituted for x in the given equation, the resultant equation is $R = \dfrac{8\left(\dfrac{2}{3}\right)}{3y}$ or $R = \dfrac{\dfrac{16}{3}}{3y}$. The value of R cannot be determined since the value of y is not known; NOT sufficient.

(2)   When $2y$ is substituted for x in the original equation, it yields $R = \dfrac{8x}{3y} = \dfrac{8(2y)}{3y} = \dfrac{16}{3}$; SUFFICIENT.

**The correct answer is B;
statement 2 alone is sufficient.**

104. A bookstore that sells used books sells each of its paperback books for a certain price and each of its hardcover books for a certain price. If Joe, Maria, and Paul bought books in this store, how much did Maria pay for 1 paperback book and 1 hardcover book?

    (1)   Joe bought 2 paperback books and 3 hardcover books for $12.50.

    (2)   Paul bought 4 paperback books and 6 hardcover books for $25.00.

Algebra Applied problems

Let p be the price for each paperback book, and let h be the price for each hardcover book.

(1)   From this, Joe's purchase can be expressed as $2p + 3h = \$12.50$. Without more information, this equation alone cannot determine the cost of 1 paperback and 1 hardcover book; NOT sufficient.

(2)   This statement is equivalent to $4p + 6h = \$25.00$. If both sides of this equation are divided by 2, it gives exactly the same equation as in (1); NOT sufficient.

Since (1) and (2) are the same equation that cannot be solved, taken together they cannot determine the cost of each type of book.

**The correct answer is E;
both statements together are still not sufficient.**

105. If x, y, and z are positive, is $x = \dfrac{y}{z^2}$?

    (1) $z = \dfrac{y}{xz}$

    (2) $z = \sqrt{\dfrac{y}{x}}$

Algebra First- and second-degree equations

(1)   Since x, y, and z are positive, both sides of the equation can be multiplied by $\dfrac{x}{z}$ to get $\left(\dfrac{x}{z}\right)z = \dfrac{y}{xz}\left(\dfrac{x}{z}\right)$, which can be simplified to $x = \dfrac{y}{z^2}$; SUFFICIENT.

(2)   If both sides of the equation $z = \sqrt{\dfrac{y}{x}}$ are squared, the result is $z^2 = \dfrac{y}{x}$. If both sides are then divided by z^2, to get $1 = \dfrac{y}{xz^2}$, and finally multiplied by x, the result is $x = \dfrac{y}{z^2}$; SUFFICIENT.

**The correct answer is D;
each statement alone is sufficient.**

106. If n is an integer between 2 and 100 and if n is also the square of an integer, what is the value of n?

    (1) n is even.

    (2)   The cube root of n is an integer.

Arithmetic Properties of numbers

(1) If n is even, there are several possible even values of n that are squares of integers and are between 2 and 100, namely, 4, 16, 36, and 64; NOT sufficient.

(2) If the cube root of n is an integer, it means that n must not only be the square of an integer but also the cube of an integer. There is only one such value of n between 2 and 100, which is 64; SUFFICIENT.

**The correct answer is B;
statement 2 alone is sufficient.**

107. For a certain set of n numbers, where $n > 1$, is the average (arithmetic mean) equal to the median?

(1) If the n numbers in the set are listed in increasing order, then the difference between any pair of successive numbers in the set is 2.

(2) The range of the n numbers in the set is $2(n-1)$.

Arithmetic Statistics

(1) From this the numbers can be written as x, $x + 2$, $x + 4$, etc. If n is odd, then the median is the middle number, which will also be the average. For example, if $n = 5$, the numbers are x, $x + 2$, $x + 4$, $x + 6$, $x + 8$. The average is the sum divided by 5 or $\dfrac{5x + 20}{5} = x + 4$, which is the middle number or median. If n is even, the median is the average of the two middle numbers, which will also be the average of all the numbers. For example, if $n = 6$, then, adding $x + 10$ to the five numbers above, the average is $\dfrac{6x + 30}{6} = x + 5$, which equals $\dfrac{(x + 4) + (x + 6)}{2}$, or the median; SUFFICIENT.

(2) The range is the difference between the least and greatest numbers. Knowing the range, however, does not give information about the rest of the numbers affecting the average and the median. For example, if $n = 3$, then the range $2(3 - 1)$ of the three numbers is 4. However, the numbers could be 2, 4, 6, for which the average (4) is equal to the median, or the numbers could be 2, 3, 6, for which the average (3.7) is greater than the median (3); NOT sufficient.

**The correct answer is A;
statement 1 alone is sufficient.**

108. If d is a positive integer, is $\sqrt{d}$ an integer?

(1) d is the square of an integer.
(2) $\sqrt{d}$ is the square of an integer.

Arithmetic Properties of numbers

The square of an integer must also be an integer.

(1) This can be expressed as $d = x^2$, where x is a nonzero integer. Then, $\sqrt{d} = \sqrt{x^2}$, which in turn equals x or $-x$, depending on whether x is a positive integer or a negative integer, respectively. In either case, $\sqrt{d}$ is also an integer; SUFFICIENT.

(2) This can be expressed as $\sqrt{d} = x^2$, where x is a nonzero integer. The square of an integer (x^2) must always be an integer; therefore, $\sqrt{d}$ must also be an integer; SUFFICIENT.

**The correct answer is D;
each statement alone is sufficient.**

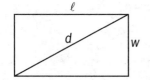

109. What is the area of the rectangular region above?

    (1) $\ell + w = 6$
    (2) $d^2 = 20$

Geometry Area

The formula for the area of the rectangular region is $\ell \times w$.

(1)   If w is subtracted from both sides of this equation, then $\ell = 6 - w$. If this value for ℓ is substituted in the equation $A = \ell \times w$, it becomes $A = (6 - w)w$, or $A = 6w - w^2$, which cannot be solved because the value of w is unknown; NOT sufficient.

(2)   When the length of the diagonal of a rectangle is known, the Pythagorean theorem can sometimes be applied to determine the length or the width of the rectangle. However, *both* the length and width cannot be determined if only the length of the diagonal is known. Since the length and width cannot be determined from this information, the area of the rectangle cannot be determined; NOT sufficient.

The Pythagorean theorem ($a^2 + b^2 = c^2$, where a and b are legs of a right triangle and c is the hypotenuse) can be applied when (1) and (2) are taken together. In this case the hypotenuse is the diagonal d, and from (2) the Pythagorean theorem yields the equation $\ell^2 + w^2 = d^2$, or $\ell^2 + w^2 = 20$. If both sides of the equation from (1) are squared, then $(\ell + w)^2 = 36$, or $\ell^2 + 2\ell w + w^2 = 36$. By regrouping and substituting the established value of $\ell^2 + w^2$, then $20 + 2\ell w = 36$, and $2\ell w = 16$. Thus, $\ell w = 8$, and the area of the rectangle is known.

**The correct answer is C;
both statements together are sufficient.**

110. Is the positive integer n a multiple of 24?

    (1) n is a multiple of 4.
    (2) n is a multiple of 6.

Arithmetic Properties of numbers

(1)   This says only that n is a multiple of 4 (i.e., n could be 8 or 24), some of which would be multiples of 24 and some would not; NOT sufficient.

(2)   This says only that n is a multiple of 6 (i.e., n could be 12 or 48), some of which would be multiples of 24 and some would not; NOT sufficient.

Both statements together imply only that n is a multiple of the least common multiple of 4 and 6. The smallest integer that is divisible by both 4 and 6 is 12. Some of the multiples of 12 (e.g., n could be 48 or 36) are also multiples of 24, but some are not.

**The correct answer is E;
both statements together are still not sufficient.**

111. If x is a positive integer and w is a negative integer, what is the value of xw?

    (1) $x^w = \dfrac{1}{2}$
    (2) $w = -1$

Arithmetic Arithmetic operations

If x is a positive integer, then $x^{-r} = \dfrac{1}{x^r}$.

(1)   Since x is a positive integer and w is a negative integer, the only values for which x^w can equal $\dfrac{1}{2}$ are $x = 2$ and $w = -1$, that is, $2^{-1} = \dfrac{1}{2}$. Therefore, $xw = (2)(-1) = -2$; SUFFICIENT.

(2)   This does not mention x, so the value of xw cannot be evaluated; NOT sufficient.

**The correct answer is A;
statement 1 alone is sufficient.**

112. If x is an integer, is y an integer?

    (1) The average (arithmetic mean) of x, y, and $y - 2$ is x.
    (2) The average (arithmetic mean) of x and y is <u>not</u> an integer.

Arithmetic Statistics + Properties of numbers

(1) From this, it is known that
$\dfrac{x + y + (y - 2)}{3} = x$, or:

$x + y + y - 2 = 3x$ multiply both sides by 3

$2y - 2 = 2x$ combine like terms; subtract x from both sides

$y - 1 = x$ divide both sides by 2

This simplifies to $y = x + 1$. Since x is an integer, this equation shows that x and y are consecutive integers; SUFFICIENT.

(2) According to this, y might be an integer (e.g., $x = 5$ and $y = 6$, with an average of 5.5), or y might not be an integer (e.g., $x = 5$ and $y = 6.2$, with an average of 5.6); NOT sufficient.

The correct answer is A; statement 1 alone is sufficient.

113. In the fraction $\dfrac{x}{y}$, where x and y are positive integers, what is the value of y?

    (1) The least common denominator of $\dfrac{x}{y}$ and $\dfrac{1}{3}$ is 6.
    (2) $x = 1$

Arithmetic Properties of numbers

(1) From this, $\dfrac{x}{y}$ can be $\dfrac{x}{2}$ or $\dfrac{x}{6}$, but there is no way to know whether $y = 2$ or $y = 6$; NOT sufficient.

(2) From this, y could be any positive integer; NOT sufficient.

If both (1) and (2) are taken together, $\dfrac{x}{y} = \dfrac{1}{2}$ or $\dfrac{1}{6}$, and again y is either 2 or 6.

The correct answer is E; both statements together are still not sufficient.

114. Is $\dfrac{1}{a - b} < b - a$?

    (1) $a < b$
    (2) $1 < |a - b|$

Arithmetic + Algebra Arithmetic operations + Inequalities

(1) From this, it is known that $\dfrac{1}{a - b}$ is negative and $b - a$ is positive. Therefore, $\dfrac{1}{a - b} < b - a$; SUFFICIENT.

(2) From this statement that the absolute value of $a - b$ is greater than 1, $a - b$ could be either positive or negative. If $a - b$ is positive, then $b - a$ is negative and $\dfrac{1}{a - b} > b - a$. However, if $a - b$ is negative, then $b - a$ is positive and $\dfrac{1}{a - b} < b - a$. For example, if $a = 7$ and $b = 4$, then $\dfrac{1}{3} > -3$, but if $a = 4$ and $b = 7$, then $-\dfrac{1}{3} < 3$; NOT sufficient.

The correct answer is A; statement 1 alone is sufficient.

115. If x and y are nonzero integers, is $x^y < y^x$?

    (1) $x = y^2$
    (2) $y > 2$

Arithmetic + Algebra Arithmetic operations + Inequalities

It is helpful to note that $(x^r)^s = x^{rs}$.

(1) From this, $x = y^2$, so by substitution then $x = (y^2)^y$, or y^{2y}, and $y = y^{y^2}$. Comparing x^y to y^x can then be done by comparing y^{2y} to y^{y^2}, or simply comparing the exponents $2y$ to y^2. If, for example, $y = 2$, then $2y = 4$ and $y^2 = 4$, and then x^y would equal y^x. If, however, $y = 3$, then $2y = 6$ and $y^2 = 9$, and so x^y would be less than y^x; NOT sufficient.

(2) It is known that $y > 2$, but no information about x is given; NOT sufficient.

If both (1) and (2) are taken together, then $2y$ is compared to y^2 (1) and from (2) it is known that $y > 2$, so $2y$ will always be less than y^2. Therefore, $x^y < y^x$.

The correct answer is C;
both statements together are sufficient.

116. If x is a positive integer, is $\sqrt{x}$ an integer?

    (1) $\sqrt{4x}$ is an integer.
    (2) $\sqrt{3x}$ is not an integer.

Arithmetic Arithmetic operations + Properties of numbers

Note that $\sqrt{xy}$ can be separated into $(\sqrt{x})(\sqrt{y})$.

    (1) Since $\sqrt{4x}$ is an integer, it follows that $4x$ must be the square of an integer. Clearly, 4 is the square of the integer 2. For $4x$ to be the square of an integer as well, x must also be the square of an integer. Therefore $\sqrt{x}$ must be an integer; SUFFICIENT.

    (2) If x is the square of an integer, for instance 4, then $\sqrt{3x}$ is not an integer and $\sqrt{x}$ is an integer. However, if x is not the square of an integer, for instance 2, then $\sqrt{3x}$ is still not an integer, and $\sqrt{x}$ is also not an integer; NOT sufficient.

The correct answer is A;
statement 1 alone is sufficient.

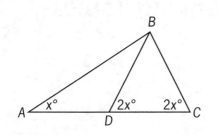

117. In triangle ABC above, what is the length of side BC?

    (1) Line segment AD has length 6.
    (2) $x = 36$

Geometry Triangles

The degree measure of an exterior angle of a triangle is equal to the sum of the remote interior angles. Note that angle BDC (with an angle measure of $2x$) is an exterior angle of triangle ADB and has an angle measure equal to the sum of the remote interior angles ABD and DAB. Thus, if angle ABD has measure $y°$, then $x + y = 2x$, or when simplified, $y = x$. Since two angles of triangle ABD are equal, then the sides opposite these angles have the same length and $AD = DB$. For the same reason $DB = BC$. If $AD = DB$ and $DB = BC$, then $AD = BC$.

    (1) If $AD = 6$, then BC must also equal 6; SUFFICIENT.

    (2) Since this gives no information about the length of any line segments, the length of side BC cannot be determined; NOT sufficient.

The correct answer is A;
statement 1 alone is sufficient.

118. If $rs \neq 0$, is $\dfrac{1}{r} + \dfrac{1}{s} = 4$?

    (1) $r + s = 4rs$
    (2) $r = s$

Algebra First- and second-degree equations

    (1) If all terms of this equation were divided by rs, the result would be $\dfrac{r}{rs} + \dfrac{s}{rs} = \dfrac{4rs}{rs}$, or $\dfrac{1}{s} + \dfrac{1}{r} = 4$; SUFFICIENT.

    (2) If $r = s = \dfrac{1}{2}$, then $\dfrac{1}{r} + \dfrac{1}{s} = 4$, but if $r = s = 1$, then $\dfrac{1}{s} + \dfrac{1}{r} = 2$; NOT sufficient.

The correct answer is A;
statement 1 alone is sufficient.

Appendix A   Percentile Ranking Tables

Table 1			
Percentages of Examinees Tested from July 2004 through June 2007 (including Repeaters) Who Scored Below Specified Verbal Scores			
Verbal Scaled Score	Percentage Below	Verbal Scaled Score	Percentage Below
46–51	99	26	42
45	98	25	37
44	97	24	35
43	96	23	30
42	95	22	28
41	93	21	24
40	89	20	20
39	88	19	17
38	84	18	15
37	82	17	12
36	80	16	10
35	75	15	8
34	70	14	7
33	68	13	5
32	65	12	4
31	60	11	3
30	57	10	2
29	55	9	1
28	50	7–8	1
27.5	44	0–6	0

Number of Candidates = 616,490
Mean = 27.5
Standard deviation = 9.0

Table 2

Percentages of Examinees Tested from July 2004 through June 2007
(including Repeaters)
Who Scored Below Specified Quantitative Scores

Quantitative Scaled Score	Percentage Below	Quantitative Scaled Score	Percentage Below
51	99	28	25
50	95	27	21
49	89	26	20
48	85	25	16
47	81	24	15
46	79	23	14
45	77	22	11
44	72	21	10
43	70	20	9
42	66	19	8
41	63	18	7
40	61	17	5
39	57	16	4
38	55	15	4
37	52	14	4
36	48	13	3
35.2	44	12	2
34	42	11	2
33	40	10	1
32	36	9	1
31	32	8	1
30	30	7	1
29	26	0–6	0

Number of Candidates = 616,490
Mean = 35.2
Standard deviation = 10.6

Table 3

Percentages of Examinees Tested from July 2004 through June 2007
(including Repeaters)
Who Scored Below Specified Total Scores

Total Scaled Score	Percentage Below	Total Scaled Score	Percentage Below
760–800	99	510	41
750	98	500	38
740	97	490	35
730	96	480	33
720	95	470	30
710	93	460	26
700	92	450	24
690	90	440	22
680	88	430	20
670	87	420	18
660	84	410	16
650	82	400	14
640	78	390	12
630	77	380	11
620	74	370	10
610	71	360	8
600	68	350	7
590	65	340	6
580	62	330	5
570	59	320	4
560	56	290–310	3
550	53	260–280	2
540	50	230-250	1
530	45	200–220	0
520	44		

Number of Candidates = 616,490
Mean = 530
Standard deviation = 118.6

Table 4

Percentages of Examinees Tested from July 2004 through June 2007
(including Repeaters)
Who Scored Below Specified AWA Scores

AWA Scaled Score	Percentage Below
6.0	89
5.5	83
5.0	61
4.5	49
4.3	26
3.5	16
3.0	7
2.5	4
0.5–2.0	3
0.0	0

Number of Candidates = 616,490
Mean = 4.3
Standard deviation = 1.2

To register for the GMAT® test go to www.mba.com

Appendix B Extra Answer Sheets

Problem Solving Extra Answer Sheets

1.	36.	71.	106.	141.
2.	37.	72.	107.	142.
3.	38.	73.	108.	143.
4.	39.	74.	109.	144.
5.	40.	75.	110.	145.
6.	41.	76.	111.	146.
7.	42.	77.	112.	147.
8.	43.	78.	113.	148.
9.	44.	79.	114.	149.
10.	45.	80.	115.	150.
11.	46.	81.	116.	151.
12.	47.	82.	117.	152.
13.	48.	83.	118.	153.
14.	49.	84.	119.	154.
15.	50.	85.	120.	155.
16.	51.	86.	121.	156.
17.	52.	87.	122.	157.
18.	53.	88.	123.	158.
19.	54.	89.	124.	159.
20.	55.	90.	125.	160.
21.	56.	91.	126.	161.
22.	57.	92.	127.	162.
23.	58.	93.	128.	163.
24.	59.	94.	129.	164.
25.	60.	95.	130.	165.
26.	61.	96.	131.	166.
27.	62.	97.	132.	167.
28.	63.	98.	133.	168.
29.	64.	99.	134.	169.
30.	65.	100.	135.	170.
31.	66.	101.	136.	171.
32.	67.	102.	137.	172.
33.	68.	103.	138.	173.
34.	69.	104.	139.	174.
35.	70.	105.	140.	175.
				176.

Problem Solving Extra Answer Sheets

1.	36.	71.	106.	141.
2.	37.	72.	107.	142.
3.	38.	73.	108.	143.
4.	39.	74.	109.	144.
5.	40.	75.	110.	145.
6.	41.	76.	111.	146.
7.	42.	77.	112.	147.
8.	43.	78.	113.	148.
9.	44.	79.	114.	149.
10.	45.	80.	115.	150.
11.	46.	81.	116.	151.
12.	47.	82.	117.	152.
13.	48.	83.	118.	153.
14.	49.	84.	119.	154.
15.	50.	85.	120.	155.
16.	51.	86.	121.	156.
17.	52.	87.	122.	157.
18.	53.	88.	123.	158.
19.	54.	89.	124.	159.
20.	55.	90.	125.	160.
21.	56.	91.	126.	161.
22.	57.	92.	127.	162.
23.	58.	93.	128.	163.
24.	59.	94.	129.	164.
25.	60.	95.	130.	165.
26.	61.	96.	131.	166.
27.	62.	97.	132.	167.
28.	63.	98.	133.	168.
29.	64.	99.	134.	169.
30.	65.	100.	135.	170.
31.	66.	101.	136.	171.
32.	67.	102.	137.	172.
33.	68.	103.	138.	173.
34.	69.	104.	139.	174.
35.	70.	105.	140.	175.
				176.

Problem Solving Extra Answer Sheets

1.	36.	71.	106.	141.
2.	37.	72.	107.	142.
3.	38.	73.	108.	143.
4.	39.	74.	109.	144.
5.	40.	75.	110.	145.
6.	41.	76.	111.	146.
7.	42.	77.	112.	147.
8.	43.	78.	113.	148.
9.	44.	79.	114.	149.
10.	45.	80.	115.	150.
11.	46.	81.	116.	151.
12.	47.	82.	117.	152.
13.	48.	83.	118.	153.
14.	49.	84.	119.	154.
15.	50.	85.	120.	155.
16.	51.	86.	121.	156.
17.	52.	87.	122.	157.
18.	53.	88.	123.	158.
19.	54.	89.	124.	159.
20.	55.	90.	125.	160.
21.	56.	91.	126.	161.
22.	57.	92.	127.	162.
23.	58.	93.	128.	163.
24.	59.	94.	129.	164.
25.	60.	95.	130.	165.
26.	61.	96.	131.	166.
27.	62.	97.	132.	167.
28.	63.	98.	133.	168.
29.	64.	99.	134.	169.
30.	65.	100.	135.	170.
31.	66.	101.	136.	171.
32.	67.	102.	137.	172.
33.	68.	103.	138.	173.
34.	69.	104.	139.	174.
35.	70.	105.	140.	175.
				176.

Problem Solving Extra Answer Sheets

1.	36.	71.	106.	141.
2.	37.	72.	107.	142.
3.	38.	73.	108.	143.
4.	39.	74.	109.	144.
5.	40.	75.	110.	145.
6.	41.	76.	111.	146.
7.	42.	77.	112.	147.
8.	43.	78.	113.	148.
9.	44.	79.	114.	149.
10.	45.	80.	115.	150.
11.	46.	81.	116.	151.
12.	47.	82.	117.	152.
13.	48.	83.	118.	153.
14.	49.	84.	119.	154.
15.	50.	85.	120.	155.
16.	51.	86.	121.	156.
17.	52.	87.	122.	157.
18.	53.	88.	123.	158.
19.	54.	89.	124.	159.
20.	55.	90.	125.	160.
21.	56.	91.	126.	161.
22.	57.	92.	127.	162.
23.	58.	93.	128.	163.
24.	59.	94.	129.	164.
25.	60.	95.	130.	165.
26.	61.	96.	131.	166.
27.	62.	97.	132.	167.
28.	63.	98.	133.	168.
29.	64.	99.	134.	169.
30.	65.	100.	135.	170.
31.	66.	101.	136.	171.
32.	67.	102.	137.	172.
33.	68.	103.	138.	173.
34.	69.	104.	139.	174.
35.	70.	105.	140.	175.
				176.

Problem Solving Extra Answer Sheets

1.	36.	71.	106.	141.
2.	37.	72.	107.	142.
3.	38.	73.	108.	143.
4.	39.	74.	109.	144.
5.	40.	75.	110.	145.
6.	41.	76.	111.	146.
7.	42.	77.	112.	147.
8.	43.	78.	113.	148.
9.	44.	79.	114.	149.
10.	45.	80.	115.	150.
11.	46.	81.	116.	151.
12.	47.	82.	117.	152.
13.	48.	83.	118.	153.
14.	49.	84.	119.	154.
15.	50.	85.	120.	155.
16.	51.	86.	121.	156.
17.	52.	87.	122.	157.
18.	53.	88.	123.	158.
19.	54.	89.	124.	159.
20.	55.	90.	125.	160.
21.	56.	91.	126.	161.
22.	57.	92.	127.	162.
23.	58.	93.	128.	163.
24.	59.	94.	129.	164.
25.	60.	95.	130.	165.
26.	61.	96.	131.	166.
27.	62.	97.	132.	167.
28.	63.	98.	133.	168.
29.	64.	99.	134.	169.
30.	65.	100.	135.	170.
31.	66.	101.	136.	171.
32.	67.	102.	137.	172.
33.	68.	103.	138.	173.
34.	69.	104.	139.	174.
35.	70.	105.	140.	175.
				176.

Data Sufficiency Extra Answer Sheets

1.	32.	63.	94.
2.	33.	64.	95.
3.	34.	65.	96.
4.	35.	66.	97.
5.	36.	67.	98.
6.	37.	68.	99.
7.	38.	69.	100.
8.	39.	70.	101.
9.	40.	71.	102.
10.	41.	72.	103.
11.	42.	73.	104.
12.	43.	74.	105.
13.	44.	75.	106.
14.	45.	76.	107.
15.	46.	77.	108.
16.	47.	78.	109.
17.	48.	79.	110.
18.	49.	80.	111.
19.	50.	81.	112.
20.	51.	82.	113.
21.	52.	83.	114.
22.	53.	84.	115.
23.	54.	85.	116.
24.	55.	86.	117.
25.	56.	87.	
26.	57.	88.	
27.	58.	89.	
28.	59.	90.	
29.	60.	91.	
30.	61.	92.	
31.	62.	93.	

Data Sufficiency Extra Answer Sheets

1.	32.	63.	94.
2.	33.	64.	95.
3.	34.	65.	96.
4.	35.	66.	97.
5.	36.	67.	98.
6.	37.	68.	99.
7.	38.	69.	100.
8.	39.	70.	101.
9.	40.	71.	102.
10.	41.	72.	103.
11.	42.	73.	104.
12.	43.	74.	105.
13.	44.	75.	106.
14.	45.	76.	107.
15.	46.	77.	108.
16.	47.	78.	109.
17.	48.	79.	110.
18.	49.	80.	111.
19.	50.	81.	112.
20.	51.	82.	113.
21.	52.	83.	114.
22.	53.	84.	115.
23.	54.	85.	116.
24.	55.	86.	117.
25.	56.	87.	
26.	57.	88.	
27.	58.	89.	
28.	59.	90.	
29.	60.	91.	
30.	61.	92.	
31.	62.	93.	

Data Sufficiency Extra Answer Sheets

1.	32.	63.	94.
2.	33.	64.	95.
3.	34.	65.	96.
4.	35.	66.	97.
5.	36.	67.	98.
6.	37.	68.	99.
7.	38.	69.	100.
8.	39.	70.	101.
9.	40.	71.	102.
10.	41.	72.	103.
11.	42.	73.	104.
12.	43.	74.	105.
13.	44.	75.	106.
14.	45.	76.	107.
15.	46.	77.	108.
16.	47.	78.	109.
17.	48.	79.	110.
18.	49.	80.	111.
19.	50.	81.	112.
20.	51.	82.	113.
21.	52.	83.	114.
22.	53.	84.	115.
23.	54.	85.	116.
24.	55.	86.	117.
25.	56.	87.	
26.	57.	88.	
27.	58.	89.	
28.	59.	90.	
29.	60.	91.	
30.	61.	92.	
31.	62.	93.	

Data Sufficiency Extra Answer Sheets

1.	32.	63.	94.
2.	33.	64.	95.
3.	34.	65.	96.
4.	35.	66.	97.
5.	36.	67.	98.
6.	37.	68.	99.
7.	38.	69.	100.
8.	39.	70.	101.
9.	40.	71.	102.
10.	41.	72.	103.
11.	42.	73.	104.
12.	43.	74.	105.
13.	44.	75.	106.
14.	45.	76.	107.
15.	46.	77.	108.
16.	47.	78.	109.
17.	48.	79.	110.
18.	49.	80.	111.
19.	50.	81.	112.
20.	51.	82.	113.
21.	52.	83.	114.
22.	53.	84.	115.
23.	54.	85.	116.
24.	55.	86.	117.
25.	56.	87.	
26.	57.	88.	
27.	58.	89.	
28.	59.	90.	
29.	60.	91.	
30.	61.	92.	
31.	62.	93.	

Data Sufficiency Extra Answer Sheets

1.	32.	63.	94.
2.	33.	64.	95.
3.	34.	65.	96.
4.	35.	66.	97.
5.	36.	67.	98.
6.	37.	68.	99.
7.	38.	69.	100.
8.	39.	70.	101.
9.	40.	71.	102.
10.	41.	72.	103.
11.	42.	73.	104.
12.	43.	74.	105.
13.	44.	75.	106.
14.	45.	76.	107.
15.	46.	77.	108.
16.	47.	78.	109.
17.	48.	79.	110.
18.	49.	80.	111.
19.	50.	81.	112.
20.	51.	82.	113.
21.	52.	83.	114.
22.	53.	84.	115.
23.	54.	85.	116.
24.	55.	86.	117.
25.	56.	87.	
26.	57.	88.	
27.	58.	89.	
28.	59.	90.	
29.	60.	91.	
30.	61.	92.	
31.	62.	93.	